CHRISTIAN-OWNED COMPANIES

What does it look like
when a follower of Jesus
runs a business?

MICHAEL ZIGARELLI

9 †o 5 Media

Copyright © 2019 Michael Zigarelli. All rights reserved.
ISBN: 978-0578614069

Gratefully dedicated in memory of
Professor John F. Cummings, 1936-1996.
My work is part of your legacy.

ABBREVIATED CONTENTS

DETAILED CONTENTS

Their People
133
They treat their employees like family

Their Poverty Plan
183
They create jobs for people who would not have one

Their Planet Protection
219
They value creation care

What does it look like when a follower of Jesus runs a business?

The exchange usually goes something like this.

Me to my business class: "What does it look like when a follower of Jesus runs a business? What do you think that means in practical terms?"

Cue the faux note-taking and other eye contact avoidance techniques, to minimize the risk of being cold-called.

Nice try, but I've been doing this longer than you've been alive. "Nathan, take a stab at it. What do you think that looks like?"

Cue the deer-in-the-headlights, frozen in the fourth row. But Nathan shakes it off. I selected him because he's mentally tough enough.

"I guess it means you're honest," he ventures.

"A good start. Probably better than the alternative. What else, Nathan?"

"Uh, maybe that you're nice to people?" The question mark is not a typo. It's often the default in a conversation like this.

"Okay, keep going. Anything more than *honest* and *nice*? Or does that satisfy their responsibility?"

Cue another awkward pause. And suddenly more note-taking.

A half-raised hand on the other side of the room rescues Nathan. "It means that you pray to make a million bucks this year," offers Brandon.

Class clown. Some chuckle at his mediocre humor.

I smile and nod to keep it light, but then push back, rephrasing to help him along.

"Now Brandon, you mentioned this semester that you've been a Christian for most of your life. And you've regaled us with stories of your work experiences. So connect the dots. What does it mean when a Christian is in charge at work?"

I go to the board and pick up a piece of chalk, signaling our anticipation while giving him a moment to think. Unfortunately, on this topic, Brandon's got nothing beyond wise cracks.

Students throw a few more darts: "It means you're closed on Sunday." "It means you can't fire people." "It means you don't lie."

"Thank you. I think Nathan already covered that. What else, folks?"

The Goal of this Study: A Data-Driven Answer

For more than 20 years, across four Christian universities—one Catholic, one Pentecostal, one Southern Baptist and one Brethren in Christ—I've asked this question to my undergraduate and MBA students. That's literally thousands of young adults and early-career professionals. And just like this hypothetical exchange, my students always hazard a guess, occasionally an educated one born of experience, but more typically something superficial.

That used to frustrate me. These were Christians in a college business program, after all. Juniors and seniors and even graduate students. Shouldn't they have thought through by now the application of Sunday to Monday?

Perhaps, but I've come to interpret their confusion as a microcosm of the broader societal confusion about the question.

In one camp are those who reduce "Christian-owned company" to "no wedding cake for gays, no birth control for employees, and no chicken sandwiches for anyone on Sunday." Since these are the only times the issue makes national headlines, the myopia is understandable. Their perception is, however, only about one-percent of the reality, and often a caricature at that.

Other camps, replete with believers, see a positive nexus between Christianity and business practice. Social justice advocates, for example, emphasize a faith-based company's responsibility to care for the poor and the powerless, including its employees. Evangelistic believers emphasize business as a platform for introducing people to God. Still other Christian business leaders I've known claim that their entire moral responsibility is to increase profits— legally and ethically—to enrich the owners and the public coffers. Turning five talents into ten, they insist, maybe eisegetically, maximizes the common good and discharges their corporate duty as disciples.

Despite their important truths, all of these latter perspectives, like those of the first camp, are a bit reductionist. Their well-intended primacy of some faith expressions comes at the expense of others. Hence the confusion, from the front lines of business to the front page of the newspaper to the front row of my classroom when the question arises: "What does it look like when a follower of Jesus runs a business?"

It was hazy to me for a long time, too, because the resources in the area tend to be single-company anecdotes from CEOs, or normative principles from someone's exegesis. Helpful for sure, but there's almost nothing that uses the standard social science methodology of looking across organizations to discover the best practices.

So I conducted this study to gain some clarity, examining the operations of 50 Christian-owned companies. They vary quite a bit by size, industry, geography, and denomination of the owners, but when they're juxtaposed, something unique emerges: an objective, data-driven answer to the question of what the Christian faith looks like in business.

It's an answer that I hope will benefit practitioners and students alike, and one that I hope demystifies the issue for a confused culture. I'll summarize that answer in a minute and unpack it throughout the book, but to better interpret it, let's take a quick look at the companies included in this research.

The Sample for this Study: 50 Faithful For-Profits

I selected these particular companies based, in part, on my familiarity with them from a couple decades of teaching and writing on the subject. To supplement my initial list, I picked the brains of trusted colleagues in the field, and gleaned from expert commentary—books, articles, blogs, news stories and so on—and from historical examples.

In the end, I converged on a sample of 50 that includes both the usual suspects and some unusual, unsung heroes. They're mostly U.S.-based companies, ranging from local to national to global in scope; from nine employees to several thousand; from eight-years-old to centuries-old. For the research purists, this may or may not be a representative sample of the half-million or so Christian-owned companies in the United States. It's certainly not representative of such companies worldwide.

That wasn't the intention, though. Rather, this is a best-practice sample—a study of some of the most innovative and most successful Christian business owners who love God and take seriously God's lordship over all things.

And notice that these are not just Christians who own a business; these are Christians who intentionally run their business by Biblical principles, as they understand them. Our aim here is simply to learn from their vast, collective experience—2,518 years of experience, to sum the ages of these companies. At the same time, you may also find yourself inspired by their devotion, their courage, and their business acumen.

One last aspect of the sample: I've narrowed this research to for-profit organizations. Why? To study those who, while adhering to the tenets of their faith, have competed on their merits without relying on charitable donations. As these companies show, it *is* possible to do that—an important implication since it dispels the myth that we can't be faithful and profitable at the same time.

Which segues us to findings, so let's get to it.

The Findings of this Study: Eight Best Practices

Perhaps the greatest value-added of this project, at least relative to other work in this field, is this: The approaches of these 50 companies form a practical framework for how to operate Christianly.

My academic colleagues, with their bent toward advancing the body of knowledge, would call it a "theory" or a "model." My practitioner colleagues, with their bent toward getting from A to B, might call it a "road map." My students would simply call it a "curriculum." Regardless the framing, this study describes eight ways that Christians live out their faith through the businesses they own. I've structured this section of the chapter, and the entire book, accordingly.

In some of these companies, we see all eight expressions of the faith. In others, we see several but not all expressions. A few of these companies implement only one or two. The point is these eight "best practices" are not mutually exclusive. Nor do they conflict with one another. Rather, they're entirely complementary, though all eight may not fit the Christology of all Christian business owners.

I hope that's enough context. Contact me if you want more. When a follower of Jesus runs a business, it looks like this:

1. Their Purpose: They Seek to Honor God in All They Do

It's Christian shorthand—a phrase that transcends Christian-owned companies. Many have formally adopted "to honor God in all we do" as part of their mission or core values. Many others, Chick-fil-A, Interstate Batteries and Altar'd State among them, adopt a close variation that includes "to glorify God." Still others imply in their mission or values statements that they put God first, without explicit reference to God.

Regardless the phrasing or the overtness, the underlying theology very similar and it serves as the primary filter for decision making. "To honor God" is essentially the *WWJD* of the corporate world.

The global company ServiceMaster has been a forerunner here. Though no longer Christian-owned or even faith-informed, their former statement of objectives has been imported in whole or part around the world: "To honor God in all we do, to help people develop, to pursue excellence, to grow profitably." It's as close to a creed as it gets among believers in business, prompting every other expression of the faith described in this book.

Though Christian-owned companies vary greatly in the paths they take, most seem to share the same starting point.

2. Their Products: They Make Products That Make a Better World

Imagine living without access to the electrical grid. No lights at night, no refrigeration for food, no fans or heat, no way to cook.

When a group of Stanford students learned that this is the daily reality for nearly two-billion people around the world, they went to work on an affordable, solar-powered light. A little more than a decade later, their company, D.light Design, has sold 20 million solar products in 65 countries, touching nearly 100 million lives.

Like D.light, many companies run by Christians express the faith through the very products they make. They see a significant need—an injustice, a crisis, a decaying world—and to honor God they start a business that addresses that need.

Another example: Arthur Guinness, a devout follower of Jesus, brewed beer not just to make a living, but to make a difference. In Arthur's world, eighteenth century Ireland, the water supply was toxic, so people turned to gin as a safer daily beverage (alcohol killed the germs in liquid). As you might imagine, the implications for society were dire. Driven by his relationship with God, Guinness offered an alternative that helped to heal and restore order to his tortured society.

Guinness was also quite generous with the proceeds, blessing both his community and his employees. That brings us to the next two expressions of the faith.

3. Their Profits: They Fund Faithful Causes

Philanthropy. It may be the most common expression of the faith among Christian business owners. Some faith-based businesses, though, were specifically created for this purpose: Make more money so we can give away more money.

For example, two faithful Harvard Business School grads launched Pura Vida Coffee, now a national brand in the U.S., to generate resources for impoverished kids and families in Costa Rica, and to take care of the coffee farmers. Similarly, the longstanding purpose of TOMS Shoes has been to put shoes on the feet of kids who have never had them, inventing along the way the "buy one, give one" business model.

Bridgeway Capital Management actually built into its articles of incorporation the mandate to give away a full 50 percent of its profits. Forever. And "Auntie Anne" Beiler founded her well-known pretzel company for this little-known reason: to fund her husband's free marriage-counseling service. It's now helped repair thousands of relationships. No charge.

The list of philanthropists is broad and varied, but their ministry strategy is much the same. To honor God, they give away money; to give away money, they need to make money; to make money, they started a business. These companies are changing the world by operating at the intersection of theology and capitalism.

4. Their People: They Treat Their Employees Like Family

There are plenty of companies, even some owned by Christians, that point to attractive wages and benefits as evidence that they love their employees. But at the same time, they maintain an oppressive culture in the name of profitability, or in Christianese, "financial stewardship." In reality, they're what the Apostle Paul called "clanging cymbals" (1 Corinthians 13:1)—loud do-gooders on the outside who don't really love people on the inside.

Other business owners, by contrast, are more holistic in their care, safeguarding the physical, psychological and spiritual needs of their employees. Broetje Orchards in Washington has long been an exemplar, not only providing year-round jobs in a seasonal business, but building houses for employees, as well as a school for their kids, a church, a gym, a grocery store, and a bilingual library for the mostly-immigrant workforce. They put their money where their love is.

At Mary Kay Cosmetics, the default for decades has been to love their people by lavishing praise on them, complementing the many other benefits of working there. That sort of encouragement and affirmation is an elusive form of love in modern organizations, but it's long been at the core of Mary Kay.

Also with an eye toward psychological care, many companies, like Tyson Foods, keep chaplains on-staff and on-call for employees who need advice, assistance, or just somebody to listen. It's not cheap—especially when you have more than 100 of them, like Tyson does—but it's an investment in care at a deeper level than mere compensation.

There are countless other manifestations, but they all flow from the heart condition of the owners. Some Christian-owned companies genuinely love employees like family.

5. Their Poverty Plan: They Create Jobs for Those Who Would Not Have One

This might be the most surprising expression of the faith. If we think about it for a minute, though, perhaps it shouldn't be. After all, the principle comes from Jesus himself: "Whatever you did for one of the least of these brothers and sisters of mine, you did for me" (Matthew 25:40).

In fact, some of these companies exist *primarily* to create jobs for what some might say are "the least of these." Lamon Luther, a furniture company in Georgia, started as one carpenter in a truck asking homeless guys to do some remodeling with him. The aptly-named Second Chance Coffee exists to employ former felons, putting them to work roasting the beans and even managing the company.

Other Christian entrepreneurs operate in impoverished countries with the express goal of generating jobs and wealth, lifting people out of poverty. Tegu is a toy company that manufactures in Honduras for this very purpose, even though making toys in China would increase their margins considerably. And Sunshine Nut Company was launched in Mozambique to create a market for cashew farmers and to give people with difficult pasts a chance to earn a living.

Keystone Custom Homes has taken all this a step further, underwriting microfinance loans to the poor around the world, equipping them to lift themselves out of poverty by starting a business. Like these other companies, Keystone offers something that is better than charity: a permanent way out.

6. *Their Planet Protection: They Value Creation Care*

God is great, God is green. Or so some would claim.

Few social movements in recent decades have gotten as much traction internationally as environmentalism. It's a priority for many Christians as well, though they tend to avoid the "Mother Earth" references, instead framing their perspective as "creation care."

The theology is simple: God gave us the Earth, so it's our responsibility to take care of it. And that applies to institutions, like businesses, not just to individuals.

Pretty straightforward. For some Christian-owned companies, that entails recycling, limiting their air and water pollution, and a general sensitivity to their potential effect on humans, animals and plants. Many businesses covered in this book are careful to do their part here.

For others, their very essence is green. Tom's of Maine, for example, has long-existed to provide all-natural products for personal care, practically inventing the category. Cardone Industries takes the same approach, having built a 5,000-employee remanufacturing business around reusing old car and truck parts. That's literally millions of vehicle parts since 1970 that would have otherwise cluttered landfills. Elevation Burger was founded on the humane treatment of the animals in their supply chain, while making every part of their operation eco-friendly. And Enviro-Stewards, a Canadian consulting company, teaches clients how to earn more money by spending less on water and energy.

Notice that for all of these companies, sustainability is not an add-on or a greenwashing marketing tactic. It's part of their triple-bottom-line of "profit, people and planet"—a theological mandate for them, not an ideological one. They honor God by stewarding his creation and preserving a healthy environment for future generations.

7. Their Principle: They Stand Firm, Regardless the Cost

It's counter-cultural. As long as Christianity has existed, it's stood as a faithful presence in a disbelieving culture.

Indeed there are exceptions, historical and contemporary, but most of the companies in this study operate in a predominantly secular and agnostic setting. So where their corporate values align with secular values, there's no problem: The company is celebrated and often rewarded by the market. But where the values collide, the company has to make a difficult choice.

Case in point: The Army, during World War II, asked Correct Craft to build boats seven days a week. The company drew the line at six days, risking the biggest contract they had ever been offered. In the end, they faced down the Army and even delivered the boats before the deadline.

A couple more examples, these with a twenty-first century flavor. When the courts insisted that Masterpiece Cakeshop create custom cakes for same-sex weddings, the owner, despite the fines and the death threats, still refused to violate his conscience. And when a new Federal law required companies to provide abortifacients in employee benefit plans, Conestoga Wood Specialties and Hobby Lobby risked everything to avoid complicity in any type of abortion. After years of uncertainty about their survival, each of these faith-based companies emerged victorious at the U.S. Supreme Court.

It doesn't happen often in American culture, but some believers in business can attest that faithful management means standing on principle, even at great potential cost.

8. Their Proselytizing: They Introduce People to God

Some Christian business owners see their company as a platform for evangelism and discipleship. For them, the Great Commission is central to their faith: "Go and make disciples of all nations, baptizing them in the name of the Father and of the Son and of the Holy Spirit, and teaching them to obey everything I have commanded you" (Matthew 28:19-20). The fact that these are Jesus's last words in the gospels only adds to the urgency of the mandate.

Their Great Commission activities take various forms. Many companies use their property as a billboard for the gospel message. Those driving by U.S. Plastic Corporation on I-75 in Ohio can't miss the message "Christ is the Answer" in enormous letters on the building side. Similarly, at night you can see the lighted cross atop a silo at DNS Animal Nutrition in Iowa from 10 cornfields away.

Another Great Commission strategy is to fund evangelism around the world. R.G. LeTourneau famously reverse-tithed, donating 90 percent of the proceeds from his earth-moving business to spread the gospel message. Through example and stirring speeches, he inspired a generation that is now paying it forward—a global movement, sometimes called "business as mission," that witnesses to the world, often in places where no church can go.

A couple more approaches: Companies like Pure Flix and Interstate Batteries create films, the storytelling medium of choice in the modern day, to communicate a memorable, penetrating evangelistic message. Other companies are more subtle about their outreach, putting a discreet scripture verse or citation on their packaging, inviting customers to investigate it for themselves (among them, In-N-Out Burger, Cookout, and Rose Acre Farms).

Overall, Christian-owned businesses run the evangelistic spectrum from overt to covert, direct to indirect, unmistakable to almost imperceptible. What these companies have in common, though, are leaders who love God and love people enough to live out the Great Commission, telling people about Jesus Christ.

The Value of this Study

My hope is that one day the exchange will go something like this.

Me to my business class: "What does it look like when a follower of Jesus runs a business? What do you think that means in practical terms?"

Hands shoot up around the room. I pick the one raised first.

"Well," Nathan starts, "it kind of a long answer. First, there's this study that says there are eight different ways they live out their faith. And then there were several studies after that, improving the theory…"

Everyone turns toward Nathan as he continues, many of them taking notes, this time for real.

Okay, it's a professorial pipedream. But then again, maybe it's not entirely implausible. If there's one thing that has come out of this project, it's an empirical explanation to the question. And I'd humbly suggest that it matters.

It matters to the Nathans and Natalies of the world who will grow up to be Christian entrepreneurs. They'll benefit from a template.

It matters to current business leaders struggling to understand how their faith applies to their company. They'll benefit from road-tested ideas.

And it matters to a society that's confused by misperceptions and misrepresentations of these companies. We'll benefit from a corrective.

There is a factual answer to this question. Let me tell you a story about what Christian-owned companies do and why they do it.

Actually, let me tell you 50 of them.

PART 1

~

THEIR PURPOSE
They seek to honor God in all they do

The ServiceMaster Company
Chick-fil-A
Hobby Lobby
Martin's Famous Pastry Shoppe
TURBOCAM International

THE SERVICE MASTER COMPANY

The Lesson

Statements of mission, vision and values are essential to guide and align organizations. ServiceMaster's tenets have long been a standard for Christian-owned companies.

It's become a creed.

Or at least as close to a creed as we see among Christian-owned companies, having been adopted by so many of them, domestically and overseas. Fittingly, it comes from a company called Service-Master, derived from "in service to the Master."

Here are the tenets, what the company once called its "corporate objectives":

To honor God in all we do
To help people develop
To pursue excellence
To grow profitably

As William Pollard, former Chairman and CEO, described them: "The first two objectives are end goals. The second two are means goals. As we seek to implement these objectives in the operation of our business, they provide us with a reference point for seeking to do that which is right and avoiding that which is wrong."[1]

End goals, means goals. Translation: Once upon a time, ServiceMaster was in business *to honor God* and *to help people develop*. That's why they existed. And they got there by *pursuing excellence* and *growing profitably*. Without the latter two, the former two don't happen. Without the former two, the latter two don't matter.

It's a template that instructs with striking clarity. Perhaps that's why companies simply lift those four objectives verbatim: ServiceMaster may have captured the immovable essence of faith-based business.

In fact, to communicate that immovability, ServiceMaster engraved the words in its corporate lobby on a wall 18 feet high by 90 feet long, in letters 12 inches high. Everything else could change about the company, but not this. These principles were etched in stone—literally.

It's a foundation that goes back to their founder, Marion Wade (1898-1973), a devout follower of Jesus who started a mothproofing company in 1929.[2] Since then, the business has expanded into home and commercial cleaning, pest control (well-beyond moths), lawn care, home warrantees and more, operating under familiar names like ServiceMaster Clean, Merry Maids, Terminix, TruGreen, and American Home Shield. Thanks to its franchise model, ServiceMaster now has 40,000 employees and franchisees, serving 50,000 customers a day across two dozen countries, earning an annual system-wide income of about $2 billion.[3]

Despite all that change, and maybe generating much of it, the four cornerstones endured. Two ends, two means.

The genius in their formula, though, may lie in what seems to be the most enigmatic element. Honoring God, pursuing excellence, growing profitably—they're all axiomatic in a faith-based environment. But in a service company, how does *to develop people* make the cut instead of something like "delighting customers" or "delivering superior service"? Beyond that, how is developing people an *end* goal, one of only two?

No less an authority than Peter Drucker helped them converge on this. In a two-day seminar he led for the ServiceMaster Board of Directors, he demonstrated to them that "Your business is simply the training and development of people. ... You can't deliver quality service to the customer without motivated and trained people."[4]

In other words, if they could get people-development right, then serving customers well would take care of itself. So would market share, EBITDA, and stock price.

It was both good strategy and good theology. Briefly, here are two of many ways they made that a reality.

With regard to training blue-collar employees, consider what happened when ServiceMaster landed a contract to clean a hospital. The ServiceMaster CEO himself visited the site and asked to meet with the hospital's professional staff—doctors, nurses, technicians and so on—to invite them to teach the cleaning staff how the medical equipment works. In response to the inevitable pushback and snide questions like "Do you expect janitors to understand radiology?" the CEO explained to the group: "No, but we do expect them to be able to see the important part they play in the mission of the hospital and its various functions. It connects them to a greater goal and inspires them to quality, cleanliness and even to those of you of the professional staff."[5]

The people-development principle is this: "People want to work for a cause, not just a living."[6] Technical training, as important as it is, does not inspire. But greater purpose, even in the most menial tasks, can supercharge motivation. It also brings life and dignity to someone created in the image of God.

Manager training was equally innovative. Forget people-skills seminars. Developing servant-leaders requires heart training—an understanding and appreciation and empathy for those we lead. So ServiceMaster created a system whereby every manager, at least one day a year, worked in the field doing the job of his or her employees.

The results were transformational. One vice-president recalled:

"I cleaned Greyhound buses for a day. I spent a long time scrubbing bugs off of windshields. I was sore for days! But I gained a new feeling for people who work hard like that every day. ... (I had) a new-found respect for them."[7]

Another manager, as he was cleaning a hospital room, was struck by how no one there thought him worth acknowledging, even when he said hello to them.[8] It was an epiphany that made him a better, more emotionally-intelligent manager.

Of course, their people-development system went much further, but for decades, it existed because it was *right*, not just because it worked. ServiceMaster, as a company that strived to honor God, invested fully in caring for and cultivating employees.

As it turned out, few people internally or externally found fault with that approach, especially given ServiceMaster's ongoing growth through the 1970s, 80s and 90s. What did irk some of them in this public company, though, was what Pollard called "the God language."

"At one of our recent shareholders meetings," he wrote, "a shareholder, while commending us for our profit performance, made the following statement: 'While I firmly support the right of an individual to his religious convictions and pursuits, I totally fail to appreciate the concept that ServiceMaster is, in fact, a vehicle for the work of God. The multiple references to this effect, in my opinion, do not belong in the annual business report. ... I urge that next year's business report be confined to just that—business.'"[9]

For a long time, shareholders like these were merely a vocal minority. Now, as ServiceMaster passes its 90th year, it seems that they have won. A group of equity investors took the company private in 2007 and then public again in 2014. In the process, they moved the headquarters from Illinois to Memphis. The new facility featured no engraved wall of corporate objectives, permanently pointing to God. Nor could you find such words on the new website or in the annual reports.

It seems that God got the boot as ServiceMaster got a reboot—new leadership, a new location, new statements of mission, vision and values. And not a whiff of "God-language" in the air.

But—and this is the point—that aroma has, for decades, wafted far and wide, informing countless corporate missions and the faithful decisions that flow from them. We'll see one such beneficiary later in this book, Cardone Industries, a large manufacturing company in Pennsylvania. A simple Internet search offers plenty of others, including many ServiceMaster franchisees who remain closely guided by the original creed: To honor God in all we do, to help people develop, to pursue excellence, to grow profitably.

That framework will always be part of Marion Wade's legacy, regardless of who's running the company or what's on the lobby wall. Even though today's ServiceMaster has cut its faith-based moorings, Wade's company left in its wake four anchors that can keep Christian-owned companies from drifting.

For Further Study

William Pollard, *The Soul of the Firm*, Grand Rapids, MI: Zondervan Publishing, 1996.

Marion Wade, *The Lord is My Counsel: A Businessman's Personal Experiences with the Bible*, Englewood Cliffs, NJ: Prentice-Hall, 1966.

Notes

1. William Pollard, *The Soul of the Firm*, Grand Rapids, MI: Zondervan Publishing, 1996, p. 19.
2. Marion Wade, *The Lord is My Counsel: A Businessman's Personal Experiences with the Bible*, Englewood Cliffs, NJ: Prentice-Hall, 1966.
3. The ServiceMaster Company, "Growth through Service: 2018 Annual Report," investors.servicemaster.com/sites/service-master.investorhq.businesswire.com/files/doc_library/file/ServiceMaster_Annual_Report_2018.pdf

4. *The Soul of the Firm*, p. 113.
5. Charles Colson and Jack Eckerd, *Why America Doesn't Work*, Dallas, TX: Word Publishing, 1991, p 157.
6. *The Soul of the Firm*, p. 45.
7. *The Soul of the Firm*, p. 54.
8. *The Soul of the Firm*, p 56.
9. *The Soul of the Firm*, p 20.

CHICK-FIL-A
CREATING A CORPORATE PURPOSE

The Lesson

When their closed-on-Sunday policy threatened to render them closed-on-every-day, the leaders didn't give up. They doubled-down, responding with a bold new mission statement.

When it comes to Christian-owned companies, this chicken restaurant is the top of the pecking order.

In fact, it's also at the top of the entire quick-service restaurant industry. The average Chick-fil-A location grosses $4.1 million annually, more than any competitor. By far. They bring in 40 percent more than the second place chain; they've tripled the per-store U.S. sales of chicken rival KFC.[1]

And remarkably, they're beating the competition with one wing tied behind their back: Chick-fil-A is closed for about two months every year—each Sunday plus a few holidays. It's total dominance.

It's also total foolishness to many industry observers. That closed-on-Sunday policy costs the company upwards of $1.2 billion in additional sales every year.[2] Notwithstanding, this is a matter of principle. Non-negotiable principle. Immovable principle. The company wouldn't change it even if their very survival were at stake.

We know because that's exactly where they were in 1982. It may be the most instructive story in the company's history.

But let's get a running start at that story by going back even further, to 1946.

Truett Cathy, a young and diligent entrepreneur, took out a small loan to open a restaurant in Hapeville, Georgia. His "Dwarf Grill" consisted of a mere ten counter seats and four tables, but Truett steadily grew the business, serving up quality food and friendly service twenty-four hours a day, six days a week.

It was in this modest setting that Truett experimented with faster ways to prepare chicken and creative ways to season it. Years later, in the 1960s, all that experimentation paid huge dividends. He developed the winning taste combination that would become the Chick-fil-A sandwich.

Truett incorporated the new company in 1967, though in retrospect he said: "I had been preparing for twenty-one years to open the first Chick-fil-A restaurant."[3]

All that preparation clearly paid off. The business was a juggernaut as Truett pioneered in-mall fast food, peddling his novel sandwich to rave reviews of hungry shoppers. By 1980, the company's annual sales would top $100 million at about 100 locations—still exclusively in malls at this point—with same-store sales increasing every year.

Direct competition was weak and hundreds of malls were on the drawing board for cities coast to coast, so Chick-fil-A made ambitious plans to add another 100 restaurants in 1981. At the same time, they broke ground on a pristine, $10 million corporate headquarters in Atlanta.

But then came the perfect financial storm.

In 1981, interest rates jumped past 20 percent, curtailing mall construction. Wendy's introduced a chicken sandwich and McDonald's launched a popular new product called Chicken McNuggets. All that demand caused chicken prices to spike.

Even worse, inflation accelerated across the entire economy, touching every part of Chick-fil-A's business. Add to that a mortgage on a new building and it's no wonder that Truett lamented that his building "began to look like a $10 million tombstone. ... It wasn't hard for me to envision a total loss."[4]

As a result, in 1982 the company experienced its first decline in same-store sales. But rather than raising prices, and rather than relaxing their "closed-on-Sunday" policy—an enormous temptation when the alternative might be "closed-on-every-day"—they steeled themselves for the battle. This company wasn't about to go like chickens to the slaughter.

Instead, the leadership started by squeezing out every bit of waste they could find. Truett even cut his salary to zero. Then he organized a two-day retreat in October 1982 for his executive team "to review where we have been, project where we were going, and chart a course for getting us there."[5]

Halfway through that retreat, Dan Cathy, Truett's eldest son (and now CEO), shifted the focus, asking the group to consider why they were in business and why they were even alive. It seemed a bit off-center to the seasoned veterans in the room, including Dan's father. This was no time for theory or theology; it was a time for practical action. But as the group reflected on Dan's questions, recalled Truett, "we were unanimous in our belief that each of us wanted to glorify God in all we say and do," including in their work and business.[6]

Now, that was not exactly new territory for these people, but it became a significant moment as the eight of them discussed how the company had never made a public pronouncement of a larger, faithful purpose. In fact, after 15 years in business, Chick-fil-A had *no formal statement of purpose at all.*

Dan pushed for just that, a public commitment of faith that would guide them in this challenging time and in every subsequent decision. "By the end of the day," said Truett, "we had developed two statements which became Chick-fil-A's Corporate Purpose: *To glorify God by being a faithful steward of all that is entrusted to us* and *To have a positive influence on all who come in contact with Chick-fil-A."*[7]

It was a bold, overt declaration—an internal rebranding that sustains them to this very day.

Indeed, at that retreat they also outlined a new promotional program and found ways to leverage their advantages in quality, service and cleanliness, all of which helped them grow by almost 30 percent in 1983. But clarifying their Corporate Purpose was the transcendent take-away. It stamped their identity like nothing else ever had.

So indelible is that identity that it's engraved on a bronze plaque at their headquarters doorway, reminding everyone daily what their true mission is. Long-time Chief Marketing Officer, Steve Robinson, described the plaque cogently: "This is our *why*."[8]

For several decades now, that *why* has influenced every aspect of their business, from their quality and consistency, to their investment in finding the right people, to their deep training regimen, to their generous charitable contributions, to their signature "it's my pleasure" response, which seems authentic even from the largely teenage staff.

And then there are the regaling anecdotes about what the company calls its "Second-Mile Service," based on a principle in Jesus's Sermon on the Mount (Matthew 5:41). As Truett explains:

> "When customers come into Chick-fil-A, they expect to be greeted with a smile. They expect delicious food delivered quickly and accurately in a clean environment. That's the *first* mile—the expectation.
>
> "Second-Mile Service is about the heart, and it goes above and beyond, making sure customers get not only what they expect, but something more that makes them say 'Wow!' … Almost every day we hear about a team member helping change a customer's tire or making the extra effort to return lost keys or a cell phone that was left behind. This is not a Chick-fil-A strategy, it is a way of life."[9]

A way of life based on a bedrock, Biblical principle. And still, years after Truett's passing, we hear of the manifestations regularly. A few examples:

- A 19-year-old Chick-fil-A employee chased down a car departing their parking lot, sprinting 200 yards around traffic to deliver a sandwich they forgot at the drive-thru.[10]

- Another 19-year-old employee saw a disabled customer struggling to eat his food, so she spontaneously sat with him, cut up the food, and fed it to him.[11]

- When a customer dropped her keys down a nearby sewer, a Chick-fil-A manager pulled off a sewer grate and lowered himself into the muck to retrieve the keys. Then he asked if he could wash them off before giving them back.[12]

- A woman on a road trip forgot her purse at a Chick-fil-A, calling the store when she was three hours away. The manager, at no charge, shipped the seven-pound purse to her by overnight express. Curiously, it weighed a little more when she received it than when she left it: The manager had filled it with six gift cards for free meals, a mountain of mints and a couple stuffed-animal cows.[13]

- A customer neglected to take his three dollars in change. Rather than throw it in the register, the cashier put the money in an envelope and brought it back to work every day, in case the customer returned. After three weeks, the customer did return and was blown away by the thoughtful gesture.[14]

- Chick-fil-A employees handed out more than 1,000 free sandwiches to motorists who were stranded for hours on a nearby, snow-covered highway.[15]

Of course, some of these are simple acts of kindness and decency, perhaps ordinary in an earlier era. But how many such stories have you heard about other quick-service restaurants? Meanwhile, barely a month goes by without a new Chick-fil-A story going viral.

Recognize, though, that in this company, these are not-so-random acts of kindness. Instead, they're the natural expression of a deliberate, God-honoring Corporate Purpose, which itself is an expression of the abiding faith of the Cathy family. And today it's culminated in Chick-fil-A becoming "America's Favorite Restaurant" according to the American Customer Satisfaction Index, a standard economic indicator.[16]

Four years in a row, actually. Maybe more by the time you read this.

The question of this book is *What does it look like when a follower of Jesus runs a business?* Chick-fil-A is the exemplar. And the inspiration. For a half century, they've demonstrated that even in a fiercely competitive market, a faith-focused business can also become the industry leader.

More than that, though, they've taught the world what (closed on) Sunday values really mean on Monday.

For Further Study

Truett Cathy, *Eat Mor Chikin: Inspire More People,* Decatur, GA: Looking Glass Books, 2002.

Truett Cathy, *How Did You Do It, Truett? A Recipe for Success,* Decatur, GA: Looking Glass Books, 2007.

Steve Robinson, *Covert Cows and Chick-fil-A: How Faith, Cows, and Chicken Built an Iconic Brand,* Nashville, TN: Nelson Books, 2019.

Dee Ann Turner, *It's My Pleasure: The Impact of Extraordinary Talent and a Compelling Culture,* Boise, ID: Elevate Publishing, 2015.

Notes

1. "Ranking The Top 50 Fast-Food Chains in America," *QSR Magazine* (undated article). www.qsrmagazine.com/content/qsr50-2019-top-50-chart
2. Douglas A. McIntyre, "Chick-fil-A is missing out on more than $1B in sales by closing on Sundays," USAToday.com, July 14,

2019. www.usatoday.com/story /money/2019/07/14 /chick-fil-a-fast-food-should-open-sundays-make-one-billion-sales/39666863

3. Truett Cathy, *Eat Mor Chikin: Inspire More People,* Decatur, GA: Looking Glass Books, 2002, p 86.
4. *Eat Mor Chikin,* p. 121.
5. *Eat Mor Chikin,* p. 122.
6. *Eat Mor Chikin,* p. 123.
7. *Eat Mor Chikin,* p. 124.
8. Steve Robinson, *Covert Cows and Chick-fil-A: How Faith, Cows, and Chicken Built an Iconic Brand,* Nashville, TN: Nelson Books, 2019, p. 2.
9. Truett Cathy, *How Did You Do It, Truett? A Recipe for Success,* Decatur, GA: Looking Glass Books, 2007, pp. 40-41.
10. Maxine Shen, "Now that's customer service! Chick-Fil-A worker sprints 200 yards across a parking lot to chase down a customer who left without a chicken sandwich," Daily Mail (UK), June 18, 2018. www.dailymail.co.uk/news/article-5858453/Chick-Fil-worker-sprints-200-yards-chase-customer-left-without-chicken-sandwich.html
11. Alexandra Deabler, "Heartwarming moment Chick-fil-A employee helps, feeds disabled man in mall food court," FoxNews.com, January 7, 2019. www.foxnews.com/food-drink/heartwarming-moment-chick-fil-a-employee-helps-feeds-disabled-man-in-mall-food-court
12. Sherae Honeycutt, "KC Chick-fil-A manager braves sewer to help metro mom get her keys," Fox4KC.com, August 2, 2018. fox4kc.com/2018/08/02/kc-chick-fil-a-manager-braves-sewer-to-help-metro-mom-get-her-keys
13. Will Maule, "Chick-fil-A Goes Above and Beyond to Return This Mother's Lost Purse," FaithWire, March 2, 2018. www.faithwire.com/2018/03/02/chick-fil-a-goes-above-and-beyond-to-return-this-mothers-lost-purse
14. Erica Chayes Wida, "Chick-fil-A cashier surprises regular customer with kind gesture," Today.com, March 19, 2018.

www.Today.com/food/texas-chick-fil-surprises-customer-kind-gesture-t125278

15. Morgan Lee, "Chick-Fil-A Hands Out Over 1,000 Sandwiches to Stranded Alabama Drivers," *Christian Post*, January 30, 2014. www.ChristianPost.com/news/chick-fil-a-hands-out-over-1000-sandwiches-to-stranded-alabama-drivers.html

16. Alicia Kelso, "Chick-fil-A Named America's Favorite Restaurant Chain—Again," Forbes.com, June 25, 2019. www.forbes.com/sites/aliciakelso/2019/06/25/chick-fil-a-named-americas-favorite-restaurant-chain--again, based on America Customer Satisfaction Index, *ACSI Restaurant Report*, 2018-2019, p. 5.

HOBBY LOBBY
REDEEMING RETAIL

The Lesson

Many business owners talk about honoring God no matter what. David Green has lived it for half a century.

He may be the most successful Christian business owner in history, at least from a financial perspective.

From an initial investment of $600 in a home-based business, one in which his kids glued frames together for seven cents apiece, David Green has grown Hobby Lobby to $5 billion in annual revenue. Now at 900 stores, it's the largest privately-owned arts-and-crafts retailer in the world, making Green one of the wealthiest private citizens in the world, with a net worth of $7.4 billion.[1]

Not bad for a kid from Oklahoma with a mere high school diploma.

But there's not much else that's "mere" about David Green. He astutely positioned Hobby Lobby to reach a massive target market: "a woman who wants to make her home better in some way."[2] And his masterstroke of competitive advantage was to reach her with *ambience*—pleasant lighting, soothing background music that's classical or Christian, spacious aisles and well-organized merchandise—all to create an "escape" or "reward" for the female shopper in an otherwise frenetic world.[3]

To that he added good value and the broadest selection of useful products, more than 100,000 in a typical Hobby Lobby store.

Remarkably, they all ship from one central hub in Oklahoma City. Think about that for a minute: Thousands of products, coast-to-coast, and no regional distribution points. Nobody does it that way. It's one of the reasons a business magazine quipped that "David Green, CEO of Hobby Lobby, does everything wrong, according to retail conventional wisdom."[4]

But David Green doesn't report to the god of retail; he reports to the God of Israel. That's why his first principle of business is this: "We are committed to honoring the Lord in all we do by operating the company in a manner consistent with Biblical principles."[5]

It's been costly. Breathtakingly so. Consider this:

- When Green contemplated closing the stores on Sunday "to give employees time for family and worship," Hobby Lobby was grossing about $100 million a year on Sundays—their highest sales-per-hour day of the week. They closed anyway since, Green discerned, it was what God wanted them to do. Paradoxically, or maybe providentially, what followed was their highest percentage-profit year ever.

- When a Hobby Lobby neighborhood deteriorated because of drug traffickers, Green decided to close the store. It was simply not safe for their employees or their customers. The company was locked-in, though, to another ten years of a building lease at $330,000 a year. Then they heard from a wholesale liquor outlet that wanted to sublease from them at the same price. An obvious solution, right? Not to Green. "That's just about the last thing this neighborhood needs," he thought. So the retail guy who does everything wrong turned down the offer and, for several years, kept paying for an empty building.

- Similarly, when the Coors Brewing Company sought to have Hobby Lobby back-haul its beer (i.e., use Hobby Lobby trucks returning from a deliveries to carry Coors products), Green declined the lucrative $300,000 a year contract. So their trucks returned empty and unprofitably on what Green considered to be this higher road.

Expensive principles indeed. But all of that *combined* was no match for their supreme test of principle.

When federal law changed in 2010 to require that businesses add abortifacients to their employee benefit policies, Hobby Lobby gently but firmly refused. The company already provided many forms of birth control in its benefit plan, but not morning-after pills since they abort a fertilized egg.

Their refusal triggered a high-profile lawsuit, a firestorm of caricatured publicity, and a $1.3 million fine for *every day* they would not comply with the new law.

Here at the crossroads, the Green family was unswerving. "We knew that this could cost us our business if we took a stand," said David in a 2017 interview, "but we decided to stand on principle."[6] In the end, the U.S. Supreme Court stood with them, but by the narrowest of majorities. Upholding their principles put the company within one vote of being shut down.[7]

They don't open on Sunday, they don't support alcohol sales, they don't facilitate miscarriages, and they don't back down when sued. We might get the impression that at Hobby Lobby, "honoring the Lord in all we do" is basically a list of thou-shalt-nots.

We would be incorrect, though. Woefully incorrect. In this company, "honoring the Lord" also produces these affirmative expressions of the faith:

- All full-time workers earn at least twice the federal minimum. Green has long been ahead of the curve on paying a living wage.

- Nurturing employees' families is also fundamental at Hobby Lobby. So besides closing on Sundays, every store also closes at 8 p.m. on Monday through Saturday to permit employees to get home to children and spouses. "If I could somehow reduce the stress on family life and help my employees be more balanced," reports Green, "I'd rather do that than bring in a little extra profit."[8]

- Hobby Lobby donates fifty percent of its pre-tax profits to charitable causes, especially evangelistic ones. It used to be a lower percentage, but according to Green, one day as they were marveling that "you really can't outgive God," Green sensed God responding: "Well, you really haven't tried."[9] So now, half of all corporate profit goes to philanthropy. This also explains why they're so bent on growth. "If we can add stores and thereby boost profits," Green explains, "we can give away that much more to make a difference eternally."[10]

- In the mid-1990s, Green was troubled while reading the December 25th edition of a newspaper, by just how little mention of Christmas was in there. So he took it upon himself to address the situation. Hobby Lobby started placing full-page ads in newspapers nationwide every Christmas and Easter, overtly sharing the message of what each day means. Green claims that "Hundreds if not thousands of people … have made their peace with God through this inspirational ad campaign."[11]

- In 2017, the company opened the 430,000 square foot Museum of the Bible, two blocks from The National Mall in Washington D.C. Throughout these eight floors, visitors can peruse artifacts and exhibits from 3,500 years of history, learning about the Bible's message and impact on the world.

All that plus undeniable financial stewardship, turning five talents into five billion. It all flows from Green's premise that the company belongs to God.

And the most authenticating evidence might be this: Because the company "belongs to God," no one in the family, not even David and Barbara Green, can draw from the net worth of the company. In fact, if the company or any part of it were to be sold, according to its legal documents, 90 percent of the proceeds would go to its nonprofit foundation to be dispersed for ministry purposes.

As David is fond of telling his family, "God didn't put any of us here to sit on a yacht."[12] No, but he's clearly anointed Mr. Green to hoist sales and navigate rough waters.

For Further Study

David Green with Dean Merrill, *More Than a Hobby*, Nashville, TN: Thomas Nelson, 2005.

David Green with Bill High, *Giving It All Away ... And Getting It All Back Again*, Grand Rapids, MI: Zondervan, 2017.

Notes

1. Luisa Kroll and Kerry A. Dolan, "The Forbes 400," October 2, 2019, www.forbes.com/forbes-400
2. David Green, *More Than a Hobby*, Nelson Business: Nashville, TN, 2005, p. 17.
3. *More Than a Hobby*, p. 43.
4. Scott S. Smith, "Hobby Lobby's David Green Goes 'By the Book,' Not Conventional Wisdom," *Investor's Business Daily*, May 22, 2017. www.investors.com/news/management/leaders-and-success/hobby-lobbys-david-green-goes-by-the-book-not-conventional-wisdom
5. www.hobbylobby.com/about-us/our-story
6. Interview with Rodney Fouts, at 7:20, published July 9, 2017. www.youtube.com/watch?v=KzRjVDlefHc
7. *Burwell v. Hobby Lobby Stores, Inc.*, 573 US 22 (2014)
8. *More Than a Hobby*, p. 132.
9. Interview with Fouts, at 13:30.
10. *More Than a Hobby*, p. 196.

11. *More Than a Hobby*, p. 162. To view their recent holiday messages, see www.hobbylobby.com/about-us/holiday-messages
12. *More Than a Hobby*, p. 195.

MARTIN'S FAMOUS PASTRY SHOPPE
Honoring God through Excellence

The Lesson

In Christian theology, excellence is a virtue. So companies like Martin's put it at the center of everything they do.

Excellence is not just a value. It's a virtue, "a necessary ingredient in the exercise of faith," according to Christian theology.[1]

In fact, to extend the ingredient metaphor, excellence is essentially the yeast that elevates every other virtue. Believers are not called to have a "satisfactory" work ethic, or to be "pretty good" at humility, or "better than most" at forgiveness. The divine calling is to excel in every area and to keep getting better.

So the same is true in the operation of a business. For the Christian-owned company, there is no such thing as "good enough," only more striving.

Martin's Famous Pastry Shoppe has long been an exemplar. We hear the striving in their mantra—"Whatever it takes, God helping us"—and we see it through their increasingly-global footprint, now at 32 countries on six continents, with annual revenues exceeding $100 million.[2]

Not exactly your neighborhood, mom-and-pop "pastry

shoppe." However, it did start that way in 1955.

Back then, Lois and Lloyd Martin would bake all week in their south-central Pennsylvania garage in preparation for the weekend farmer's markets. Their 1954 Dodge Coronet, with the backseat removed, served as their delivery vehicle.

From that humble beginning, the business grew, led by the popularity of their "potato rolls"—rolls made by replacing some of the wheat flour with potatoes, creating a lighter and more flavorful product. After the couple started distributing through grocery stores, they had to buy a new house to keep up with demand. They converted the back of it to a bakery and the front to a restaurant, serving 130 items. Most were baked goods, which is how the company got its name.

By the late 1970s, the business again relocated to gain capacity. Potato rolls remained their signature; indeed, they were such a distinctive that in 1987 the family closed the restaurant to focus on them entirely. Martin's potato rolls were becoming a sandwich sensation far beyond the rural hills of Chambersburg, impressing even the roll connoisseurs of Philadelphia and New York.

It's here that we learn a profound lesson in the pursuit of excellence: *Martin's preserved the simplicity to excel.* Cutting the product line by more than 90 percent—and it remains at only about a dozen products today—allowed the company to funnel all of its resources toward the best possible product and delivery system. In short, they chose to do fewer things with more excellence, strengthening their competitive advantage.

It's the same approach that enabled world-class companies like McDonald's and Apple to break through. Simplify. *Focus.* Be the best at one thing, ceding everything else to the competition. Wise strategy delineates what you won't do, not just what you will do.

So to this day, Martin's is a bread and roll company. That's it. And through that laser focus they've become the bestselling bread of any kind in the Northeast, and the number-one branded hamburger roll in the entire country, despite not having expanded much beyond the Mississippi. They're dominating in New York City, accounting for one out of every four rolls sold,[3] and they're a differentiator that helped take the stratospherically-successful Shake Shack restaurant to that altitude.

In a moment that revealed how far the company had come, a family member showed Lois Martin a picture of Michelle Obama eating a Shake Shack burger, made with a Martin's roll, asking her: "Grandma, did you ever think the First Lady of the United States would be eating your roll?" Lois replied with a grandmotherly chuckle: "Oh nooo, dear! We were just trying to feed our family."

Now they're feeding families around the world. More and more each year. In 2013, Martin's didn't even track international sales. Five years later, it was ten percent of their business.

That's the yeast of excellence. Faithful excellence. Consider how it leavens these other priorities at Martin's.

With regard to the products, they're made with the finest flour, real cane sugar, and milk to enhance the flavor and the nutritional value. The company could cut costs by about 75 percent if they used whey, corn syrup and water like many other brands, but they're in the business of offering a premium product.

With regard to their employees, they offer a lavish benefit package with a high-end health care plan, tuition assistance, and a six percent contribution to employee pensions. The disposition of second-generation President Jim Martin, the man behind most of the historic growth, is that Martin's should be the employer that best takes care of people's needs.

With regard to charity, the company tithes 13 to 14 percent of its profits every year. They step up generously in crises as well. When a hurricane devastated Houston in 2017, Martin's, who was not even selling in Texas at the time, sent two truckloads of bread— about 45,000 loaves.

With regard to financial stewardship, the company maintains a conservative debt-to-equity ratio, it re-invests most of its profits back into the business, and it's content with a philosophy of slow, steady growth.

And with regard to sharing their faith, the company is gently intentional. Martin's maintains a pluralistic workforce, but on their corporate campus, every welcome mat says "Jesus Christ is Lord," and inscribed on the lobby wall is Mark 8:36: "For what will it profit a man if he gains the whole world, and loses his own soul?" The employee handbook also cites scriptures to illuminate the core values.

Similarly, Martin's serves pluralistic societies, but they print on every package "May God bless all our customers with goodness and health!" and they introduce website visitors to that guiding maxim: "Whatever it takes, God helping us." The witnessing, it seems, both inside and outside the company is nuanced but steadfast. Or, as social media manager Julie Martin puts it: "You have to be careful and yet not ashamed" in your communication of beliefs and values. It's a judicious approach that similar companies might want to adopt.

Overall, and this is the point, Martin's insists on high standards. Relentlessly high, in everything they do, from products to people to profit-distribution to pointing people toward God. But seemingly, it's simply an echo of the down-home diligence of Julie's grandparents, Lloyd and Lois.

And maybe that's what distinguishes Martin's Famous Pastry Shoppe the most—not their world-renowned potato rolls, but the God-honoring pursuit of excellence that gives rise to them. To be faithful, this company shows, is to become exceptional.

For Further Study

Martin's YouTube Channel: www.YouTube.com/user/MartinsPotatoRolls

Website: PotatoRolls.com

Notes

1. Ronald Youngblood, Editor, *Nelson's New Illustrated Bible Dictionary*, Nashville, TN: Nelson, 1995, p. 1296.

2. Much of this story, except where otherwise noted, comes from conversations with Martin's executives in 2019, as well as from its website, PotatoRolls.com.

3. PR Newswire, "Martin's Potato Rolls and Bread are New York City's Favorite," July 19, 2018. www.prnewswire.com/news-releases/martins-potato-rolls-and-bread-are-new-york-citys-favorite-300683352.html

TURBOCAM INTERNATIONAL
SETTING CAPTIVES FREE HALF A WORLD AWAY

The Lesson

If all he did was create 1,000 jobs or contribute to the Space Station, Marian Noronha would have quite a legacy. But along the way, his company also helped end slavery in Nepal.

Could the end of slavery in Nepal really begin at a Burger King in New Hampshire?

Natu Ram thought he would be a slave his entire life. His father was a slave. His grandfather was a slave. But Natu and his son are no longer in bondage because a man named Marian Noronha, Founder of TURBOCAM International in Barrington, New Hampshire, bought his freedom[1] ... and the freedom of dozens more Nepali families.

TURBOCAM, an acronym for TURBOmachinery Computer-Aided Manufacturing, makes precision parts used by other companies in the creation of their products. In particular, they serve the industrial, automotive, propulsion, and aerospace markets, producing a million parts a year, sold as far away as Taiwan.

Actually, farther. You can also find Marian's parts on the Space Station.

43

But you'd never know any of that from the company's mission statement: "TURBOCAM exists as a business for the purpose of honoring God, creating wealth for its employees, and supporting Christian service to God and people." And yes, the themes in that statement trace their roots to the modest setting of a Burger King restaurant, where in 1981 Marian and some friends brainstormed what it would mean for a company to operate on Christian principles.

Fast-food, in fact, may have been a step up for him at the time. When he moved from India to Canada in the late-1970s, Marian arrived with a mere six dollars in his pocket. Five of those were Canadian dollars, but he retained one U.S dollar, representing his hope of someday living in the States.

Eventually, Marian did cross the border, working for a Vermont company that built wind turbines. He later shifted to CAD/CAM programming in Boston where he honed the skills to launch TURBOCAM in 1985.

A few orders from General Motors gave him some traction, but things really took off when he bid on a contract to build turbines for Boeing, a company with a star-spangled insistence of buying American. They found that in TURBOCAM. NASA did too, requesting a component that other suppliers were simply unable to manufacture.

Quality and innovation gave Marian his edge, and they always have. Indeed, his company's motto has long been "Innovate with Grace." Perhaps that explains why they've enjoyed turbocharged growth to nearly 1,000 employees. It's a classic rags-to-riches tale.

However, *where* those riches flow may be the real story here. Of course, there's the reinvestment in the business, enabling TURBOCAM to sustain its competitive advantage. But then, emanating from the mission statement, it's been Marian's goal to generate "wealth for [his] employees" and to "[support] Christian service to God and people."

On the employee side is a long list of benefits, including generous profit sharing and a no-layoff policy during their significant business downturns of 1999 and 2009.[2] Additionally, despite needing to operate seven days a week to satisfy demand, Marian gives everyone Sunday off. His creative, both/and solution was to launch, in 2000, an automated division that builds products without people. Everything is completely unmanned, so Sunday is a productive day for the company, even without anyone in the plant.[3]

It's all culminated in TURBOCAM winning statewide recognition as a model employer.[4] They've won *international* recognition, though, for their mission-based commitment to "Christian service."

Most notable has been their work in Nepal. In 1999, after reading a story in the *London Telegraph* about the plight of Nepali slave families,[5] Marian and a few others set off to that remote country to learn more. What they found were generations of families that owed so much money to their masters—they had been charged for every scrap of food, every aspirin, every garment, and so on—that they accumulated a debt they could never repay. The slaves were also too illiterate to know when a master had added a zero to the end of that bill, perpetuating their confinement.

Worse still, their debts passed to their children, who inherited a life sentence of servitude. And the cycle continued.

With the assistance of some local churches, Marian decided to help directly, paying off the debt of seven families, in essence, buying their freedom. Then he paid the debt of 35 more families in 2000.

He wondered, how many slave debts should his company cancel in the coming years? Hundreds of thousands remained in captivity.

The answer turned out to be *zero*. Inspired by Marian's successful approach, a groundswell of protest ensued in Nepal, demanding that all slaves be freed. In Marian's words, their redeeming of slave families "created enough of a ruckus in the community that eventually, with some folks ... demonstrating down in front of the King's palace, the King declared that slavery was illegal and that was the end."[6]

An extraordinary development, but that *wasn't* the end of the need. The legions of newly-freed families had nothing—no place to live, no jobs, no communities, no schools. So Marian and his TUR-BOCAM employees stepped up to support the transition of at least some of them, creating three towns: ViswasNagar, AshaNagar and PremNagar, meaning Faith Town, Hope Town and Love Town. Here they resettled former slaves by providing land, chlorinated water systems, livestock, microfinance loans and business training, to empower them to become self-sufficient, forever breaking the hold of poverty.

And over the next several years, TURBOCAM helped build six schools to educate more than 1,000 children. For the older kids, much of this included skills-intensive vocational training, permanently elevating their standard of living.

Beyond that, Marian saw a perfect opportunity to introduce these people to Jesus. The redemption these people had experienced was analogous to the gospel message: "You have been set free from slavery," he would tell them. "The same way, you can be set free from your sin."[7] And in the same way that you did nothing to be forgiven your financial debt, you don't need to do anything to be forgiven your sins by God.

Since they *felt* the gospel tangibly in their release, Marian surmised, they might understand the gospel spiritually.

Many have. Among them, all 42 families originally freed by Marian chose to be baptized, an outcome that's at the heart of TUR-BOCAM's mission "to honor God." Marian puts it this way on the company's website: "I started this company as a means of making a living, while also spreading the Good News of salvation through Jesus Christ."[8]

Today, his business ministry continues as Marian still leads TURBOCAM while traveling the globe to speak about how business can transform lives and communities. He's also leveraged TURBOCAM to care for the impoverished of India, South Africa and Haiti, all in the name of "Christian service to God and people."

Meanwhile, back in Nepal, the redeemed have become the redeemers. Natu Ram is now a leader in his community, serving on many boards, including the local school board. His son is a teacher in one of the TURBOCAM schools, and both men have a vision for developing what they say their community needs most: not just farmers and pastors, but doctors, teachers, engineers, pilots and social workers.[9] Their vision is gradually coming to fruition.

It's a vision, though, that Marian Noronha seemed to have a generation ago. Yes, he's built a phenomenal company that delivers components from Earth to the Space Station. But more than that, he's built a company that delivers people from bondage, from New Hampshire to Nepal.

For Further Study

Movie: "Captives," June 2013. Available on DVD and online at www.turbocam.com/videos

TURBOCAM Corporate, "Innovate with Grace," www.youtube.com/watch?v=htSYBU7vlZI

Website: www.Turbocam.com

Notes

1. "Captives," June 2013, Part 3 at 11:00, www.turbo-cam.com/videos
2. TURBOCAM International, "Why TURBOCAM?" www.tur-bocam.com/why-turbocam and "Innovate with Grace," www.youtube.com/watch?v=htSYBU7vlZI
3. "Innovate with Grace," at 6:15.
4. "Innovate with Grace," at 4:45.
5. "TURBOCAM Chosen as One of the Best Companies to Work for in NH," January 13, 2014. www.turbocam.com/announce-ments/turbocam-chosen-as-one-of-the-best-companies-to-work-for-in-nh. For all of its awards, see www.turbo-cam.com/awards

6. Caroline Lees, "Today's Offer in Nepal's Slave Market: Buy One Get One Free," *London Telegraph*, March 15, 1998, p. 28.
7. "Marian Noronha's Powerful Story," www.youtube.com/watch?v=A31UQ-5VM6c at 8:00
8. "Captives," Part 1 at 6:30. www.turbocam.com/videos
9. TURBOCAM International, "Why This Mission?" www.turbocam.com/why-this-mission, accessed October 10, 2019.
10. "Captives," Part 3 at 11:15. www.turbocam.com/videos

PART 2

~

THEIR PRODUCTS
They make products that make a better world

Guinness Brewing Company
D.light Design
Eventide Asset Management
CapinCrouse
The C12 Group
Big Idea Productions

GUINNESS BREWING COMPANY

The Lesson

Influenced by John Wesley, Arthur Guinness brewed quality beer to bring health and wealth to an increasingly sick society.

How does a beer company make it into a book that highlights exemplary Christian-owned companies?

For starters, much of Guinness Brewing Company's 250-year history involves "wealth gained through faith-inspired excellence and then used to serve others for the glory of God," writes Stephen Mansfield, the company's biographer.[1]

The business traces its roots to Arthur Guinness (1725-1803) of Dublin, a devout Christian who parlayed a 100-pound inheritance into the largest enterprise in Ireland. More specifically, the story goes that John Wesley, founder of the Methodist tradition, profoundly influenced Arthur through his admonition to "gain all you can, save all you can, give all you can."

In fact, this seems to be precisely what Arthur did as a businessman and philanthropist. Consider how he cared for his employees. "From the beginning of their corporate and family history, the Guinnesses had embraced their obligation to the needy of the world. This began at home, with their own employees. … Accordingly, the Guinness brewery routinely paid wages that were 10 to 20 percent higher than average, had a reputation as the best place to work in Ireland, and, as important to many employees, allowed workers two pints a day of their famous dark stout."[2]

Even into the twentieth century, the company kept offering benefits that would rival some of the most paternalistic companies of today. How unusual it would be for a factory worker in the 1920s, for example, to have access to an on-site health clinic, company doctors available for house calls, company dentists, pharmacists, nurses, a masseuse, and a consultant to ensure healthy conditions in workers' homes? How unusual would it be to have the majority of the funeral expenses paid for employees and their family members, mortgages available from the company, a company-funded pension with no contribution from workers, and an annual all-expense-paid trip to the countryside for employees and their families?[3]

Arthur Guinness's generosity also extended to the community as the company supported a variety of charities, gave vast amounts to the poor, and built parks, schools, and hospitals. Arthur also famously founded the first Sunday schools in Ireland.[4]

Their cause of caring for the less fortunate continued for generations to come.[5] And all of it was made possible by the quality and competitive advantage of his product. Guinness had produced a porter as good as those in London, and he was wise enough to focus on it, foregoing ales and other popular products. Eventually he expanded beyond Ireland, even penetrating the London market.[6] Later in life, Arthur began brewing variations on the dark beer theme—innovations that would survive long trips overseas and become a direct precursor to the beers brewed today.[7]

But still, how is brewing beer God-honoring?

Understand it in cultural context. In the days before people understood micro-organisms, water made people sick or even killed them because it was polluted with sewage. Many found alcohol to be the safer choice (not necessarily knowing why, but it killed the germs that made water dangerous). In particular, in the U.K., the masses turned to gin as a dietary staple.

However, this "Gin Craze," as it is now labeled by historians, decimated Arthur's world. People in England and Ireland fed gin to infants when they cried. They gave it to children to help them sleep. They consumed it to the point of living intoxicated, indolent and untamed lives. Poverty and crime became rampant, especially in the cities.

A solution, from an individual and societal perspective, was to replace gin with lower-alcohol-content beer. In other words, beer was essentially health food at the time, so for Arthur Guinness and many of his peers, brewing beer was "something of a moral mandate. ... His chosen profession was a service to his fellow man."[8]

The point: Not only was Arthur's generosity toward employees and community an expression of his Christian faith, *the product itself* was an expression of the faith. Indeed, in historical context, brewing beer may have been the most contributory aspect of his ministry.

Centuries later, this global corporation that serves ten-million pints a day is no longer Christian-owned-and-operated, but its legacy remains a formidable and faithful one. "[W]hat distinguishes the Arthur Guinness story is not just that he brewed good beer and sold great amounts of it," concludes Mansfield. "What distinguishes his story is that he understood his success as forming a ... calling of God beyond just himself and his family to the broader good he could do in the world."[9]

For Further Study

Stephen Mansfield, *The Search for God and Guinness: A Biography of the Beer That Changed the World,* Nashville, TN: Nelson Books, 2009.

Stephen Mansfield, "God and Guinness: How the Faith of Arthur Guinness Inspired the Vision for His Beer," *Relevant Magazine,* March / April 2010, pp. 70-74.

Notes

1. Stephen Mansfield, *The Search for God and Guinness: A Biography of the Beer That Changed the World*, Nashville, TN: Nelson Books, 2009, p. xvi.
2. *Ibid.*, p. xix.
3. *Ibid.*, p. xix-xxi.
4. *Ibid.*, p. 38.
5. *Ibid.*, p. 72.
6. *Ibid.*, p. 66-69.
7. *Ibid.*, p. 71-72.
8. *Ibid.*, p. 53.
9. *Ibid.*, p. 59.

D.LIGHT DESIGN
A BRIGHTER FUTURE FOR MILLIONS
IN THE DEVELOPING WORLD

The Lesson

Entrepreneurs who choose to do so can make products that make the world better. At D.light Design, they've made it better 100 million times and counting.

The problem was pervasive. Their invention was ingenious.

2004. While he was working for the Peace Corps in Benin (Africa), one of Sam Goldman's neighbors, a 12-year-old boy, was badly burned. He had accidentally knocked over a kerosene lamp that was lighting his hut.

Around the same time, Xianyi Wu, during summer break from college, was also living among the poor. As he tells it, "I grew up in a Christian family, and in the Bible, Jesus is always hanging out with the poor. ... And I wondered 'Why does he hang out with them?' I had to go and find out for myself."[1]

So Xianyi served for a few months in East Timor (southeast Asia), teaching English and working in a medical clinic.

One day a boy came into his clinic with terrible kerosene burns. Same circumstances as Sam's neighbor. As Sam and Xianyi learned, these boys were among the nearly two-billion people around the world who use fuels like diesel and kerosene *indoors* for lighting because they have no other source of energy. They're completely off the electrical grid, so they live at continual risk of respiratory disease and burns—or worse, as gas fires sometimes consume entire huts, killing everyone inside.

For the privilege of that risk, they pay up to one-third of their income to buy these fuels. It's their only alternative to living in darkness 12 hours a day—until, that is, people like Sam and Xianyi came along, as well as their friends Ned Tozun and Erica Estrada.

The four of them met as Stanford University students in a graduate course called "Design for Extreme Affordability." As a project team, the two engineers and two MBA students set out to invent a rechargeable, solar-powered light for the poor. Xianyi suggested the name D.light, which was not only about lights, but was also inspired by Psalm 37: "Delight yourself in the Lord and he will give you the desires of your heart."[5]

D.light's goal was straightforward: Consumers of energy would become their own producers of energy. Charge a light by day, use it at night. No electrical grid necessary.

It was a radically simple idea, but was it economically feasible, especially in a world where many in their target market live on one or two dollars a day?

The team raised an initial $10,000 to find out, mostly from friends and family, as well as from Ned's church. With that modest capital, they built a better prototype than the one from class ("our first design was actually quite lousy" Xianyi told *Christianity Today*),[2] and they took it directly to the end-users in places like India, Cambodia and Myanmar.

Xianyi tells of one experience when they left the light with a villager. When they asked her a few days later what she thought of the light, her emotion was palpable: "It's *amazing*! Before this, we would sit in the dark killing mosquitoes at night, and we felt hopeless. But with this light, we were able to do our chores, the kids were able to study, we were able to read, we were able to do so many other things. And this has given us hope!"[3]

Indeed, at night, light can turn a house into a home. Xianyi and his friends knew they were onto something big with solar lighting.

World-changing, in fact—what *The Economist* would later call the next great invention to "quickly improve the lives of the world's poorest people."[4]

While still out field-testing, Xianyi opened his email one day to find a picture from Sam and Ned: a $250,000 check made out to their company. Xianyi scoffed, "Photoshop!" and went to bed.

The next morning he called the guys to ask about the joke and they told him that the check was real. They had actually won a prestigious business plan competition! It became a springboard to visibility, credibility and four million dollars in venture capital to launch the company worldwide.

Interestingly, they structured themselves as a for-profit because nonprofits in that industry did not have a rigorous enough business approach to be sustainable. They wondered: "What would happen if we leveraged capitalism and great design to reach more people?"[5]

They would soon find out. By manufacturing in China and taking advantage of the declining costs of solar technology and LED bulbs, they were able to deliver a robust product for about five U.S. dollars, which included the margins for D.light, the distributors and the retailers. Over the next several years, with Sam and Ned at the helm, D.light pieced together a network of more than 100 distribution partners and more than 25,000 distribution outlets on six continents.

And sales? As of this writing, D.light has sold 20 million solar products in 65 countries, touching nearly 100 million people, and reducing carbon dioxide emissions by tons.[6] They've become a top solar lighting brand, an exemplar in the off-grid solar movement.

They've also broadened their product line to rechargeable solar-powered fans with built-in LED lights, as well as lights with USB charger ports. Their products are getting better and better as well—weather-proof and built to last at least five years, with full two-year warranties.

D.light can make that kind of promise because the leadership team has been as focused on quality as they have been on cost containment. Quality is both their value proposition and their social purpose, since it dignifies the person who owns the product—even if the product did only cost five bucks. To some customers, that's a sacrifice of food or medicine. So to D.light, yes, they absolutely owe the customers quality. To them, this is a moral issue, not just a competitive advantage.

It's an inspiring story, though the impetus behind it all may be even more inspiring. Xianyi captured it well in his cogent TED talk. "We can send a man to the moon. We can send a bunch of robots to Mars. I'm sure we can solve the needs of our fellow human beings here on planet Earth."[7] He then quotes the Gospel of Luke as the theological mandate: To everyone who has been given much, much will be expected (Luke 12:48).

Like his colleagues, he sees business as the practical vehicle. "Just like the approach we at D.light take with user-centered products, businesses should be about providing goods and services with the view of adding value to people, and thus society at large, and not focused solely on profit maximization. I wish more Christians believed this."[8]

This is the essence of social entrepreneurship, from a Judeo-Christian perspective. D.light Design is business reframed: a few college kids with a love for the poor, showing everyone the light—customer and capitalist alike.

For Further Study

Chris Horst, "A Designer Lighting the Way to Justice," *Christianity Today*, June 11, 2013. www.christianitytoday.com/thisisourcity/silicon-valley/designer-lighting-way-to-justice.html

TED Talk, "Shedding a Little Light on Poverty: Xian-Yi Wu at TEDxWanChai," August 7, 2013. www.youtube.com/watch?v=vALLndCrp9E

Website: www.dlight.com

Notes

1. "Shedding a Little Light on Poverty: Xian-Yi Wu at TEDxWan-Chai," August 7, 2013. www.youtube.com/watch?v=vALLnd-Crp9E at 2:10.
2. Chris Horst, "A Designer Lighting the Way to Justice," *Christianity Today*, June 11, 2013. www.christianityto-day.com/thisisourcity/silicon-valley/designer-lighting-way-to-justice.html
3. "Shedding a Little Light on Poverty," at 6:40.
4. "Lighting the Way," *The Economist, Technology Quarterly*, September 1, 2012, pp. 10-11.
5. "A Designer Lighting the Way to Justice."
6. www.dlight.com/social-impact
7. "Shedding a Little Light on Poverty," at 14:30.
8. "A Designer Lighting the Way to Justice."

EVENTIDE ASSET MANAGEMENT
INVESTING FOR THE COMMON GOOD

The Lesson

It's a myth that we have to choose between what's profitable and what's ethical. For companies and investors alike, Eventide shows that we can make money while making a difference.

He got his M.D. from Harvard and at the same time a Ph.D. in Chemistry. They were an impressive complement to his MIT engineering degree. Then he went into … investing?

But whatever six-figure debt Finny Kuruvilla might have accrued along the way, it was long ago repaid by his seven-figure salaries. Along with Robin John—a fellow Bostonian, believer, and buddy from high school—Finny launched Eventide Asset Management in 2008, now one of the top performers in the country.

It was not in the original plan, though. At least not their plan.

A couple years earlier, each was becoming increasingly restless with his chosen path. Finny was in health care with dreams of changing the world, and Robin was in public accounting, struggling to see any connection between his work and his faith. Robin had even enrolled in seminary classes in case the calling was to the clergy, but he felt no peace about that direction.

The two friends prayed together for guidance, once a week for six months, "and that's really how Eventide came about," recalls Robin. "We wanted to use our backgrounds, our giftings, our education to honor God."[1]

It's not that the world needed another mutual fund. What it did need, they say God revealed to them, was a mutual fund that invested exclusively in ethical companies, channeling capital toward those that were doing things right.

From a theological standpoint, explains Robin, the guys thought of it like this: "There are business models that are God-pleasing and those that are God-displeasing."[2] Not only should the exemplars be elevated and celebrated, people of conscience should have an easy way to invest in them, thereby advancing the common good.

Eventide, you see, was not just a company. It was a cause.

So they created an audacious vision statement: "Investment that makes the world rejoice."

They created a faithful mission statement: "To honor God and serve our clients by investing in companies that create compelling value for the global common good."

They created a promotional tagline: "Investments designed for performance and a better world."

They created screening criteria to identify companies that take proper care of six stakeholders: customers, employees, supply chain, host communities, the environment, and society at-large.

And they rooted it all in Old and New Testament exegesis: Don't join forces with those who reap ill-gotten gain, even by passively sharing in their gains (Proverbs 1:10-19),[3] and Jesus's command to love your neighbor as yourself (Matthew 22:39)[4]—in particular, those six stakeholder neighbors.

Radical stuff, especially for this industry. *Christianity Today* captured the typical Wall Street reaction: "Theology as a foundation for picking stocks? Are these guys for real?"[5]

A fair question. Their philosophy seems to put them at a clear competitive disadvantage. Possibly a fatal one. After all, the other funds optimize results by selecting from the full universe of investment options. Eventide would select from only the small subset that satisfies its six, stringent criteria.

Robin has a couple retorts.

First, he says, because their approach significantly reduces the number of companies they have to evaluate, it allows them to analyze each one in greater depth and to make better-informed decisions.[6] Second, and more fundamentally, businesses that *create* value for stakeholders—the businesses in which Eventide invests—will prosper over time, whereas businesses that *extract* value from stakeholders, though they may prosper in the short-term, ultimately will have a day of reckoning. In other words, Eventide holdings, on average, should be superior long-term investments.[7]

Well, nice theory gentlemen. If you want my life savings, most would say, you're going to need more than ideas and idealism.

How about a decade of data? Their fund performance seems to be validating the theory, empirically and emphatically. Since inception in 2008, their flagship Gilead Fund (the Hebrew word means "mountain of witness"), where Finny now manages almost three billion dollars in assets, has returned more than 15.5 percent annually.[8] By comparison, the S&P 500 since then has an annual return of 10.1 percent.

And on its ten-year anniversary, Morningstar ranked the Gilead Fund in the top one-percent of its mid-cap growth category (515 funds) for total returns.[9] No wonder Gilead just won another award (to join accolades from *The Wall Street Journal, The New York Times,* and *Bloomberg*), this time from *Investor's Business Daily* as one of the best mutual funds for 2019.[10]

Nice theory, indeed. Who wouldn't take 15.5 percent? As they like to say at Eventide, "What's right is also what's smart."[11]

It's also what gets attention. Despite their crowded industry, Eventide consistently gets lots of positive press. One might say it's becoming a "mountain of witness" to both responsible business management and responsible stock ownership—a faithful way to make money while making a difference.

Perhaps that's even enough to make the world rejoice.

For Further Study

Jeff Haanen, "Investments for the Kingdom," *Christianity Today*, November 23, 2016. www.christianitytoday.com/ct/2016/december/investments-for-kingdom.html

Podcast: "Biblically-Responsible Investing," Center for Christianity in Business, Houston Baptist University, November 18, 2016. hbu.edu/center-for-christianity-in-business/2016/11/18/biblically-responsible-investing-w-robin-john-ceo-eventide-funds

Web site: www.EventideFunds.com

Notes

1. "Biblically-Responsible Investing," Center for Christianity in Business, Houston Baptist University, November 18, 2016. hbu.edu/center-for-christianity-in-business/2016/11/18/biblically-responsible-investing-w-robin-john-ceo-eventide-funds at 3:09
2. "Biblically-Responsible Investing" at 9:45.
3. "Proverbs 1 and the Ethics of Investing," Eventide Asset Management, October 16, 2018. www.youtube.com/watch?v=l4yIjSgxlBs
4. Jeff Haanen, "Investments for the Kingdom," *Christianity Today*, November 23, 2016. www.christianitytoday.com/ct/2016/december/investments-for-kingdom.html
5. "Investments for the Kingdom"
6. "Biblically-Responsible Investing" at 31:00.
7. "Our Approach to Investing," Eventide Asset Management, July 27, 2018. www.youtube.com/watch?v=0S282IYih8k at 0:50.
8. As of this writing, other classes of shares for the Gilead Fund are higher than 15.5 percent—up to 18.2 percent. For the most

current numbers, see Eventide's "Fact Sheet" available at www.eventidefunds.com/our-products

9. "Eventide Gilead Fund Completes First 10yrs Top 1% in Mid-Cap Growth Funds," June 11, 2018. markets.businessinsider.com/news/stocks/eventide-gilead-fund-completes-first-10yrs-top-1-in-mid-cap-growth-funds-1027360201

10. "Eventide Gilead Fund Named One of the 2019 Best Mutual Funds by Investor's Business Daily," April 18, 2019. www.eventidefunds.com/news/eventide-gilead-fund-named-one-of-the-2019-best-mutual-funds-by-investors-business-daily

11. "Our Approach to Investing" at 1:00.

CapinCrouse
Helping Nonprofits Help More People

The Lesson

Poor management leads to poor performance. When that happens in a ministry, there may be even more at stake. For 50 years, CapinCrouse has been on a mission to prevent that.

It all started at Madison Square Garden.

In 1961, Richard "Dick" Capin (pronounced kay'-pin) was a young CPA attending his first post-season NCAA basketball game, something he had always wanted to do. Now he was finally there, in the Garden nonetheless.

But amidst the chants and cheers, it was a voice from the Garden of Eden he would hear most clearly in that place.

"Go Cross go! Go Cross go!" shouted the student body of one of the teams, Holy Cross. As Dick recalls, it was at that very moment that "all of a sudden, the Lord began to speak to me. ... God put in my heart that one soul is worth all the world, and *that cross* is the only answer for the souls of the world."[1]

It was jarring. He walked out of the arena and onto the streets of New York, where he contemplated God's message, ultimately asking God to allow him to share the message of the cross with the world. It would mean leaving accounting, he discerned, and becoming a missionary in Asia.

But God had much more to say to Dick. As one biographer writes: "as he traveled the world, he saw men and women doing office work they hardly understood ... which took away from their call to take Christ to a dark and sinful world."[2]

Ministry leaders didn't understand accounting and financial management, and their clumsy handling of it distracted from their mission. Worse still, since they couldn't properly account for the funds, it undermined their ability to raise desperately-needed new money. And even worse than that, lack of basic systems was creating chaos for them, putting many on the verge of insolvency.

It was a revelation to Dick: Ineffective management created ineffective ministry around the world.

He helped them out where he could, designing and implementing systems to fortify the ministries and relieve missionaries from day-to-day operations.[3] After years of assisting ad hoc, God's call on his life was clearer than ever: "God showed a need for an accounting firm, one especially equipped to assist Christian ministries."[4]

Of course, the man to whom God revealed this was himself "especially equipped," in both skill and will. Dick returned to accounting in the U.S. in the late 1960s and within a few years, he was in a position to build that firm. Partnering with a recent accounting graduate, C.E. Crouse, who had just returned from his own stint as a missionary in Asia, the two set out to provide accounting and consulting services to faith-based nonprofits.

The demand was overwhelming and through the 1970s and 1980s, CapinCrouse grew steadily. Headquartered in Greenwood, Indiana, they started opening offices near major metropolitan cities. Today they have 15 offices nationwide, serving 1,500 nonprofit clients who operate in 60 countries. Their church clients host more than 500,000 church attendees each week; their higher education clients serve 100,000 students a year; their rescue mission clients serve 13,000 meals a day.[5]

It's all aligned by one mission, though—the original mission that God placed on Dick Capin's heart: to serve "organizations whose outcomes are measured in lives changed."[6] It was never about company growth, it was never about profit. It was always about helping those who help others—"empowering nonprofits," as their tagline says.

The mission has also supercharged their workforce. Among the many benefits of working for CapinCrouse, as one of their recruiting videos portrays, is the nature of the work itself. One by one, employees turn to the camera and reveal what they do:

"Today, I will help … an organization that educates students in China … an organization that provides rehabilitation services for those struggling with drug and alcohol addiction … a relief organization that offers pharmaceuticals to the needy … an organization that rescues women and girls from abuse and exploitation … an organization that provides relief to a poverty-stricken nation."[7]

It's enough to get you out of bed on a rainy Monday morning. They know it's raining harder somewhere else. Or, as they like to say in this company, "it's not about doing accounting, but about doing ministry through accounting."[8]

Dick is in awe of what it's become. "I remember thinking it would take me about five years to put a firm together and then I'd be returning to a role more directly hands-on in evangelizing the nations. I had no idea the scope God had in mind."[9]

Good thing, perhaps, because the vision was even more daunting than strengthening his clients. What God had in mind for Dick was to positively influence *every* Christian ministry, whether or not it was a client. The need was everywhere.

Dick began to do that in 1979 by helping found the Evangelical Council for Financial Accountability (EFCA) and serving as a board member, the treasurer and eventually, as board chair. The EFCA is an accreditation body—a standard-setter for biblical accountability of nonprofits—that has effectively shepherded all U.S. ministries away from the wild west of financial practices, toward good stewardship.

All? Yeah, pretty much. Even if a Christian nonprofit is not accredited by the EFCA, they now operate in a world where there is an EFCA-inspired expectation that ministries will be run professionally and transparently, with full integrity in fundraising, operations and board governance.

Plain English: Leaders like Dick Capin raised the bar for ministry stewardship and effectiveness by providing tools for these ministries to succeed. Christian nonprofits—whether churches or schools or outreach organizations or foundations—are now better managed and more credible to prospective donors, keeping the money flowing toward their worthy causes and keeping integrity violations to a minimum.

Plainer English: Christian ministries around the globe are more effective today because of Capin-led organizations like the EFCA and CapinCrouse. It's inarguable.

It's also incredible for a humble man like Dick. "I sit back in amazement that God could take a young man from a small town in southern Illinois … and use what he had gifted me with."[10] And while it may not be the most captivating story in a book like this—the more intriguing stories tend to be of companies making a more direct impact—the indirect influencers like CapinCrouse are just as integral to change.

That's because bad management is a disease. It debilitates. It disables. If left untreated, it destroys an organization.

But behind the scenes, giving God all the glory, CapinCrouse offers a cure, in turn empowering nonprofits to cure a broken world.

For Further Study

Bob Kelly, *Giving Account: Life Lessons of Businessman and Accountant Dick Capin*, Greenwood, IN: CapinCrouse, LLP, 2012.

"The CapinCrouse Story: Building on Our Legacy," July 16, 2018. Vimeo.com/202384263

Websites: CapinCrouse.com and EFCA.org

Notes

1. "The CapinCrouse Story: Building on Our Legacy," July 16, 2018. Vimeo.com/202384263 at 0:45.
2. Bob Kelly, *Giving Account: Life Lessons of Businessman and Accountant Dick Capin*, Greenwood, IN: CapinCrouse, LLP, 2012, p. 54.
3. "Our History," CapinCrouse.com/who-we-are/about-capin-crouse/our-history
4. *Giving Account*, p. 55.
5. "The CapinCrouse Story: Building on Our Legacy" at 0:00.
6. "Our Mission and Values," CapinCrouse.com/who-we-are/about-capincrouse/our-mission-and-values
7. "What Will You Do Today?" Vimeo.com/187215862
8. "Our History," CapinCrouse.com/who-we-are/about-capin-crouse/our-history
9. *Giving Account*, p. 55.
10. "The CapinCrouse Story: Building on Our Legacy" at 4:40.

THE C12 GROUP
BUILDING GREAT BUSINESSES
FOR A GREATER PURPOSE

The Lesson

Business owners often mentor their people, but who mentors them? The C12 Group designed a system that grows both an owner's business and his or her walk with God.

He's arguably the Steve Jobs of business consulting, at least to many Christians. He has simply built a better product than anyone else.

But let's back up to the 1990s.

The problem was this: Christian business owners had trouble finding solid advice about how to run their businesses faithfully. The solution was this: Monthly events where owners could hear engaging speakers and network with one another.

Except that it didn't work very well.

In 1992, Buck Jacobs,[1] a successful businessman, left the corporate world to work for an organization that used this very model — a meal, a speaker or a video, and some fellowship time. The organization had been growing steadily since the late 1970s, with about 100 chapters across 30 U.S. cities. However, their donations-driven model, though viable from a financial perspective, didn't produce results that really mattered.

A least that was Buck's conclusion after being on the inside for a while.

Attendance was patchy, as was the business owners' voluntary financial support, and more importantly, there didn't seem to be much progress in business acumen or spiritual maturity. According to Buck, participants seemed unchanged by these meetings, as were their companies. So what was the point?

The dysfunction mattered to Buck. There was a lot at stake. When leaders change, companies change. When companies change, their stakeholders may change—employees, customers, suppliers, the community. Maybe even entire societies. And since these were presumably God's companies that Buck was serving, it was too big a responsibility to squander.

He had some ideas, though. Increase their skin in the game—make it fee-for-service rather than donations-based. And offer a confidential space for transparency, hard questions and customized business coaching from wise advisors. Plus, unleash the permanent change that only accountability can provide.[2]

More specifically, Buck envisioned about a dozen Christian business owners in a classy facility for a monthly, all-day retreat. During the first half of the day, they'd discuss read-ahead material about faith-based management. During the second half, they'd tackle one of the members' specific challenges, giving that person a brain trust to solve problems and supercharge their business.

As members grew more comfortable with one another, Buck surmised, the questions would get more uncomfortable—penetrating questions about their treatment of employees, their integrity in finances and advertising, their business tithing, as well as more personal questions about their anger or lust or parenting or the extent to which they're really honoring God with their lives.

No softballs, no sacred cows, no condemnation. Nothing's off limits and nothing leaves the room.

From Buck's perspective, this was simply a Jesus model: a group of 12 disciples sharpening one another to elevate their companies, their leadership, their families and their walk with God. As such, it was also a genius model. Buck started seeing genuine transformation in his pilot testing, something so elusive in his current employer's approach. People were growing, businesses were growing, group members kept investing.

The point is this: Buck Jacobs had designed a superior system of personal and professional development for Christian business owners. It was a masterpiece.

But then his organization rejected it.

Maybe they just didn't buy-in to the model. Or maybe there was too much inertia in their own system. Regardless, Buck did what entrepreneurs do when they see demand with no supply: He set out on his own, launching a for-profit business to build these groups around the country.

It was a leap of faith at age 54, especially with a daughter headed to college and another two behind her. Then again, Buck and his wife Bonnie are people of deep faith.

Originally calling it "The Christian 12 Group"—later streamlined to "C12"—Buck formed a board of directors, wrote a business plan, and crafted a mission about changing the world through faithful business owners.

And, as Buck predicted, it took off. What began as a few guys around some tables in Florida became, group by group, city by city, state by state, year by year, the nation's largest network of Christian CEOs, business owners and executives. According to *Forbes*, on the 25th anniversary of C12, it had grown to 250 franchises serving about 1,800 business owners, who themselves served tens of millions of employees, customers and vendors.[3]

During that time, C12 has itself been a profitable business. Members pay an executive-sized fee—several thousand dollars a year—to be part of a group, and most of them maintain membership for years because there's more value in this than anything else they've tried. For them, C12 is more than a CEO roundtable or a business Bible study. It's a personal consulting team that advances their businesses while also helping them become better people. They emerge more successful in every sense of the word, including in the most important sense: doing what God has called them to do in life.

Again, it's the product design. Better design equals better results.

The same is true for the organization as a whole. The design makes the difference. Buck didn't lead all the C12 groups, of course. He franchised them, offering franchisees an exclusive, business-rich territory to create multiple groups of business owners and, more recently, of "key players" (Christians near but not at the top of their organization). The franchisees—typically former business owners or Fortune 500 executives—facilitate the monthly peer-advisory groups while also coaching each group member one-on-one. In fact, it seems they're the lynch pins in all this. The group leader's efficacy drives the product efficacy, which in this case drives the transformation of businesses and lives.

A few quotes from C12 members capture the transformational power of this system:[4]

- "C12 has changed the entire direction of my company. We have made the transition from a greedy, profit-centered company to one that is Christ-centered."

- "The accountability has kept me from making some incredibly painful and costly mistakes. It also keeps me focused to use this business as a platform for ministry."

- "C12 members are brutally honest, but in a loving way. This is one of the reasons C12 is such a high priority in my life. There is nothing like it."

- "I have never felt so close to God in my entire life and I credit a major part of that to the inspiration that C12 gives me on a monthly basis."

- "I got in it initially because I thought I'd get some good business advice … but I never anticipated that a total, holistic, personal development would happen because of it."

We see a pattern in just these five responses. It could be fifty or five hundred responses and we'd see the same pattern: business change, life change. C12 groups set the bar high and members rise to the level of excellence expected of them.

Like any good visionary, Buck Jacobs saw that before it happened. Or, he'd say, God showed it to him. Either way, to quote their incisive motto, The C12 Group continues "building great businesses for a greater purpose."

For Further Study

Buck Jacobs with Kenneth R. Overman, *I, Radical: God's Radical Business through an Ordinary Man*, 2014.

Jerry Bowyer, "Does God Belong in the Boardroom? 1,800 CEOs Say Yes," *Forbes*, August 12, 2016. www.forbes.com/sites/jerrybowyer/2016/08/12/does-god-belong-in-the-boardroom-1800-ceos-say-yes

Website: www.C12group.com

Notes

1. Some of this story derives from a personal interview with Buck Jacobs in 2004.
2. Buck Jacobs with Kenneth R. Overman, *I, Radical: God's Radical Business through an Ordinary Man*, 2014. p 113.
3. Jerry Bowyer, "Does God Belong in the Boardroom? 1,800 CEOs Say Yes," *Forbes*, August 12, 2016. www.forbes.com/sites/jerrybowyer/2016/08/12/does-god-belong-in-the-boardroom-1800-ceos-say-yes
4. Testimonies gleaned from www.theC12group.com (cached) and www.C12group.com

BIG IDEA
PRODUCTIONS
A TRIUMPHANT AND TRAGIC (VEGGIE)TALE

The Lesson

Phil Vischer's creative genius birthed a special company.
His executive team's creative forecasting killed it.

This is a story of a children's film producer who refused to sell out. But his videos sure did.

In 1990, Phil Vischer had a big idea: Produce a Christian counterpart to the secular, Saturday morning cartoons. Teach kids values without sacrificing fun. Help turn around a dying culture!

If that didn't work, he at least wanted to provide his own kids with an animated, Biblically-based program.

One problem, though. With almost no budget, Phil's computer animation would be limited. Special effects were out. So were elaborate characters. Even arms, legs and clothes were a stretch. What possibly was left?

Vegetables. More specifically, talking vegetables.

So Phil and his partner, college buddy Mike Nawrocki, created a twelve-second clip of "Larry the Cucumber" bouncing around on a kitchen counter—a unique calling card as they sought funding for a full video.

Alas, though, no takers. No surprise either. After all, these weren't just talking vegetables; these were *religious* talking vegetables. Big ideas don't get much more bizarre than this.

But Phil's family and friends didn't see it that way. His parents took out a second mortgage, his sister loaned him her son's college fund, and a couple from church invested their retirement savings. Capital in hand, Phil launched Big Idea Productions in 1993 out of a spare bedroom and began to market through Christian magazines the first "VeggieTales" video, "Where's God When I'm S-Scared?"

He received about 500 orders ... which didn't even pay for the ads. Phil persevered, though, and caught a break in 1994 when Word Publishing agreed to distribute VeggieTales to Christian bookstores. The Veggies got rave reviews, but still, disappointing sales.

Later that year, an even more enticing offer from a different distributor: Phil could place his loquacious legumes in every Walmart in America. Larry would become a friend to millions and Phil would become a millionaire.

Just one catch: To close the deal, Phil had to delete both God and the Bible from his stories.

The situation epitomized the word *dilemma.* Phil's response epitomized the word *principled.* They were broke at the time, so it clearly was tempting. But how could they teach God's truth and edit out God? Big Idea couldn't, so they didn't. They declined the offer and pressed on toward their mission to "promote biblical values and encourage spiritual growth."

In 1995, word-of-mouth advertising pushed video sales to 130,000. So the video distributors revised their offer: "We don't mind the theism, but could you take the Bible verse off the end?"

"No deal," said Phil. "Our teaching has a Biblical base and we don't want to cut that off."

The buzz grew louder. Sales snowballed. Pastors were wearing Veggie ties to the pulpit. Big Idea distributed its two-millionth video in 1997. And back came the suitors, this time ready to do business on Phil's terms. "We want them just as they are. How soon can we get them?" [1]

Phil chose Lyrick Studios as his distribution partner, and in 1998, the company sold 6.2 million videos, making VeggieTales the bestselling Christian video series ever.

Predictably, perhaps, Big Idea then turned to bigger ideas. Could they become The Christian Disney, providing Biblically-based entertainment on that scale? Maybe that had been the calling ever since high school when Phil was making videos in his basement, rather than going to the prom.

But he was an artist and a Bible school dropout, not an MBA who could run a large, complex organization. So, flush with cash at that point, he hired people who could—an all-star executive team, in fact, from places like PriceWaterhouse, GE, Kraft and Coca-Cola. Then Phil did his best to stay out of their way.

Revenue grew to $44 million in 1999 (by comparison, it was $1.3 million in 1996) and Big Idea began work on their first full-length, animated movie, based on the story of Jonah. Meanwhile, the new executive team staffed the company to maintain momentum and accelerate growth. Big Idea's marketing department, for example, swelled from one person in 1998 to 30 people in 2000.

The broader plan was to take the company to more than 300 employees in the next year, which would have been fine had they hit their wildly-ambitious revenue projections. But in January 2000, Big Idea missed their sales forecast by 80 percent; that is, they sold *one-fifth* what the new executive team had projected. By the end of the year, sales were still horizontal while expenses were going vertical. The cost of the Jonah movie kept spiraling as well, now triple its original budget of seven million dollars.

"I had made a huge mistake," wrote Phil years later. "I was running the company blind."[2]

Now, eyesight restored, he started benching his all-stars—firing the President, the head of marketing, and the sales VP. Phil's CFO left in protest. In May 2001, Phil had no choice but to layoff 15 percent of the company (leading one employee to circulate an email asking "Where's God When I'm F-Fired?").

Phil also sought a different distributor, one that would give them more visibility and better representation with the retailers.

Their deal with Lyrick Studios was merely verbal—it had never been˜ signed—so Phil switched to Warner Brothers. But that prompted a costly lawsuit, which then prevented the company from borrowing desperately-needed capital.

Declining sales, mass layoffs, an expensive lawsuit, cash drying up: Perhaps the Jonah movie could save the company in 2002?

Its first weekend alone grossed $6.5 million, on its way to $25 million overall—a new record for Christian films at the time. However, even that couldn't prevent the company from being swallowed by its whale of a financial crisis. In fact, the final tally showed that the Jonah project didn't even pay for itself.

Then, the coup de grace in 2003: The verdict in federal court. Despite the distributor agreement having never been signed, a jury decided that Big Idea violated its "contract" with Lyrick Studios—a contract based on a document that clearly said it was not binding. Worse still, the jury gave Lyrick everything it asked for: $11 million in damages plus legal fees.

In Phil's epitaphic words, "Big Idea Productions was dead."[3] And it was sent off in a makeshift casket, apparently: "Every character I created, every song I had written, every story I had told was packed up in a box and sold to the highest bidder."[4]

There's an epilogue to this as well—a tragic, Shakespearean epilogue. In August 2005, the Fifth Circuit Court of Appeals unanimously overturned the Lyrick Studios verdict. They said the decision was plainly wrong in light of the facts, as was the financial judgment against Big Idea.[5]

Redemption? Yes. Resurrection? No.

Phil explains: "The bankruptcy sale had taken place; the assets had been sold to cover the debt. None of that could be reversed."[6] Big Idea Productions, though cleared of any wrongdoing, was still dead.

And while this is a case study in both principled and unprincipled management, edifying too is Phil Vischer's reaction to it all. Rather than being bitter with Lyrick, with his executive team, with himself, or with God, Phil has peace about it.

Why didn't God show up in the courtroom to rescue Big Idea?

Phil says it's not for him to know. Why didn't God help him become the Christian Walt Disney and change the culture? It's not for Phil to know.

Phil's posture is humble, not huffy. Reverent, not resentful.

"If I'm a Christian," he shrugs with a smile, "if I've given Christ lordship of my life, then where I am in 20 years is none of my business. Where I am in five years is none of my business. Where I am tomorrow is none of my business. The only thing that *is* my business is 'what has he asked me to do today, and am I doing it? Am I walking with him? Am I sharing his love with every person I encounter?'"[7]

Not exactly a garden-variety response. But it's a deeply instructive one for disappointed disciples everywhere. Despite the injustice, the broken dreams, and the lost fortune, Phil Vischer has modeled how to be one cool cucumber about it all.

For Further Study

Phil Vischer, *Me, Myself, & Bob: A True Story About Dreams, God, and Talking Vegetables*, Nashville, TN: Thomas Nelson, 2006.

Notes

1. Carolyn C. Armistead, "Vegetarian Humor...Bob the Tomato and Larry the Cucumber Reflect Christian Values," *Chicago Tribune*, February 15, 1998, "Tempo" section, p. 1.
2. Phil Vischer, *Me, Myself, & Bob: A True Story About Dreams, God, and Talking Vegetables*, Nashville, TN: Thomas Nelson, 2006, p. 171.
3. *Me, Myself, & Bob*, p. 196.
4. 100 Huntley Street interview with Phil Vischer, published July 16, 2009. www.youtube.com/watch?v=aJw_njstsNg at 1:01.

5. *Lyrick Studios, Inc. v. Big Idea Productions, Inc.*, 420 F.3d 388 (5th Cir. 2005).

6. *Me, Myself, & Bob*, p. 259.

7. 100 Huntley Street interview, at 4:20.

PART 3

THEIR PROFITS
They fund faithful causes

Domino's Pizza
Auntie Anne's Pretzels
TOMS Shoes
Pura Vida Coffee
Altar'd State
Barnhart Crane & Rigging
Bridgeway Capital Management
4 Rivers Smokehouse

DOMINO'S PIZZA

The Lesson

With great success comes great temptation. Tom Monaghan succumbed to that, until an even greater power gave him a way out.

Four-year-old Tom stood before his father's casket. It wasn't fair. It didn't make sense. Why would God take his daddy? And why, of all times, on Christmas Eve?

He reached in to shake his father, screaming "Daddy, wake up! Wake up!" Tom's family led him away as he kept shouting to his dad, his hero. *"Wake up!"*[1] Even the mortician was moved by the scene.

His father's passing changed Tom's life forever. So did his mother's subsequent decision to send Tom and his younger brother to a foster home. Psychologically, she just couldn't handle them.

Two years later, after moving from home to home, the boys landed in a Catholic orphanage. There it became clear that Tom wasn't going to be an academic superstar, but he did earn a reputation for efficiency. Tom could iron a pile of laundry faster than anyone at the orphanage, and with the next heap, he'd try to beat his own record.

It would lay the foundation for a business built on speed.

When Tom was 12, his mother finally brought the boys back

home. Tom was different, though, having been influenced by the nuns and priests for so long. In fact, their impression was so indelible that by ninth grade, Tom decided he too wanted to be a priest. But his mischievous side would be his undoing. The seminary expelled Tom for pillow fighting, talking in study hall, and not writing to his mother often enough.

Not exactly "high crimes and misdemeanors," but in the 1950s it was enough to get a seminary kid paddled out the door.

Tom did eventually complete high school, albeit graduating last in his class,[2] and then enlisted in the military to earn college money. In 1959, at age 22, Tom finally enrolled at the University of Michigan.

Soon thereafter, he bought a failing pizza restaurant to fund his education—despite having no idea how to make pizza.[3] Hundred-hour weeks gave him plenty of practice, though, and his enormous effort stabilized the business. However, it became clear that Tom was going to have to choose: college or company?

Tom chose the latter and in a masterstroke, focused the company for both excellence and lower cost, slashing the menu to just pizza and just the most popular toppings. He also focused on the target market he knew best: college students.

But it was another masterstroke that led to explosive growth: pizza delivered in 30 minutes or less. Here again was that penchant for productivity, dating back to the orphanage. It was also a penchant for pragmatics. What good are fresh ingredients and perfectly cooked pizza, Tom reasoned, if the food arrives cold?

Hard work plus low cost plus a niche plus a tasty product delivered fast. Tom Monaghan, it seemed, had developed a hand-tossed recipe for success.

So he opened two more stores in college towns. And then a few more. And then a lot more. Three decades later, in 1990, Domino's Pizza boasted nearly 5,000 franchises and 54 percent of all the pizzas delivered in the United States.

Of course, there were plenty of bumps in the road—like the trademark infringement suit from Domino Sugar, and the ongoing allegations that Tom's speeding drivers caused accidents. Then there was the strident, late-80s boycott by the National Organization for Women. Tom's offense? Donating to pro-life causes. For several years, a few cents of Tom's proceeds from every pizza made their way to right-to-life organizations.

Like the other challenges, Domino's navigated the boycott, undeterred and virtually untouched financially. When the dust settled from the contribution kerfuffle, Tom's net worth was still close to a billion dollars.

In a way, the Tom Monaghan story unfolded like a Charles Dickens novel—rags-to-riches for a grieving-but-gritty orphan boy. But there's another dimension to the story, one that unfolded more like a Gospel parable. It might be told like this:

Once there was a poor man who became very rich by delivering pizzas. And as he did, he denied himself nothing, buying houses, helicopters, planes, yachts and hundreds of classic cars. He splurged on twelve thousand dollar watches, seven thousand dollar vases, and a 2,500-acre golf resort. He even bought the beloved baseball team of his youth, the Detroit Tigers, for $53 million.

Along the way, the man also did many good things externally, donating lots of money. He was a Christian, after all. But internally, the man had never really surrendered his life to God. The man's heart was hard and his extravagant living reflected that—until, that is, another man named C.S. Lewis performed some CPR.

Studying Lewis's book, *Mere Christianity*, the man read about something called "pride."[4] He had certainly considered the sin before, but this time his eyes were opened—literally as well as figuratively—as the man lay awake all night taking inventory of his life, wrestling with the icy awareness that his prodigal lifestyle had been nothing more than "to get attention, to have people notice me."[5]

Regardless his generosity and his professed faith, the man realized that his god was really himself and his reputation. He had become the world's pizza delivery king while only paying lip service to the King who had delivered him.

End of parable; beginning of total transformation. For Tom Monaghan, C.S. Lewis's insight was as shocking as Tom's moment at the casket. "I realized that I had more pride than any person I know," he said of the epiphany. "I'm the biggest hypocrite there is."[6]

It was not just a call to awareness, but to action. "None of these things I've bought, and I mean none of them, have ever really made me happy," admitted Tom. "So anything I've got that gives me pleasure only for selfish reasons, I'm selling."[7]

Thus began in the early 1990s what the *Wall Street Journal* called "an extraordinary renunciation of material assets."[8] Labeling it "a millionaire's vow of poverty,"[9] Tom halted construction of his 20,000 square foot dream house, which was one-third complete, and sold the helicopter, the yacht, the plane, the resort, and even the baseball team, earmarking much of the money for the church.

And in 1998, he sold his company to Bain Capital for one billion dollars. All the money he made through Domino's would go to build an intentionally–Catholic university in Florida,[10] and to a plethora of other faith-based causes.

So although Domino's Pizza is no longer a Christian-owned company, its story offers a valuable lesson in Christian entrepreneurship. Diligence, quality, serving wants and needs better than anyone else—these are God-honoring virtues, and lucrative ones at that.

The story also offers a valuable lesson in Christian discipleship. Tom Monaghan, still one of the world's great philanthropists, now chooses to live in a college dorm[11] and often says that his goal is to die broke.

He's well on his way, but as a result, he'll probably die richer than he ever was.

For Further Study

Joseph Pearce, *Monaghan: A Life,* Charlotte, NC: TAN Books, 2016.

Notes

1. Joseph Pearce, *Monaghan: A Life,* Charlotte, NC: TAN Books, 2016, p. 24.
2. "Tom Monaghan In 30 Minutes Or Less," *Entrepreneur*, October 10, 2008. www.entrepreneur.com/article/197674
3. *Monaghan: A Life*, p. 56.
4. *Monaghan: A Life*, pp. 146-157. See also the chapter "The Great Sin" in C.S. Lewis, *Mere Christianity*, New York: MacMillan Publishing Company, 1952.
5. "The private penance of Tom Monaghan," *The Detroit News*, November 17, 1991, p. 1A.
6. *Ibid.* See also Dottie Enrico, "Roots of ambition: Childhood experiences of orphaned, adopted ignite drive to thrive," *USA Today*, September 5, 1997, p. 1B.
7. *Ibid.*
8. Richard Gibson, "Domino's Pizza to be sold for $1 billion: Founder to turn attention to philanthropy," *The Wall Street Journal Europe*, September 28, 1998, p. 11.
9. *Monaghan: A Life*, p. 156.
10. See www.AveMaria.edu/campus/about-ave-maria
11. "Tom Monaghan," Giants for God, www.youtube.com/watch?v=KscTniDGOC0 at 5:57.

AUNTIE ANNE'S PRETZELS
PURPOSE OUT OF PAIN

The Lesson

Anne Beiler started a little pretzel company to support her husband's free marriage counseling service. To date, they've served thousands of couples by serving millions of customers.

They were living the good life, at least as it's defined in Pennsylvania's Amish country.

Anne and Jonas Beiler, raised Amish, married when she was 19 and he was 21. Their goals were modest: a quiet, peaceful life, except for the noise of their children. According to Anne, "In my early teens, my whole dream was to be a wife and a mom and to have my own family. That was my goal. ... 'Career' is not really in the vocabulary of Amish people, so I really had no dreams or plans beyond family life."[1]

The couple helped start a church in Lancaster County and served as the youth pastors. Soon they were pastoring children of their own, daughters LaWonna and Angela. Their life was becoming just what they imagined it would be.

And then everything changed.

One September morning, as 19-month-old Angela was toddling

across the yard, she was struck by a farm vehicle. Compounding the tragedy, Anne's sister was behind the wheel.

Anne was in her kitchen at the time. "Screaming," she would later write. "That's all I remember. Horrendous screaming." And the voice of her father outside. "I had never heard that voice before, full of panic and too-late despair. Then another round of screaming, this time women's voices. *No*, I thought, *not Angie*."²

Anne's father ran into the house. "In his arms he cradled a tiny bundle wrapped in child's pajamas." Angie was gone.

None of it made sense. "Growing up," recalls Anne, "I always believed that if I love God and keep his commandments, he would bless me and life will be wonderful."³

It was. Then, suddenly and inexplicably, it wasn't. "The first half of the 1970s presented us with five years of happy marriage and our first two daughters. The second half became a long walk through the kind of darkness I never knew existed."⁴

In fact, that darkness included more than just the accident. There were ripple effects. Anne sought counsel from their pastor, but he took advantage of her vulnerability, seducing her, luring her into what would become a six-year affair that Jonas knew nothing about. When Anne finally confessed to her husband, it shattered him. "The look on his face said it all for me," Anne lamented, certain it was over.

Out of desperation, Jonas met with a counselor and received breakthrough advice: "I don't want to set you up for failure and more devastation, but if there is a chance you can salvage your marriage, it will be because you're able to love your wife the way Christ loves you."⁵

"That changed my life forever," explains Jonas. It gave him fresh perspective, prompting him to tell his wife: "I do want you to be happy. I'll do whatever I can to help you. ... Just tell me if you want to go. I'll help you find a place and help you pack your bags, but you have to take the girls with you (they had another daughter at that point) because they need their mom."⁶

Anne was overwhelmed. Astonished. Jonas's unmerited, unqualified grace offered a spark of hope. Within days the couple vowed never to talk about divorce again, vowing instead to make it work. To this day, decades later, they have.

It's a captivating story. Ruin, then restoration. Heartbreak, then daybreak. But what does any of this have to do with those irresistible soft pretzels at the mall?

Only everything. You see, after experiencing the power and potential of marriage counseling, Jonas wanted to do that for others—in particular, those from the Amish-Mennonite tradition because, he says, "they're mostly quiet when they go through hard times." So he and Anne started counseling couples in their home while, to support the family, Anne started selling food at farmer's markets.

More specifically, she sold pretzels.

The thinking was this: If she could pay the bills, Jonas could counsel full-time, charging couples nothing for his services. That would be the game plan for this new team. Anne puts it poignantly, almost proverbially: "Out of our pain, our purpose was born."[7]

Another surprise: Even though Anne had never baked a soft pretzel before, hers became bestsellers at the farmer's market. Revenue grew. Anne bought another store that year. In the three years that followed, the business increased to 12 stores, then 35, and then 50. They found an angel investor—a chicken farmer who gave them $1.5 million on a handshake.[8] By 1995, a mere seven years after peddling her first pretzel, Auntie Anne's had expanded all the way to Jakarta, Indonesia.

This despite Anne Beiler's admitted ignorance about entrepreneurship. "(I was) in a world I knew nothing about. Business? Zero. Franchising? Below zero. Nothing. I didn't even know what the word meant."[9]

She knew how to work hard, though. She knew how to be diligent, how to persevere. Amish values run deep. "Without that experience (growing up), I would probably never have been able to fulfill the mission of Auntie Anne's because it was intense, it was hard work, and it was nonstop."[10]

Deeper still is where those values came from. Throughout the launch and expansion, Anne says, "I knew it was not about us. It was about God. It was about his plan. It was about Auntie Anne's becoming a company of excellence."[11]

The proof is in the proliferation. When Anne sold the business in 2005 to Sam Beiler, the company's President and C.O.O. (and her second cousin), it had grown to 850 locations in 43 states and 12 other countries. Currently, Auntie Anne's has about 1,500 locations worldwide, with about $200 million in system-wide revenue.

Indeed, it is a company of excellence.

And more importantly to Anne, it is a company of benevolence, enabling Jonas and his team of counselors to bless thousands of couples, families and individuals with free services. *Thousands.*

That was their purpose from the beginning: start a company to fund a ministry. You could say that Auntie Anne's Pretzels is a faithful twist on what a business can be.

For Further Study

Anne Beiler with Shawn Smucker, *Twist of Faith: The Story of Anne Beiler, Founder of Auntie Anne's Pretzels*, Nashville, TN: Thomas Nelson, 2008

"Interview with Anne Beiler," Right Now Media, www.youtube.com/watch?v=HSlrkv6TuVw

Dinah Eng, "Auntie Anne's: Soft Pretzels Out of Hard Times," *Fortune,* July 22, 2013. Fortune.com/2013/07/08/auntie-annes-soft-pretzels-out-of-hard-times

Notes

1. "Interview with Anne Beiler," Right Now Media, www.youtube.com/watch?v=HSlrkv6TuVw at 2:10.
2. Anne Beiler with Shawn Smucker, *Twist of Faith: The Story of Anne Beiler, Founder of Auntie Anne's Pretzels*, Nashville, TN: Thomas Nelson, 2008, p. 9.

3. "Interview with Anne Beiler" at 4:20.
4. *Twist of Faith*, p. 9.
5. "Interview with Anne Beiler" at 8:30.
6. "Interview with Anne Beiler" at 9:00.
7. "Interview with Anne Beiler" at 13:20.
8. Dinah Eng, "Auntie Anne's: Soft Pretzels Out of Hard Times," *Fortune*, July 22, 2013. Fotune.com/2013/07/08/auntie-annes-soft-pretzels-out-of-hard-times
9. "Interview with Anne Beiler" at 13:50.
10. "Interview with Anne Beiler" at 1:47.
11. "Interview with Anne Beiler" at 14:00.

TOMS SHOES
BUY ONE, GIVE ONE

The Lesson

They invented a new business model that gives back as much as it takes in, reducing hardship around the world. Now dozens of other companies have followed in the footsteps of TOMS Shoes.

His name is not even Tom. It's Blake, and he's been a serial entrepreneur since his teenage years.

First, it was tennis lessons. Blake was a tennis stud in his youth, so when his dad suggested he get a summer job, Blake signed up a bunch of kids for $25-an-hour and taught them in batches. Slightly more lucrative than a lemonade stand.

Blake later had successful forays opening a billboard company that advertised on the side of buildings, a college laundry service that eventually grossed $1,000,000 a year with more than 40 employees, and an online driver's education course. That last one zoomed to the top of the Los Angeles market after he cleverly hired some Abercrombie & Fitch models to promote it.

But the idea that would make Blake Mycoskie a household name, even if everyone thought his name was Tom, was TOMS Shoes. You buy one pair, we give one pair to a child who has none.

Ironically, this company that would do so much for the poor began because of a sport for the rich.

In 2006, Blake, then in his mid-20s, was in search of a polo camp. He had ridden plenty of horses growing up in Texas. Now a California boy, the only polo instruction around came with a California price tag.

He stumbled upon an affordable option down south. Way south in Argentina. It would be a providential trip, regardless the distance, one that would change his life and change the way many do business.

The story goes like this. While in Buenos Aires, Blake overheard a conversation—in English, to his delight—between two women who were collecting shoes from wealthy neighborhoods and distributing them in poor neighborhoods. Blake, not just an entrepreneur but an extrovert, introduced himself and before long he was joining them in their volunteer work.

After an exhilarating day playing with kids and putting shoes on their feet, he told his polo coach how remarkable it was. But the straight-faced coach responded with a sobering question: Who's going to give them the next pair?

It gave them both piercing clarity. Something needed to be done.

That coach became the co-founder of TOMS Shoes, though his name isn't Tom either. It's Alejo, and his question prompted Blake's brilliant "one-for-one" idea. Blake and Alejo could pay a shoemaker in Argentina to make several pairs, Blake could sell half of them to his friends in L.A., and then they could give away the other half to kids back in Argentina.

He wanted to call them "Tomorrow's Shoes," but that wouldn't fit on the shoe label. So he shortened it to TOMS.

Exhilaration aside, it didn't sound like much of a business model. The shoes would have to sell at a significant premium to pay for the giveaway pairs. Plus, no one Blake knew wore these kind of shoes, called alpargatas, which looked more like slippers.

But just like the laundry service and the online driving school and some of Blake's other unlikely successes, there was no business plan required. Just a touch of luck in this case.

Or maybe a touch of God's hand.

Back in the States, a reporter was intrigued with Blake's buy-one-give-one model, as well as his cause. Just like that, a prominent article appeared in the *Los Angeles Times* hyping the company and their alpargatas.[1] By 4:00 that afternoon, Blake's fledgling website had fielded 2,200 orders. And there was Blake, in his apartment with a mere 60 pairs.

Vogue magazine soon followed. They loved the cause. They loved the shoes. They didn't mind the price. Orders tumbled in from Bloomingdale's, Macy's and plenty of others. Clearly, Blake had some shoes to make and he accelerated production in Argentina.

Within a year, Blake had sold 10,000 pairs, so it was time to make good on his promise by returning to Argentina with a group of employees and family members. They rented a bus and traveled the countryside, distributing 10,000 pairs to kids, many of whom never had shoes before.

He described the moment in his bestseller, *Start Something That Matters*: "The kids ... would start clapping with joy when they spotted the bus rolling into town. I broke down in tears many times. *Oh, my God*, I thought, *this is actually working*. At each stop I was so overcome with emotion that I could barely slip the first pair of shoes on a child without crying with love and happiness. Just nine months ago this started with a sketch in my journal and now we were about to provide 10,000 pairs of new shoes to children in need."[2]

Blake vividly recalls villages that looked like trash dumps, streets filled with glass and garbage, houses barely upright—and notwithstanding, kids filled with joy. "When I returned from that shoe drop, I was a different person," he wrote.[3] So were those who joined him on the trip, redoubling their efforts to make this company work.

Perhaps most interesting, at least from a business perspective, is that they made this trip even though the company was still unprofitable. Despite all the demand and all the free publicity and all the buzz, TOMS was not yet making money. Still, they delivered on their promise.

To Blake, a Christian businessman, it was simply a Biblical mandate: "TOMS represents a lot of different biblical principles," he said at Willow Creek's Global Leadership Summit in 2010. "But the one I go back to again and again is in Proverbs where it says 'give your first fruits and your vats will be full.' We didn't start a business—a shoe company—make a bunch of money and then start giving. Day One, we started the business so we could give away shoes, and for the first couple years, we were not profitable. We were losing money and still giving away shoes. And because we did that and stayed true to our one-for-one model, we've been incredibly blessed."[4]

Three years after launch, the company finally earned a profit. Then the serial entrepreneur went to work with his next idea: restoring eyesight to people around the world.

Their website explains why: "285 million people worldwide are blind or visually impaired. 80% of them don't have to be. So, we devoted part of our business to helping restore sight to people in need."[5] They did it by diversifying, selling eyewear and donating an eyesight correction (glasses, medical care, a surgery, etc.) for every pair sold.

Blake's next focus would be clean water, such a dire need around the globe. TOMS started selling coffee and for every bag of TOMS beans sold, they'd give a week of clean water to a person in one of the countries from which the beans were sourced. For every individual cup they sold, they gave a day of clean water.

Around the same time, Blake also made an important midcourse correction in his one-for-one shoe model. Hearing the valid criticisms of those who said his shoe drop, though generous, was costing jobs by putting local shoemakers out of business, the company started manufacturing shoes in the countries they were serving, thereby creating jobs. Now, 40 percent of TOMS Shoes are made in the countries where they're also freely distributed.

In other words, the company has come full circle back to its first charitable days of both making and distributing in Argentina.

There are many charitable days ahead for the company, too, though it's now a partnership. With the company valued at $625 million, Blake sold 50 percent of it to Bain Capital, earmarking much of his windfall for new social enterprises. The serial entrepreneur has become a serial philanthropist as he invests in others who have an audacious business vision—those with an altruistic dream but inadequate funding to pursue it.

The recipients have an experienced role model to follow in Blake, as well as a novel, twenty-first century business model that really works. The evidence is the nearly 100 million pairs of shoes given away around the world. It's the 770,000 free eyesight restorations for those who were impaired. It's the 720,000 weeks of safe, clean water for those who would otherwise drink from a toxic river.[6]

The evidence is also in the dozens of other contributory businesses that are now following the one-for-one approach, among them FIGS, Warby Parker, Roma Boots, SoapBox and Love Your Mellon.

TOMS Shoes is a profound and inspirational story, one that will be told for generations to come. And it's all because a guy named Tom, I mean Blake, had the courage to reimagine what a company could be.

For Further Study

Blake Mycoskie, *Start Something That Matters*, New York: Spiegel & Grau, 2012

Global Leadership Network, "Blake Mycoskie – The Global Leadership Summit, 2010," www.youtube.com/watch?v=f5OCcD4qbk8

Website: www.toms.com

Notes

1. Booth Moore, "They're Flipping for Alpargatas," *Los Angeles Times*, May 20, 2006. www.LAtimes.com/archives/la-xpm-2006-may-20-et-stylenotebook20-story.html
2. Blake Mycoskie, *Start Something That Matters*, New York: Spiegel & Grau, 2012, p. 15.
3. *Start Something That Matters*, p. 16.
4. Global Leadership Network, "Blake Mycoskie – The Global Leadership Summit, 2010," www.youtube.com/watch?v=f5OCcD4qbk8 at 24:50.
5. "How Your Purchase Creates Change," stories.toms.com/impact
6. "How Your Purchase Creates Change," stories.toms.com/impact

PURA VIDA COFFEE
GREAT COFFEE, GREAT CAUSE

The Lesson

When a nonprofit structure falls flat, a for-profit structure may be the answer, generating sustainable revenue to change more lives.

Here's a recipe for an extraordinary cup of coffee. Start with two Harvard Business School grads, mix in some Microsoft money, and top it off with overflowing compassion for the poor. The result is Pura Vida, which of course means "pure life," but for street kids in Costa Rica, it means so much more.

It's a simple story about a complex problem.

Chris Dearnley and John Sage entered business school in the fall of 1987, a bit daunted by their limited business background. Chris had been an economics major at Wheaton; John chose American Studies and History at Stanford. But as grad students, they connected over case studies and caffeine, as well as a mutual love for God, praying together regularly for each other's professional and spiritual growth.

God seemed to answer both prayers, developing them considerably during those two years. After graduation, though, they went their separate ways, John to Microsoft just as it was becoming the most profitable tech company in the world, and Chris to San Jose.

Not the San Jose in Silicon Valley; the one in poverty-stricken

Costa Rica. Unlike his crimson classmates, Chris swapped the American dream for what many would consider a Central American nightmare.

Over the years, the friends stayed in touch, John sharing about his launch of the now-ubiquitous Microsoft Office and Chris sharing about his launch of an obscure church plant. Indeed, both men were change agents in their own contexts; however, in 1997 their conversation turned to changing the world.

At their annual golf-weekend, John admitted to an ongoing existential crisis, driven by 100-hour workweeks and some personal family tragedy. He had even considered ditching it all to go to seminary and become a minister. At this point in his life, John was long on cash but short on vision.

Chris, meanwhile, told stories of the kids touched by his ministry. His church was making progress with several issues: malnutrition, substandard housing (six to a bed and gaping holes in the roof), kids' dental problems because they had no toothbrushes, and the rampant drug abuse.

But funds were drying up quickly. He basically had the opposite problem from John: Chris was long on vision but short on cash.

That weekend, Chris also gave a bag of Costa Rican coffee to John. When John learned that the bag cost only four dollars, the light bulb went off. Coffee of this quality would sell for ten or eleven bucks in the United States.

John recalls the epiphany of that conversation: "In that moment, God birthed the vision. 'What if we started our own little company to sell Costa Rican coffee over the web and used the bags to share the story of your work with children? The profits could provide sustainable funding for your ministry.' Without any hesitation, Chris grabbed on to it: 'We could call the company *Pura Vida*, which is how Costa Ricans greet one another.' I was so excited! It seemed the perfect combination of all my interests: technology, business, coffee and ministry, so I was ready to get going."[1]

Right there at poolside, they did the proverbial back-of-the-napkin calculations. The two Ivy-League MBAs agreed that the idea was viable.

They put it to the test in 1998. Wanting the company to be accountable to the rigors of the marketplace, they structured Pura Vida as a for-profit, channeling all of the excess to their nonprofit, Pura Vida Partners. It was a clever configuration, giving them access to both investors and donors.

John initially underwrote the venture, joining Pura Vida full-time a year later. His salesmanship opened doors in Seattle, Denver and Los Angeles, at first by selling to large churches that wanted to support the Cost Rican mission, but then by experimenting with other models, like wholesaling, private label and online sales.

Not surprisingly, the business grew rapidly, allowing them to fulfill a promise to improve the living conditions of their coffee growers. Pura Vida used certified fair-trade beans, meaning it voluntarily paid higher-than-market rates—a "living wage"—to the farmers. To date, that's generated $16 million in revenue for farmers, above commodity prices.[2]

So, on the front end of the ministry the company took care of their growers, and on the back end they took care of kids and others in their community. In fact, the consistent infusion of cash saves lives while at the same time, gently pointing people toward the God who loves them.

Pura Vida also gave these kids practical skills and a potential way out of poverty. Chris explains how that started: "With a grant from Microsoft, we created four computer centers and the impact was tremendous—way beyond just computer knowledge. The kids gained self-esteem and experienced the joy of learning. ... It's opened up a whole new world beyond their neighborhood and given them a vision of who they can become."[3]

Hope. It's as fundamental a need as the food, health care, shoes and clothing—and toothbrushes—Pura Vida provides.

In 2007, with the company finally approaching profitability and stability, John felt comfortable turning over his role to a more experienced industry professional. Chris followed in 2008, ultimately transferring ownership to one of their larger investors (but not before Pura Vida again proved its merits, winning a taste-test in the U.S. House of Representatives among fair-trade coffees, including

Starbucks, Seattle's Best, and Green Mountain, giving it the exclusive right to sell in the House.)[4]

More specifically, John went back into consulting work in Seattle and eventually became the chief of staff at the Bill & Melinda Gates Foundation, continuing his work in philanthropy. Chris remained in Costa Rica and still leads the church he planted in the 1990s. He's also the Executive Director of a local nonprofit which runs three community centers to bring hope and opportunity to 600 at-risk youth every year.

They had a remarkable decade running Pura Vida, demonstrating that it's possible to build a social enterprise in a developing country and scale it into a national brand, all to benefit the poor. It's sustainable, too. To this day, the company's mission remains almost the same and their tagline is as true as ever: Great Coffee, Great Cause.

It's the natural result of two great guys following a great God.

For Further Study

Steve Rundle and Tom Steffen, "Pura Vida Coffee," in *Great Commission Companies: The Emerging Role of Business in Missions*, pp. 206-222. Downers Grove, IL: InterVarsity Press, 2011.

Websites: PuraVidaCreateGood.com, FundaVida.org

Notes

1. "Founders' Story," www.PuraVidaCreateGood.com/history
2. "Our Mission," www.PuraVidaCreateGood.com/our-mission
3. Clark Baker, "Pura Vida is Way Cool: Conversations with Chris Dearnley and John Sage," Center for Christian Ethics at Baylor University, 2004. www.Baylor.edu/ifl/christianreflection/FoodandHungerinterviewBaker.pdf, p. 74

4. Melissa Allison, "Pura Vida Wins Support of the House," *The Seattle Times,* February 7, 2008. www.SeattleTimes.com/business/pura-vida-coffee-wins-support-of-the-house

ALTAR'D STATE
STANDING OUT, FOR GOOD

The Lesson

Altar'd State epitomizes the good that can be done through a business. What looks like a clothing store is really a wealth-creating entity transforming communities, customers and employees.

It's an oasis in the secular temple we call the mall.

Just a few doors down from the immodesty of Forever 21 and the impudence of Victoria's Secret is a women's clothing store with an impactful mission: "Serving as an inspiration, empowering others, by giving more than we receive, we stand out for good to glorify God."

Rich ideals. But it started with a bankruptcy.

Aaron Walters and Brian Mason were friends and colleagues at a large clothing store in Knoxville when it tanked in the recession of 2009. Aaron went off to Laguna Beach, California; Brian remained back east.

After landing a dream job running a company, Aaron says "I was making more money than I could ever spend, living in one of the prettiest places in America, and I was ... miserable, dreading getting out of bed and going to work."[1] Drilling down, he recalls: "I felt this emptiness, like there had to be something more to my life than my next promotion, my next pay raise, what house did I live in and what car did I drive? ... I think God was always tugging on my heart saying 'What are you going to do with your talents?'"[2]

How about launching a social enterprise? Possibly even changing the world?

Months later, he abruptly quit his job, sold everything he could sell, including his beloved Ford Bronco, cashed out his stock, and met up with Brian in Arkansas to brainstorm a business that would give back generously—a business that would make a real difference. Appropriately, they would call it Altar'd State.

Note, Altar'd with an –ar not an –er. The pun worked well, since their goal was to use the company *as* an altar *to* alter lives.

They opened their first store in Knoxville in November 2009, a small, Christian-themed retail store and coffee shop. It was an uphill battle for years. Their first six months they lost $82,000, a huge sum for them at the time.

But they were nothing if not resilient. The duo reached out to more than 300 banks across the country for financing. They suffered rejection after rejection from mall and shopping center owners who didn't understand their mission. Determined to grow, they opened a second store in Birmingham, Alabama, not because Birmingham was strategic, but because no other property owner in the country would have them.

The relentlessness paid off. A decade later, they have more than 100 stores in 34 states, offering tops, sweaters, jackets, shorts, skirts, footwear, jewelry, bags and gift items—all of it accessorized by Christian décor. The background music, too, is Christian but instrumental.

The prayer request journal in the dressing room is another subtle touchpoint of the faith. Some who write in it, anonymously, are not so subtle, though. "People write their deepest, darkest secrets— things they really want guidance on and help with," says Mary Beth Fox, chief marketing and merchandising officer. Managers share those prayer requests with their team as they join together to intercede.

Mary Beth shares another tidbit. She's gathered many since coming on board in 2011. "We get feedback from guests saying 'I was having this really rough day ... but everywhere I looked in this store was something that helped me in spirit and guided me to get through this time."[3]

It's exactly her hope. "We want her to leave feeling better than when she came in." Indeed, Mary Beth sounds more like a minister than a marketer.

So does her boss Aaron, though sometimes he has a congregation of one: "A goal is to build a company that my mother would be proud of."

That vision has likely come to fruition. Brilliantly, though, they've not positioned Altar'd State as a store for mothers. Nor for daughters. It's "a mother-daughter store" according to Aaron. "A mother and a daughter can come in and shop, they can experience our store and enjoy the fitting rooms together. Maybe the daughter buys a little bit more product or apparel for herself, but we also have product that fits a fashion-forward mother."[4]

So Altar'd State is not just "faith meets fashion." It's also "daughter meets mother," a store full of young women with cool moms checking price tags, and occasionally mirrors.

It's also "employee meets enjoyment." The company was recently honored as a "Great Place to Work," with 4 out of 5 of their 2,000+ employees testifying to the quality of their environment.[5] That may have something to do with their daily devotionals as a staff, or their contributions to the community, or just the congeniality of everybody there. A company with a mission to give back tends to attract selfless people who care about each other.

Here's how they give back, or at least the highlights.

Aaron reports that philanthropy is their number one priority, and it ranges from 17 to 25 percent of profits.[6] Mary Beth adds that they have key performance indicators that ensure they give back at the same rate or better than their growth in sales.

For local philanthropy, they coined the term "Mission Mondays" to describe their practice of giving 10 percent a store's net proceeds every Monday to a community cause selected by each store—veterans, pet adoption, food banks, pediatric illness. The list is endless, with different causes each month at every store.

Their partnership with Compassion That Compels is representative, funding "compassion bags" for women battling cancer. In the bag—a large tote decorated with the scripture "be strong and courageous" (Joshua 1:9)—are items like an extra-soft blanket, a devotional guide and journal, organic tea, a travel mug and a Chick-fil-A gift card. Besides writing a check to the charity, some Altar'd State stores keep compassion bags at the register because, as Mary Beth explains, "you would not believe the number of times a month that a lady comes into our store and she just spills it—tells us that she's going through this tough time. She just got bad news that she's battling cancer and we hand her a compassion bag and she knows somebody cares about her."[7]

They care globally as well, specifically in Peru. Sounds random, but their generosity in that country is an outgrowth of a mission trip that Aaron took several years ago with some employees.

"I was talking to a young lady in the sixth grade," he recalls from the first Peru trip, "and I asked her a typical American question: 'What do you want to be when you grow up?' She just started crying."

The girl told Aaron she didn't know what she would do because in her village, schooling ended after the sixth grade. They didn't have money to build beyond that. Without even thinking, Aaron responded: "Don't worry about it. We'll build another school for you."

On the bus, his translator asked him: "Do you realize what you just said?" Aaron did, sitting there pensively, wondering whether that was a wise decision.

Years later, there's no doubt. That young lady graduated from the high school built by the company, and so have many others. Altar'd State has now completed five schools in Peru, with another 14 under construction, and they continue to send employee teams there for mission trips.[8]

Mary Beth captures their philosophy well: "Instead of *telling* people we're Christians, we *show* them we're Christians." In financial terms, they've shown them with more than $10 million so far. But it's just a down payment. The goal, Aaron recently told a room full of college students, is "to donate $1 billion before I retire."[9]

Since he's only in his early 40s, he just might get there. That's the sort of thing that can happen when your business is an altar.

For Further Study

"The Center for Entrepreneurship Hosts Aaron Walters," *Sam Houston State University*, March 28, 2019.
www.youtube.com/watch?v=AJ0lGuu_SXU

Website: www.AltardState.com/our-story

Notes

1. "The Legacy Centre Speaker Series with Aaron Walters," The Legacy Centre, November 5, 2013.
   www.youtube.com/watch?v=sfK5Ho5iXoM at 1:00.
2. "God's Love in Action: Altar'd State and Compassion That Compels," *Jesus Calling Podcast*, May 22, 2019.
   www.youtube.com/watch?v=ZdMJt6s2UZI at 1:05 and 1:45.
3. "God's Love in Action" at 11:30.
4. Stephie Grob Plante, "The Massive, Secretive Christian Clothing Chain You've Never Heard Of," *Racked*, September 9, 2015.
   www.racked.com/2015/9/9/9280177/altard-state-christian-fashion-stores
5. "Altar'd State," *Great Place to Work*, www.greatplacetowork.com/certified-company/7010389
6. "God's Love in Action" at 4:12.
7. "God's Love in Action" at 9:00.
8. "God's Love in Action" at 5:15.
9. "The Center for Entrepreneurship Hosts Aaron Walters," *Sam Houston State University*, March 28, 2019.
   www.youtube.com/watch?v=AJ0lGuu_SXU

BARNHART CRANE & RIGGING
STARTING AT THE FINISH LINE

The Lesson

Recognizing that business success can led to spiritual failure, the Barnhart family created safeguards to keep them faithful ... and at the same time, bless millions around the world.

Picture a lengthy vehicle with 700 tires, transporting an 1,800-ton recycling bin. Imagine the system of cranes required to safely install a nuclear reactor. Or to lower a drill, 60-feet in diameter, to dig a tunnel beneath Seattle.

That's the business of Barnhart Crane & Rigging, based in Memphis. CEO Alan Barnhart likes to describe it matter-of-factly: "We pick up and move heavy stuff. We're a bunch of engineers with a bunch of big toys."[1]

Big toys that can lift and transport just about anything: cargo onto barges, jumbotrons in a stadium, wind turbines, the walls of dams. And often they can do it cheaper and safer than the competition. It's how they've gone from a small, mom-and-pop business to grossing hundreds of millions of dollars every year as a coast-to-coast operation.

The inflection point occurred when mom and pop left for a trip around the world. Having launched the business in 1969, by 1986 it was time for their dream trip. They'd be gone seven years: Did the boys, Alan and Eric, want the business or should they sell it?

Alan was about to take his new bride Katherine to Saudi Arabia to launch a business-as-mission venture, an engineering company whose covert purpose was to share the gospel in a closed country. They prayed hard about the options, often voting one-to-one at the end of those prayers, but in the end they both saw the family business as simply another mission field.

Eric joined Alan as a partner and the second generation officially took over. They had all of ten employees at the time.

But here's where the story becomes especially instructive. Not exactly unique, but close, since not many business owners do this: *The partners started at the finish line.* That is, they determined how much money would be enough for their families to live in reasonable comfort and they targeted that salary, committing to give away anything beyond that number.

To make sense of that decision, we need to shift into reverse for a minute, back to Alan's college years.

Public universities are not known for strengthening a young man's faith, but Alan's time at The University of Tennessee did just that. Living with a group of sold-out believers, Alan became increasingly devoted to following Jesus.

After graduation, some of those well-meaning friends encouraged Alan to drop engineering for more traditional Christian ministry work. But Alan's gifts were in the mechanical realm, and in business, so he rebuffed that advice.

Mostly, anyway. Agreeing with his friends that corporate life could be toxic to the soul, Alan undertook a deep personal study of scriptures to examine what it says about money and business.

He discerned two things. First, it's inarguable that everything we have, including a business, belongs to God. We are stewards managing God's property.

Second, business success can lead to spiritual failure. Alan's study left him with a genuine fear that affluence would distract him from God and tempt him to trust in money. That sort of admonition transcends scripture, he found, but it's particularly prevalent in the teachings of Jesus.

So with that in mind, he put safeguards in place when assuming leadership of the business. One was the aforementioned salary cap—the financial finish line. To avoid materialism, he never wanted to earn more than an upper middle-class salary. Alan thought about it this way: "If God chooses to prosper the business beyond what it takes to generate that amount of money, we're not going to see it as a call to increase our lifestyle. ... Instead, we're going to see it as an opportunity to take that money and use it to help others."[2]

Another safeguard was accountability. Recognizing that church people tend to rebuke some sins but not others, like the lavish use of money, he asked some church friends to hold him to the standard of modest living. Later, he invited the same accountability from leaders in the business.

Then there was this safeguard for corporate giving: It would be done as a group. No unilateral channeling of funds. We earn it together, we allocate it together.

Pretty mature stuff for a 25-year-old. It helped that his wife shared his wisdom and convictions. Alan's brother embraced the safeguards as well.

At first, though, it seemed that the whole thing might be moot. After all, profits were small and the company's promotional literature was limited to a one-page listing of their cranes, along with a seven-digit phone number. They were so local that they didn't even need the area code.

But at the end of their first year, the brothers had $50,000 to give away. And then $150,000 the next year. In fact, business grew at an average rate of 25 percent a year for the next couple decades, with giving growing proportionally. Their formula was basic: 50 percent of earnings went back into the business; 50 percent went to Christian ministries.

By 2005, the company was giving away one-million dollars a year. As business quintupled over the next few years—and profits accelerated even faster—their philanthropy jumped to one-million dollars *a month*. To date, Barnhart's cumulative giving is deep into nine figures.

The company is reasonably private about where the money goes, not looking to gain visibility or acclaim for their generosity. But Alan has said that 95 percent of it goes to international causes, in particular, he says, to places where "Christian infrastructure" is least established—the Muslim, Hindu and Buddhist worlds.

The funding also tends to focus on evangelism. "We want the gospel attached to everything we do because that's what leads to the ultimate Reality of life," explains Alan.[3]

So some of the largest recipients have been the microfinance group Hope International (founded by Keystone Custom Homes, pp. 199-204), the Seed Company (a Bible translation organization), and Strategic Resources Group (an umbrella organization for Christian ministries in the Middle East). Barnhart also gives domestically, for example in the areas of urban restoration and helping women escape trafficking.[4]

Meanwhile, despite their hundreds of millions in net worth, the Barnhart families continued to live their same lifestyle. Alan reports that it's had a profound effect on his six children, who have not grown up as "rich kids," but instead, have benefitted from hearing the word "no." And although they've never been to Disney World, Alan has taken the family to Vietnam, Cambodia, India, Africa and other places where they all gain a clearer perspective on the plight of the poor and the opportunities to serve.

"It's been a life of joy and adventure," Alan beams. "To be a kingdom investor has been so much more fulfilling" than being a material consumer.[5]

To ensure that joy will continue after they're gone, and to perpetuate the pipeline of charitable resources, the Barnharts, in 2007, signed over the ownership of the company to the National Christian Foundation, an organization that works with entrepreneurs who want to donate all or part of their business in the form of nonvoting stock.

In plainer English, the Barnharts run the company, but they no longer own it. Their descendants won't own it either.

Imagine that—simply renouncing hundreds of millions of dollars. How does someone do that?

In their case, since the Barnharts have believed from the outset that the business was never theirs, it was a natural next step. Alan is didactic about it all when he gives his testimony: "I don't think that God is at all impressed with zeros and commas. ... I don't think he wants our money. He wants us."[6]

It seems God has certainly gotten the Barnhart family, and in the process, complete ownership of a remarkable crane company—one that lifts both payloads and people.

For Further Study

Brief version of Alan's Story, from Generous Giving:
Vimeo.com/99540117

Longer version of Alan's story, from The C12 Group:
www.youtube.com/watch?v=iWcyW6BAa4c

Website: www.BarnhartCrane.com

Notes

1. The storyline of this chapter is drawn from Alan's testimony before a few different groups, including those in the "Further Study" section above and from Biola University, "Alan Barnhart: Becoming Kingdom Investors," September 24, 2103. www.youtube.com/watch?v=2G1BNGcwHzk
2. "Alan Barnhart: Becoming Kingdom Investors" at 16:50.
3. "Alan Barnhart: Becoming Kingdom Investors" at 38:00.
4. Liz Essley Whyte, "Giving It All," *Philanthropy*, Spring 2014, www.philanthropyroundtable.org/philanthropy-magazine/article/spring-2014-giving-it-all

5. "Alan Barnhart: Becoming Kingdom Investors" at 25:00.
6. "Alan Barnhart: Becoming Kingdom Investors" at 28:00.

BRIDGEWAY CAPITAL MANAGEMENT
GIVING BACK HALF

The Lesson

With the right business model, it's possible to give away half your profits and still remain competitive. With the right heart, it's possible to use that money to save lives half a world away.

It's an investment company that invests in changing the world. An unusual business, but that's because it's run by an unusual businessman.

Even back in high school, everyone knew John Montgomery was different. In eleventh grade, when schools were still significantly segregated in his hometown, he insisted on transferring from his private school to an inner-city public school. "It gave me a broader worldview," John told CNBC decades later, "and it's something I'm thankful for."[1]

He was also different in his approach to building a business, launching an investment company without ever having worked in the industry. At age 37, John had completed graduate degrees from MIT and Harvard Business School, where he learned computer modeling and statistical methods, and applied them to portfolio management. As a hobby, he continued to calibrate his investment models for a few years after school.

They were good models. Marketable models. Eventually he quit his day job, wrote a business plan and founded Bridgeway Capital Management in Houston.

His investors did quite well—further validation of his stock-picking models—but it would be three years before Bridgeway broke even. Once it crossed that line, though, it never looked back. Their system of "statistically-driven, evidence-based investing" was both wise strategy and effective marketing. A quarter century later, Bridgeway manages $8 billion in assets.

But that's not even the best part of the story.

John Montgomery may have been most different in what he included in Bridgeway's articles of incorporation. Before starting the company, he and his wife worried about how the likely profitability of the venture might change them. "I had a concern that having too much money would suck me into a lifestyle that I didn't really aspire to, either as an individual or a Christian," recalls John.[2] Hedging against that temptation, John mandated that half of Bridgeway's after-tax profits be given to charitable causes.

Forever. The give-back-half pledge is something that's actually audited because it's in the very fabric of their business. So John created a vehicle, Bridgeway Foundation, to ensure the firm delivered on its 50 percent commitment.

Some of the money is distributed each year to every employee—they're called "partners" at Bridgeway, having banished the word employee—to donate as he or she sees fit. No restrictions.

Some of the money is allocated to partner groups; that is, workers who have an affinity for the same cause. Among the group causes so far are potable water, education, microfinance, disaster relief and homelessness.

Some of the money funds local service projects by partners, and global service trips as far away as Africa, Central and South America and even China. Family members can go, too, with half of their expenses paid by Bridgeway.[3]

John rejoices over the opportunities. "Everybody is called to a different area. ... My personal passion is peacemaking and ending genocide. It's a life calling on my part and it's a big deal to me."[4]

How big? Big enough that it's bothered him since learning about the Holocaust in eighth grade. And 25 years after that, big enough to embed in his firm's mission statement: "A world without genocide. Partnering to create an extraordinary future for our clients, community, and world."

Again, uniqueness is baked right in at Bridgeway. John's business is a platform for something so much more. And it's succeeding. Their efforts to neutralize warlord Joseph Kony, for example, have helped reduce the number of displacements, kidnappings and killings by 95 percent in Africa's longest running rebel war. "I have a life vision of seeing the last genocide before I die," he explained at a Gordon College chapel.

Closer to home, he also has a life vision of seeing an end to lying, cheating and stealing in his field. Or at least in his firm. "Integrity" is core value number one at Bridgeway. Many companies say that, of course; at this firm, they live it out by keeping one question constantly in front of them: "What's in the best long-term interest of the current investors?" Note: "current investors," not prospective new business.

Sometimes that can be expensive. Then again, if integrity were cost-free, everyone would have it.

This is expensive, too. For integrity purposes, they completely avoid "soft money" transactions, a standard industry practice of channeling client business to certain brokerage firms in exchange for something from those firms—money, proprietary research, etc. To Bridgeway, there's too much potential conflict of interest there, so they simply won't participate in it, despite how lucrative it would be.

And since you can't really teach integrity in the workplace, gauging an applicant's integrity is central in Bridgeway hiring process. They look for examples in the past where an applicant demonstrated unusual integrity. They put applicants in a role-play dilemma where they have to choose between telling a small lie and being disloyal to the company. They dig deep with references about the issue as well. "We're continually trying to move in the direction of the highest standard of integrity that we can," John said when interviewed at Wharton.[5]

Then there's this enigmatic practice at Bridgeway: their seven-to-one salary ratio. No one can earn more than seven times the lowest paid person at the firm. That's not so much an integrity issue as it is a culture-building tool: "It sends a signal that we're about something else (than getting rich),"[6] insists John. It also prevents the us-against-them mentality that's so toxic in other firms, creating a more collaborative climate.[7]

People advised John that he won't be able to attract good people with a salary cap, or if he did, he'd train them up and then lose them. It hasn't worked out that way. Quite the opposite, in fact, says John. "We're trying to create an amazing place to work for people serious about the service we provide — investment advisory services — and giving back at the same time. On my team, we've lost one investment manager in 20 years."

John goes further, admitting that Bridgeway's president "could easily make twice as much elsewhere." But quality of life might be different working at another firm. Available family time might be different. Opportunities to give back might be scaled back significantly. Is the higher pay worth the trade-offs?

Apparently not to Bridgeway partners. Besides the impressively-low turnover rate, John recounts with a smile that "we hear stories from spouses about Bridgeway and what it's meant in their lives, and that's when you think, 'We really have something here.'"[8]

The salary cap has had other, ancillary benefits as well, not the least of which is keeping their costs lower. Some of that savings gets passed on to clients in the form of below-industry-average trading fees. John, the quant-methods guy, shrugs at the basic math: "If you're successful in our industry, you have the revenues, and if you're also lower cost, then you have very strong profits."[9]

Which brings us full circle to why they've been able to give back so much.

John likes to pass along something God has taught him about generosity through the journey: "It's just fun. If more business people could … see how powerful it is for the business and how fun it is, corporate philanthropy would just skyrocket."[10]

And perhaps atrocities around the world would continue to descend.

For Further Study

"Investing for Social Impact," The Wharton School at The University of Pennsylvania, March 19, 2015. Knowledge.wharton.upenn.edu/article/why-bridgeway-capital-gives-away-half-of-its-profits-to-charity

"A Conversation with John Montgomery," Gordon College, April 13, 2015. www.youtube.com/watch?v=j-G9vdNCAxo

Websites: www.Bridgeway.com and www.BridgewayFoundation.org

Notes

1. "Firm Donates 50% of Profits Every Year to Charity," CNBC, December 23, 2016. www.cnbc.com/video/2016/12/23/firm-donates-50-of-profits-to-charity-every-year.html at 3:00.
2. "A Conversation with John Montgomery," Gordon College, April 13, 2015. www.youtube.com/watch?v=j-G9vdNCAxo
3. "Our Commitment to Giving Back," Bridgeway Capital Management, www.bridgeway.com/giving-back/our-commitment
4. "Investing for Social Impact," The Wharton School at The University of Pennsylvania, March 19, 2015. Knowledge.wharton.upenn.edu/article/why-bridgeway-capital-gives-away-half-of-its-profits-to-charity at 18:25.
5. "Investing for Social Impact" at 7:10.
6. "Investing for Social Impact" at 16:00.

7. "Bridgeway Capital Management," Center for Faith and Work, LeTourneau University. www.youtube.com/watch?v=PaVI9fKog_A at 0:59.
8. "Investing for Social Impact" at 16:45.
9. "Investing for Social Impact" at 10:50.
10. "Investing for Social Impact" at 13:45.

4 RIVERS SMOKEHOUSE
BARBEQUE MINISTRY

The Lesson

John Rivers, founder of 4 Rivers Smokehouse, has a mind for business and a heart for community. His thriving company shows what's possible when you put them together.

It all started with a phone call—the kind of call that every parent fears.

The woman on the other end was crying. "Mr. Rivers, Mr. Rivers. I'm so sorry about your daughter."

"What do you mean? What's wrong with my daughter?"

"Well, her brain tumor!"

John Rivers, CEO of a billion-dollar health care company, was in his office at the time and had no idea what this woman was talking about. Twenty panicked minutes later, he finally reached his wife, Monica. Their kindergarten-age daughter Cameron was fine. No tumor, no hospital visit, no health issues whatsoever.

It must have been some sort of mix-up. The doctor's office had called the wrong number.

But maybe, in a sense, it wasn't a wrong number. In light of what happened next, maybe it was divinely-orchestrated instead. You see, John was haunted by the notion of another family battling 24/7 the horror he experienced for a mere 20 minutes. "I couldn't explain how much it had shaken me," Rivers says. "I told (Monica), 'We're going to find this family and we're going to pour into them one way or another.'"[1]

Within a week, John had found them. Curiously, the little girl with brain cancer had almost nothing in common with Cameron — they didn't share the same doctor or school. They didn't even live in the same city. It made John wonder whether God was somehow behind the errant call.

So John offered to help them financially. He had the means. The family was grateful, but they would have none of it. Then an idea struck him. John offered to host a barbeque fundraiser at the family's church, with all of the proceeds going to the girl's treatment. The family agreed.

It was a good fit, since John was a barbeque aficionado. For about two decades, ever since experiencing brisket for the first time, he had been perfecting his grilling technique. He visited dozens of barbeque restaurants during his extensive travels, sometimes even getting tours and studying the chefs. And he had hosted plenty of backyard parties, treating guests to his low 'n slow creations. So the opportunity to give back this way excited him.

Until, that is, 450 people RSVP'd to show up. "I've only cooked in my backyard," he thought restlessly. "I'm not a chef; I'm a business guy."

Somehow, though, the business guy delivered that day on both quantity and quality. They raised a ton of money and brought a community together. Exhausted he realized something: he was also exhilarated, something conspicuously absent from his day job.

As a result, John did more of it, volunteering his smoker and his services wherever he saw a need. Calling it "barbeque ministry," he would later reflect: "I was doing this on weekends and I was alive, and then I'd go to work during the week and I wasn't alive."[2]

Eventually, he took a giant leap of faith, from pinstripes to pitmaster, retiring so he could volunteer full-time. Within two years, John had served barbeque to almost 50,000 people. He had also developed the culinary skills to make barbeque a commercial venture. Chick-fil-A CEO Dan Cathy helped him think through the business model and pro formas and in 2009, John launched 4 Rivers Smokehouse, five years after that fateful phone call.

In the decade since starting up, John has been featured in national newspapers and cooking magazines. He's been invited to grill on television shows, at food festivals and in upscale restaurants. His company has won countless awards and John has even published his own cookbook.

Meanwhile, his business has grown to 15 locations throughout Florida and Georgia, despite the saturated food service market. Their value proposition? "We put a tremendous amount of effort into ensuring consistency ... (but) at the end of the day, what people remember is the way they were treated."[3]

Indeed, they're treated as special under John's roof. Valued. Appreciated. He's been insistent on hiring people who have a heart for customer service.

But the real heart of 4 Rivers Smokehouse continues to be *community* service. Regardless the publicity and the growth and the impressive P&L's, this venture is still, first and foremost, a barbeque ministry.

Their tagline testifies to it: "Family owned, locally made, community focused."

Their mission statement testifies to it: "We exist to use our God-given gifts to support the local community through exceptional products, steadfast customer service, and uncompromised integrity."

Their generosity testifies to it: They donate to about 500 organizations every year.[4] "We take the majority of our funds," explains John, "and we put them back into the community."[5]

Even their name testifies to it. "4 Rivers" doesn't just represent the four members of the Rivers family. It's a Biblical reference to the water flowing out of the Garden of Eden that branches into four rivers, nurturing various lands (Genesis 2:10).

An apt analogy and one that continues to guide John: "My dream wasn't to create a lot of restaurants. It was to create a company as an example—to show that you could run a successful business and use that business to make a difference in the community.

Every brisket sandwich that we serve allows us to help one other person out there."[6]

It's food for thought. 4 Rivers shows how a company can cater to the common good.

For Further Study

The 4 Rivers Story, 4rsmokehouse.com/about

Taylor Berglund, "4 Rivers: Great Ministry and Great Brisket," *Charisma Magazine,* November 17, 2015. Ministryto-daymag.com/outreach/22309-more-than-brisket

"John Rivers' Testimony—Leadership Prayer Breakfast," www.youtube.com/watch?v=m3grwkdY1i8

Notes

1. Taylor Berglund, "4 Rivers: Great Ministry and Great Brisket," *Charisma Magazine,* November 17, 2015. Ministryto-daymag.com/outreach/22309-more-than-brisket
2. "John Rivers' Testimony—Leadership Prayer Breakfast," www.youtube.com/watch?v=m3grwkdY1i8 at 2:10.
3. "4 Rivers: BBQ with a Purpose," www.youtube.com/watch?v=6S8rdn5DVLY at 1:25.
4. "4 Rivers: Great Ministry and Great Brisket," *Charisma Magazine.*
5. "Rosen School of Hospitality Tribute to John Rivers," www.youtube.com/watch?v=ei2vOzgQPVk at 2:30.
6. "4 Rivers: BBQ with a Purpose" at 1:40.

PART 4

THEIR PEOPLE
They treat their employees like family

H.J. Heinz Company
Broetje Orchards
Mary Kay Cosmetics
Wegmans Food Markets
World Wide Technology
Walker Manufacturing
Polydeck Screen Corporation
Tyson Foods

H.J. HEINZ COMPANY

The Lesson

Many know Henry Heinz as a nineteenth century food pioneer. But he was also a management pioneer, a brilliant light in some of the darkest times of the Industrial Revolution.

Imagine wondering, as you fill your grocery basket, whether those products will make your family sick. Or maybe even kill them.

We don't give much thought to that today, but 150 years ago, it was top of mind for shoppers buying the first mass-produced foods.

Now imagine that a brand came along during that era that you could trust—transparent packaging so you can see the food; production processes that limited contamination; consistent quality and purity for your family. How much more would you be willing to pay for that assurance? And how much of an advantage would that company have over less trusted competitors?

That, in simplified form, is how Henry J. Heinz went from peddling horseradish in 1875 to creating the largest food company in the world by the time of his death in 1919.

Here's how it all started. As a child, Henry was fascinated with his mother's gardening, so he learned the art himself. By age 12, he had his own plot and even a horse-drawn cart to sell his vegetables to local customers. At 17, he was selling homemade horseradish, based on his mother's recipe, earning about $2,400 that year—more than $67,000 in today's dollars. Later Henry formalized that into a business, which did well until The Panic of 1873, a financial crisis that prompted both an economic depression and Henry's bankruptcy.

But a resilient Henry Heinz reorganized in 1875 with a couple partners and a second product that at the time was called "catsup." Adamant about quality and purity, his new company made profitable strides, generating $44,474 the first year (about $1.1 million today). Five years later, the company grossed $284,000 ($7.1 million today), and in 1888, the mastermind of the business bought out his partners, changed the business name to the H.J. Heinz Company, and continued innovating toward his "57 Varieties."

Of course, Henry faced plenty of competition at the time. Industrialized foods were becoming commonplace in the late nineteenth century, but so were the gastrointestinal diseases that came with mass production. Untested preservatives, poor refrigeration, excessive shelf time, unsafe handling of the food by employees and grocers—it all culminated in a society being poisoned by its own food.[1]

Henry Heinz, though, had always been committed to doing it better. To this German Lutheran, who also spent plenty of time in Presbyterian, Methodist and Baptist churches, "quality was not just a platitude or marketing ploy. ... (It was) a moral compact with customers" who were increasingly anxious about adulterated food.[2]

So he invested even more heavily in food safety, starting with freshly-laundered uniforms for employees every day. No germy street clothes allowed on the factory floor. Henry also insisted on proper hygiene for factory workers. Female food handlers got free manicures regularly, to reduce the spread of bacteria. Grocers got tutorials from Heinz sales reps about how to keep foods from becoming moldy. And on a larger scale, Henry integrated vertically, purchasing his own farms to control the purity of the food from its origin.

It all minimized the chance of foodborne illness and at the same time, elevated quality well-beyond most of the competition.

Henry's faith-driven "moral compact" extended to his employees as well. To appreciate his methods, though, we should again set the table with some historical context.

In Pittsburgh, Heinz's home base, the immigrant population doubled from 1880 to 1900, with the greatest waves arriving from Germany, Ireland, Italy, Poland and Scandinavia, seeking a better life. They didn't always find one. Often the men came over first, working in brutal settings like steel mills and coal mines, and living in slums, trying to save enough to bring their families to America.

Meanwhile, the women who sought employment, both immigrants and locals, seldom had skills to work in teaching or nursing, and "most office clerks and salespeople were men. (So women worked) as a household domestic, or as a scrubwoman, or as a prostitute or at manual labor in some trade—in laundries, in garment and glass factories, in stogy factories, in packaged food plants."[3]

It was exactly this dynamic—more laborers than jobs—that culminated in the abysmal working conditions of that time. Employers had all the power and a line of applicants waiting to take the job of anyone who fell short of their dehumanizing and often dangerous standards. In fact, employees "died by the thousands," writes one researcher about that era, "in industrial accidents, in epidemics, and from tuberculosis, pneumonia, and typhoid fever."[4] No laws or courts offered protection until decades later.

It all makes the employment practices of Henry Heinz that much more striking. He didn't merely treat employees as human beings; he treated them as family.

The Heinz factory was state-of-the-art and physically comfortable—sanitary, ventilated, temperature-controlled, well lit with electric lights, and fireproofed with alarms and iron doors. Over time, he shifted workers' six-day schedule to five-and-a-half days and, eventually, to five. The company's wages were about average, but Heinz also offered piecework, allowing his mostly-female labor force to earn substantially more than they could elsewhere. Against convention, Henry Heinz also was among the first industrialists to promote women into supervisory roles.

But what really set his workplace apart was that, as one corporate biographer concludes, "his employee benefits were the best of the period."[5] Perhaps that sounds trivial, given the factory norms at the time, but how many employees even *today* receive the kind of benefits provided by Heinz in 1900?

Henry's offered his workforce free, on-site physicians and dentists; employee pensions; spotless lunchrooms and restrooms; an employee swimming pool and gymnasium; a rooftop garden for noontime relaxation; a reading room where employees could borrow books; free courses in dressmaking, cooking, drawing, singing, English, and how to become an American citizen; lectures in the evenings for personal development; group carriage rides in the summer, during work hours nonetheless, through the parks and the downtown area.

Heinz also built the first auditorium in the country intended primarily for employees—a place to enjoy concerts, plays, or an opera. The five-story, 1,500-seat, 2,000-light facility included a large dome made of stained glass, with paintings and inspirational phrases adorning the walls. Four times a year they removed the seats, waxed the floor and held dances for employees and their dates. On December 24 every year, at two p.m., employees came together in that space to celebrate Christmas, an event where the company also gave everyone a gift, usually something Henry had seen on his travels: umbrellas, scarves, handkerchiefs, or music boxes.[6]

And, again, all this in the era where the typical factory owner resembled Ebeneezer Scrooge, on December 24 and every other day. Tellingly, "there was no labor trouble at Heinz—and there were no unions—for sixty-five years," long after the death of its founder.[7]

A New York reporter once asked Henry whether the company got its money's worth for all the services to employees. Henry replied: "I have never given that side of the matter any thought. We are fully repaid when we see our employees enjoying themselves and spending their noons and evenings in a manner profitable to themselves." When pressed, Henry did appease the reporter, adding: "it is good business as well. It pays; it increases my output."[8]

A moral compact with customers and another with employees. And beyond that, there were Henry's legendary, philanthropic contributions to the city of Pittsburgh and, in his later years, to Christian missions work, sometimes in conjunction with his friend from Philadelphia, John Wanamaker (see pages 259-264 of this book). A crown jewel of that work was a faith-based, educational and recreational facility for Pittsburgh's poor children, similar to the missionary priorities of another in-state contemporary, Milton Hershey (pages 185-188).[9]

They were all a reflection of the compact that Henry saw between God and man, an abiding love of God that includes the free gift of salvation through Jesus. It was so central to Henry's life that he even testified to it in death: "I desire to set forth, at the very beginning of this Will," his testament began, "the most important item in it, a confession of my faith in Jesus Christ as my Savior."

As a blessed man, Henry Heinz gratefully passed along that blessing to employees, customers and communities, all of whom still benefit from it 100 years later.

For Further Study

Quentin R. Skrabec, Jr., *H.J. Heinz: A Biography*, Jefferson, NC: McFarland & Company, 2009.

Robert C. Alberts, *The Good Provider: H.J. Heinz and His 57 Varieties*, Boston: Houghton Mifflin, 1973.

Notes

1. Much of the story up to this point comes from Gabriella M. Petrick, "'Purity as Life': H.J. Heinz, Religious Sentiment, and

the Beginning of the Industrial Diet," *History and Technology*, Volume 27 Number 1, March 2011, 37-64.

2. "Purity as Life," p. 37.
3. Robert C. Alberts, *The Good Provider: H.J. Heinz and His 57 Varieties*, Boston: Houghton Mifflin, 1973, p. 135.
4. *The Good Provider*, p. 135.
5. Quentin R. Skrabec, Jr., *H.J. Heinz: A Biography*, Jefferson, NC: McFarland & Company, 2009, p. 8.
6. *The Good Provider*, pp. 136-141.
7. *The Good Provider*, p. 141.
8. *The Good Provider*, p. 144.
9. *H.J. Heinz: A Biography*, p. 197. For more information about the continuing work of this organization, called Sarah Heinz House, visit www.SarahHeinzHouse.org

BROETJE ORCHARDS
THE MOST GENEROUS EMPLOYER IN AMERICA

The Lesson

What would Jesus do if he owned an orchard? The compassion of Ralph and Cheryl Broetje might be a close approximation.

They grow five percent of all the apples consumed in the United States. And then they spend most of the proceeds caring for their employees.

In 1968, Ralph and Cheryl Broetje bought an orchard in southeast Washington. Their goal was simple, albeit a bit unorthodox: Make enough money to help the people of India.

Especially the kids.

You see, back when he was 15, Ralph heard a missionary speak of the suffering of India's children and began thinking about what he could do. The question remained with him for years, but after marrying Cheryl, he also had an answer: They could start a business.

It was an unmitigated disaster. The Broetje's first foray into fruit farming was a cherry orchard. A few weeks after they bought the land, the cherries froze and they lost the whole crop. In the second year, rain ruined the crop, and in the third year, fruit flies destroyed it.

For the Broetjes, money did not grow on trees. Instead, debt did.

Bushels of it. They thought it might be wise to get out before things got even worse. Cheryl recalls their plight: "We were just trying to keep the trees alive, basically."[1]

But the man who sold them the orchard was a devout Christian willing to be lenient with their mortgage payments. And Ralph's old Sunday school teacher showed up to assist with the farm—and to keep before Ralph that vision of having an orchard that would someday feed kids in India.

The couple decided to persevere and after a few more years, the cherry crop blossomed, allowing them to pay their creditors and even expand into apple growing.

That was the real turning point. Ralph and Cheryl would steward that land into one of the largest privately-held apple orchards in America: more than 6,000 acres, nearly 3,000 employees at harvest time, shipping seven million boxes of apples a year.

They did it as an openly faith-based company. Operating under the brand name "First Fruits," based on the Biblical tradition of offering God the first and best of the harvest, they crafted a mission that was also Biblically-inspired: "To be a quality fruit company committed to bearing fruit that will last." It comes from the company's cornerstone verse in the gospel of John: "You did not choose me, but I chose you and appointed you to go and bear fruit—fruit that will last. Then the father will give you whatever you ask in my name. This is my command: Love each other" (John 15:16-17).[2]

Along the way, though, a surprising opportunity emerged to "Love each other." It wasn't focused on families across the globe, but families across the backyard. Cheryl explains how their extraordinary ministry to employees began:

> "We were just finally becoming profitable when we experienced a radical shift in our labor force, away from white, U.S. migrant families to Latino immigrants. So at that point the vision morphed. We realized that if we ever hoped to help kids in India, these new employees would have to become our first focus of mission."[3]

It didn't matter, Cheryl continues, that the challenge seemed overwhelming: "They came with nothing. We didn't share the same language, culture or religion. They had never done the kind of work we were asking them to do. How do you run a business ... when you can't even talk to your people?"

However, since their youth, Ralph and Cheryl were taught to have compassion on strangers. So they embraced the cultural shift. Cheryl recalls their thinking: "How can we say we're committed to God if we're not equally committed to those who are being excluded from the dream of God?"[4]

The couple went all-in on the new calling, taking mission trips to Mexico to understand why people would leave their homeland. They concluded that their new workers were, in fact, economic refugees coming to America to give their kids hope and a future.

It prompted the Broetjes to create even more jobs. They built a warehouse to expand into packing and shipping. And as they got to know the warehouse employees, mostly women, they learned, as Ralph said, that "they've got everybody and everything going against them."[5]

Except the Broetjes. Ralph and Cheryl would step into every gap they found.

For example, when they heard about a woman locking her young kids in their apartment while she worked—and the kids almost dying from a neighboring fire—the Broetjes built a child care center. Initially they hired some of the female workers to oversee the facility. Now all the teachers there have an early-childhood certification.

When they learned that many employees were living in substandard housing, and that their families were bitten at night by rats, the Broetjes took out a multi-million dollar loan to build employee housing—100 homes offered at highly-subsidized rents. They also added a gym, a grocery store, a bilingual library, and a nondenominational church to their little community.

When they learned that employees' kids were dropping out of school because of the gangs there, the Broetjes built their own school among the new houses, and a ranch for troubled youth—a space where they could turn their life around. Additionally, they provided college scholarships as an incentive to finish high school.

When they learned that the female employees avoid smiling because their teeth are so bad, they upgraded their health care program to address that issue, among others.

When they realized that many worker families spent almost no time together as a family unit—fathers started early in the morning and mothers picked up second shifts—the company invested in a new, state-of-the-art packing facility that could eliminate evening work, while still preserving jobs.[6]

And in a defining moment, in May 2006, after a 90-second hail storm damaged almost every tree on their farm—hundreds of thousands of them at that point—the Broetjes faced a tough decision. The insurance company agreed to pay for the damage, declaring it a 100 percent loss, provided the company left everything untouched and sent everybody home for the season.[7]

A standard request, perhaps, but the implications for the workers, all of them immigrant families at that point, were dire: No work, no income, relocating the family, a different school for kids. Shutting down would mean a complete upheaval of workers' lives, so the Broetjes continued to operate. They chose to keep everyone employed, harvesting all they could, while risking forfeiture of the insurance money.

It's difficult to overstate that risk. It was a leap of faith, though. Warehouse manager Ron Appleby put it this way: "We came up with 'Let's go ahead and pick the fruit and really forget about the insurance money and hope that God is watching over us.'"[8]

In the end, the workers nurtured the orchard back to health and the company somehow managed to break even that year, while continuing to pursue a partial settlement with the insurance company.

It's in adversity, not comfort, that we know who we really are. Plain and simply, this is who the Broetjes are: possibly the most generous employer in America.

They continued that compassionate ministry right up through

the sale of their business in 2019. The purchase price remains un-disclosed, but public records put the real estate transaction alone at $288 million. The terms keep unchanged most of the company leadership, the operation, and the care for the employees.

And India? Over the decades, Broetje Orchards has sent millions of dollars to nonprofits in that country, responding to the original calling from Ralph's teenage years. Beyond that, he and Cheryl took an even more personal approach: six of their nine children are adopted from India.

Broetje Orchards offers an inspirational model of what a Christian-owned company can be. It's not just that Ralph and Cheryl built a massive business by growing fruit. It's that they were in the even bigger business of growing people, putting the "dream of God"—and the American dream—within reach for those new to America.

For Further Study

Faith@Work Summit, "Shaping Workers: Calling, Valuing, Training & Empowering: Cheryl Broetje," January 25, 2015. www.youtube.com/watch?v=Me11A3NNV9Q

Sarah Stanley, "Broetje's Big Garden," *Religion & Liberty*, November 20, 2017. Acton.org/broetjes-big-garden

Website: FirstFruits.com

Notes

1. Stan Friedman, "First Fruits: Broetje Orchards puts people before profits," *Christian Century*, November 18, 2008, p. 22.
2. First Fruit Farms, "Our Story," firstfruits.com/our-story

3. Faith@Work Summit, "Shaping Workers: Calling, Valuing, Training & Empowering: Cheryl Broetje," January 25, 2015. www.youtube.com/watch?v=Me11A3NNV9Q at 2:30.
4. "Shaping Workers" at 5:22.
5. "First Fruits: Broetje Orchards puts people before profits," p. 23.
6. Kenman L. Wong and Scott B. Rae, *Business for the Common Good: A Christian Vision for the Marketplace*, Downers Grove, IL: IVP Academic, p. 252.
7. "Shaping Workers" at 0:10.
8. "First Fruits: Broetje Orchards puts people before profits," p. 22.

MARY KAY COSMETICS
PRAISING PEOPLE TO SUCCESS

The Lesson

With "The Golden Rule" as her foundation, Mary Kay Ash built a company that would give employees "unlimited opportunity." To help them get there, she used a time-honored approach available to every leader.

It wasn't fair and she wasn't going to take it anymore.

Mary Kay Ash was a direct sales professional with enough skill to train her colleagues. But after training several men who all got promoted ahead of her, enough was enough.

She didn't sue; the law wasn't on her side at the time anyway. She didn't wait around hoping the company would become more enlightened. No, Mary Kay shattered the glass ceiling on her own by starting a business. And in doing so, she created the same opportunity for other women who had the potential and the pluck, if not the path.

Curiously, her world-renown corporation began as a book to teach women how to succeed in sales. It became clear, though, that the ideas might instead form a plan for a new kind of direct sales business. So in 1963, she launched her cosmetics company in Dallas.

The company grew rapidly as legions of women signed up to become "independent beauty consultants"—saleswomen eager to be their own boss. In fact, Mary Kay hired more than 800 of them in the first year, she reached a million dollars in annual sales within three years, and she went public within five years[1] (she took the company private again in 1985). Indeed, Mary Kay had tapped into a pervasive desire for autonomy and opportunity, not to mention cash.

Boatloads of cash. This was not just some second-income-earner side gig for a few hours a month, though anyone could approach it that way. Rather, the goal was to give women the platform and tools to run their own business full-time, with limitless upside potential.

Many did, and top salespeople became multimillionaires, sporting a diamond bumblebee pin and making sales calls in their motorized bonus, the iconic pink Cadillac.[2]

In addition to her prescient business model, Mary Kay managed the entire operation on her terms—terms very different from what she had experienced as an employee. Terms that are other-focused and intentionally Christian. According to *The Story of Mary Kay Inc.*, "Above all else, what sets Mary Kay apart is strict adherence to the principles on which Mary Kay Ash and her son, Richard Rogers, formed the Company. ... The first is simply the Golden Rule: 'Do unto others as you would have them do unto you.' The second is a simple listing of life's priorities: 'God first. Family second. Career third.'"[3]

She was challenged often about the God language, but remained steadfast. For example, in a 1979 interview with the program *60 Minutes*, the correspondent asked her: "Do you think that's really fair, in terms of marketing, to inject God into it?"

Her response: "I really feel that our company is where it is today and has been blessed beyond all belief by the fact that God is using our company as a vehicle to help women become the beautiful creatures that he created."

"But do you think in a sense you're using God?"

A rogue retort, but Mary Kay's reply epitomized her gentleness and humility: "I hope not. I sincerely hope not. I hope that he's using me instead."[4]

That kind of meekness belies her relentless zeal for the mission—a mission to "establish a company that would give unlimited opportunity to women." And by that she means the women she employs, not those who buy her products.

Notice how unusual this is for a business. Their mission is not foremost about the customer or the financials. It's about the employee, the saleswoman, "the beautiful creatures that (God) created." *They* are why the company exists. They are the mission God placed on Mary Kay's heart, and their good is what she pursued single-mindedly for almost 40 years.

Equally instructive is how she did that—her Biblically-inspired leadership philosophy. Mary Kay did not just give sales consultants a platform, a product, and some training. She built peak performance by building up people from the inside out. Encouragement and praise. Positive reinforcement. That's her number one secret to success.

Mary Kay puts it simply in her book, *The Mary Kay Way*: "I believe praise is the best way for a leader to motivate people. At Mary Kay we think praise is so important that our entire marketing plan is based on it."[5]

She then reveals the why behind the what: "For most women, the last bit of applause they received was when they graduated from high school or college. ... A woman could work day and night caring for her family, and the only time she is likely to hear a comment is if she *stops* doing it!" In sharp contrast, the basic posture at her company is "here's what you're doing right," despite what they might be doing wrong.

Mary Kay tells a story that captures this perfectly. Outside of her office door, she heard one of her top managers enthusiastically praising a new beauty consultant, commending the woman for having a $35 show. "Even then," she writes, "a $35 show was not so good," so she wandered into the conversation.

The sales manager jumped at the chance. "Mary Kay! May I present my new team member? Last night she had a $35 class! Her first two shows she didn't sell anything, but last night she sold $35. Isn't that terrific?"

That's the lens and the logic at this company. "By receiving praise for each small achievement," Mary Kay explains, "an individual gains confidence to try harder. Thus little successes pave the way to bigger successes."[6]

It happens on a macro scale as well. Their *Applause* magazine — the title is telling — is one vehicle. "Its main purpose, aside from sharing product news, is to give recognition," writes Mary Kay.[7] Sales Directors supplement this with their own local newsletters, including as many consultants' names as possible in each edition. Then there's the company's annual convention, with tens of thousands in attendance, that invests much of the time recognizing people at center stage.

Praise is the default condition at Mary Kay, the cultural norm. It's become a way of life because it was in their founder's DNA.

Now, some would argue that the success of this approach is context-specific. That is, the same default might not work as well in other places.

Then again, it might.

Recently, *Harvard Business Review* published a synopsis of the social science research on the subject under the title "The Feedback Fallacy." Their conclusion? "If we continue to spend our time identifying failure as we see it and giving people feedback about how to avoid it, we'll languish in the business of adequacy. To get into the excellence business ... managers need to help their team members see what's working, stopping them with a 'Yes! That!' and share their experience of what the person did well."[8]

The article goes on to tell the story of another Dallas legend, Cowboys Coach Tom Landry, who used the same motivational approach as Mary Kay Ash. Rather than having the team review film of what they were doing wrong, as every other NFL team did, Landry's staff created highlight reels of each player doing things right. From now on, Landry told his team, "we only replay your winning plays."[9]

Twenty consecutive winning seasons and two Super Bowl rings later, some think that Landry — another devout Christian — may have been onto something. Catch them being good.

It's not just a Dallas thing, and given Landry's testosteronic environment, it's not just a woman thing.

It's not just a pragmatic thing either. Affirmation is deeply Biblical, rooted in both the Old and New Testament (e.g., Proverbs 11:25 and 31:31, 1 Thessalonians 5:11, Hebrews 10:24-25). In other words, there's a scriptural case that affirmation is just the right thing to do—an on-your-side disposition that's, in fact, a form of love. Women and men alike are starving for it, which explains their dedication and diligence when they receive it.

Stated more succinctly, Mary Kay's exegesis is this: "Praise people to success."[10] She got a lifetime of "amens" from that four-word sermon.

Mary Kay Ash passed away in 2001, but her posture of positivity lives on in thousands of daily interactions among millions of sales consultants generating billions in annual revenue ... and through countless changed lives.

For Further Study

Mary Kay Ash, *The Mary Kay Way*, Hoboken, NJ: Wiley & Sons, 2008.

The Story of Mary Kay Inc., 2013, www.marykaymuseum.com/images/museum/TheStoryOfMaryKay.pdf

Notes

1. *The Story or Mary Kay Inc.*, 2013, p. 5. www.marykaymuseum.com/images/museum/TheStoryOf-MaryKay.pdf
2. Many are familiar with the Pink Cadillac award for top performers, though it has recently changed to Mini Coopers. But the Diamond Bumblebee is considered the "most cherished"

performance award at the company. The analogy is poignant. A bumblebee does not have the aerodynamics to fly, according to engineers, but it clearly does fly, symbolizing women who can fly to new heights that others think is impossible for them. See www.marykaymuseum.com/highlight_1970.aspx

3. *The Story of Mary Kay Inc.*, p. 4.
4. Mary Kay, Inc., "60 Minutes Rewind." www.youtube.com/watch?v=nrWz_MzKAMk, at 5:45.
5. Mary Kay Ash, *The Mary Kay Way*, Hoboken, NJ: Wiley & Sons, 2008, p. 29.
6. *The Mary Kay Way*, pp. 30-31.
7. *The Mary Kay Way*, p. 35.
8. Marcus Buckingham and Ashley Goodall, "The Feedback Fallacy," *Harvard Business Review*, March-April 2019, pp. 92-101.
9. "The Feedback Fallacy," p. 98.
10. This is the title of Chapter 4 of *The Mary Kay Way*.

WEGMANS
FOOD MARKETS
Caring for the People
Who Care for the Customers

The Lesson

Rooted in genuine compassion for employees, Wegmans has grown into one of the most admired companies in America.

Colleen Wegman, President and CEO of the company that bears her family name, likes to tell the story of how her grandfather, Robert Wegman, developed his business philosophy.

"When he was a young boy," she recalled in a college commencement address, "growing up in Catholic school, he was taught that there was only one thing important in life, and that was to get to heaven. He asked the nun, 'Well, how do you get to heaven?'

"The nun replied: 'Always help others. If you do that, you're on your way!'

"That became his guiding principle, and also became our favorite quote from my grandfather. In fact, helping others has become both our family mission and our company mission. My hope every day is that we are making a difference by helping others."[1]

Of course, not all Christians share that salvation theology, but it was a cornerstone for Robert Wegman, who in 1950 assumed leadership of the Rochester, New York grocery chain founded by his father and uncle. Robert's first order of business as president? Raise everyone's salary.

It was a sign of things to come: 56 years of servant-leadership. Fittingly, when you now walk into any of the 101 Wegmans Food Markets along the east coast, you'll see not only a wonderland of 70,000 attractively-displayed products, but also a large placard of Robert Wegman and the nun-of-his-business motto: "Never think about yourself; always help others."

As Robert signaled in 1950, foremost among those "others" were his employees. Today, with a labor force of about 50,000, Wegmans still maintains that their people are their primary stakeholders.

So do many other companies, but the proof is in the periodicals. Few companies can claim they've made *Fortune's* list of the "100 Best Companies to Work For." Fewer still—only twelve, actually—can claim they've made the list *every year* since its inception in 1998.

Wegmans is among that distinguished dozen, and it regularly makes not only the top 100, but the top five.[2] When it earned the first-place ranking in 2005, Robert Wegman remarked, tellingly, "This is the culmination of my whole life's work."[3]

Notice, the culmination wasn't the stores or the sales or even the customer accolades. It was the satisfaction of his people.

Awards like these naturally follow when your business philosophy is "always help others"—and when you're serious about core values like care, excellence, community, respect and empowerment.[4]

The practical outworkings are impressive, too: lavish health benefits, competitive pay, flexible scheduling, a positive climate, promotion from within, and a line of other perks that stretches into Aisle 12. Add to that a college scholarship program that has, since 1984, paid $110 million in tuition benefits for more than 35,000 employees, and it's no wonder that 94 percent of Wegmans employees agree that "this is a great place to work."[5]

That's 19 out of 20. In retail jobs, nonetheless.

The upshot is, according to *Consumer Reports*, 90 percent of the customers say that are "completely satisfied" with their Wegmans experience, ranking them second among 96 U.S. grocery chains.[6] That's 18 out of 20 in a pretty discerning crowd, and in some ways, that's the point. Current Chairman Danny Wegman—Robert's son and Colleen's father—put it this way: "When our people feel cared about and respected, they turn around and make our customers feel that way, too."[7]

Now, a cynic might argue that caring for employees is just a competitive advantage strategy with no moral basis. But the bigger picture at Wegmans suggests it's more than that. Employee care is part of a broad ethic of altruism that extends well-beyond their sliding front doors. Wegmans' philanthropy is simply legendary in upstate New York. They've given tens of millions to Catholic schools to educate at-risk and financially-challenged youth; tens of millions more to the Diocese of Rochester and other nonprofits for early childhood education, among other needs;[8] and millions of pounds of healthy food to all the communities in which they operate.[9]

In the Catholic social tradition, the underlying theology here is called "subsidiarity." Basically, it means that issues should be handled at the local level as much as possible.[10] Focus on the needs right in front of you—your people, your neighborhood, your city—before you try to address other needs.

However, you won't find fancy theological terms in Wegmans' corporate documents, promotions, or social media. Unlike some Christian-owned companies, Wegmans' leadership doesn't usually connect the dots from their priorities to God or Scripture or the Vatican. At least not publicly.

It's probably fair to say they neither convey nor conceal where their values come from. They just live them out, generously and consistently serving employee, customer and community alike.

And increasingly, that blessing is returned to them. In fact, in 2019, Wegmans finished first in the highly-regarded Harris Poll of corporate reputation.[11] So when it comes to most admired companies, that puts them atop not just the grocery business, but atop all businesses in the United States.

Whether that means the leadership is on their way to heaven, we can't really say. But they certainly seem to be reflecting it to more and more people.

For Further Study

"Wegmans Food Markets," *Fortune,* Fortune.com/best-companies/2019/wegmans-food-markets

Wegmans: Family-Owned Since 1916 (Wegmans Company History). www.wegmans.com/content/dam/wegmans/pdf/media/wegmans-company-history.pdf

Website: www.Wegmans.com

Notes

1. Commencement address to St. John Fisher College Class of 2017, as reprinted in *Rochester Business Journal,* June 9, 2017. RBJ.net/2017/06/09/colleen-wegman-key-principles-for-business-and-life
2. "Wegmans Food Markets Inc.," *Great Places to Work,* www.greatplacetowork.com/certified-company/1000459
3. Wegmans: Family-Owned Since 1916 (Wegmans Company History). www.wegmans.com/content/dam/wegmans/pdf/media/wegmans-company-history.pdf
4. "Company Overview," www.wegmans.com/about-us/company-overview.html
5. "Wegmans Food Markets Inc.," *Great Places to Work,* www.greatplacetowork.com/certified-company/1000459
6. Tobie Stanger, "The Brave New World of Grocery Shopping," *Consumer Reports,* August 2019, pp. 46-54.

7. "Love What You Do at Wegmans," jobs.wegmans.com/benefits

8. Mike Latona, "Major Gifts Make a Major Difference," August 4, 2014. CatholicCourier.com/articles/major-gifts-make-major-difference

9. Pamela N. Danzinger, "Why Wegmans Food Markets Gets the Love of Customers," *Forbes*, March 3, 2018. www.forbes.com/sites/pamdanziger/2018/03/03/why-wegmans-food-markets-gets-the-love-of-customers

10. Peyer Jesserer Smith, "Wegmans Among Businesses Putting Catholic Social Teaching to Good Use," *National Catholic Register*, May 2, 2017. www.ncregister.com/daily-news/wegmans-among-businesses-putting-catholic-social-teaching-to-good-use

11. "Wegmans Ranked #1 for Corporate Reputation in the 2019 Harris Poll Reputation Quotient Study," March 6, 2019, www.wegmans.com/news-media/press-releases/2019/wegmans-ranked--1-in-the-2019-harris-poll-reputation-quotient-st.html

WORLD WIDE TECHNOLOGY
DOING BUSINESS BY THE GOOD BOOK

The Lesson

Managing by Biblical principles has taken World Wide Technology from start-up to "Silicon Valley in St. Louis." David Steward, with an unshakable faith, never had any doubt.

They've now surpassed $11 billion in annual revenue. That's on par with Chick-fil-A. And their culture may be just as healthy, too.

In 1990, David Steward launched World Wide Technology (WWT). After netting about $250,000 from two companies he founded in the 1980s, the St. Louis sales specialist—once the companywide "Salesman of the Year" at Fed Ex[1]—ventured into a field he thought was poised for explosive growth: information technology.

Think internet, wifi, cybersecurity, cloud storage, customized software, and mobile devices. Or in business terms, WWT offers a comprehensive IT ecosystem for clients around the world, accelerating workflow, saving time, reducing costs, and overall, delivering a competitive advantage through technology.

It's how you get to billions in income each year. It's also how you become known as "Silicon Valley in St. Louis."

The start-up timing was perfect, for sure. How would you like to have been on the ground floor of the digital revolution in 1990? But David Steward wasn't just lucky. He was prescient.

He'll also tell you he was blessed. The very first line in his book *Doing Business by the Good Book* is this: "When I founded World Wide Technology, I wanted to run a company based on the teachings of the Bible."

As he did, the results followed.

David lists in that book the 52 Biblical principles he's applied. Woven through all of them, though, is his philosophy that as a leader, he's first a servant. David unashamedly says as much on the company's website: "I believe we are put on this earth to serve others. As the founder and chairman of WWT, my job is, and always has been and always will be, to serve the men and women who work here and help them succeed."[2]

Similarly, in his book he calls serving employees "his biggest job as CEO and owner."[3] It's taken various forms.

For example, in the early days, David ensured that everyone got paid, even though often he did not.[4] That's just who he is. Later on, he crafted a mission statement that's equally telling: "Create a profitable growth company that is also a great place to work." Of all the priorities he could juxtapose with "profitable growth," he selected employees.

Consequently, WWT offers one of the best benefit packages anywhere. Employees rave about how generous it is, even for the tech industry. It includes:

- Exceptional health insurance for employees and families, 90 percent paid by the company
- An insurance premium that hasn't budged in over a decade, despite skyrocketing costs
- A no-cost health clinic on-site
- A dollar-for-dollar match in their 401(k), up to six percent
- Paid time off starting at 17 days ... plus 10 holidays
- Paid maternity and paternity leave, tuition reimbursement, and even affordable pet insurance

Then there are the personal touches, like David signing cards for employee birthdays and Christmas. And the many family events, sometimes in suites for professional baseball, football and hockey games, with a buffet of first-class food. "We treat our people as though they are family, and we treat their families like family, too," says David.[5]

Perhaps it's no surprise, then, that the company has won so many awards from *Fortune* magazine—WWT is number 56 in *Fortune*'s latest list of "100 Best Companies to Work For"[6]—and from Glassdoor, a job search website that historically ranks WWT as a top 20 place to work.[7]

It's also no surprise that David has won so many awards from business and civic groups for his leadership. He calls it "Golden Rule Leadership," treating people the way he'd want himself and his family to be treated, a philosophy taught by Jesus.[8]

And David's not shy about communicating where it comes from: "A definite spiritual atmosphere prevails at World Wide Technology. Everyone here knows I live and manage by the Word of God, and there is an undercurrent of Christian counsel and ministry."[9]

Having said that, there's the same diversity at WWT that you'll find in the tech industry generally, an inclusivity one might anticipate in the largest African-American owned business in the country. David himself had to overcome so many hurdles in life; he's not about to erect them for others.

Instead, he's simply built a nurturing, energizing culture. In fact, ninety-three percent of his employees say "I'm proud to tell others I work here."[10]

But in a way, it's not been complicated to get the culture right. The DNA of the leader usually becomes the DNA of the company. And the DNA of WWT is WWJD.

As it has been from the beginning. "I was certain I would ultimately succeed," recalls David about the founding. "My confidence wasn't based on a wealth of business acumen or a string of successes under my belt. I felt this way due to my unshakable faith in God. Having this faith, I believed with all my heart and soul that he would see me through."[11]

Five thousand jobs, countless satisfied clients, and eleven billion dollars a year later, it seems that God has indeed.

For Further Study

David L. Steward, *Doing Business by the Good Book*, New York: Hyperion, 2004.

Notes

1. David L. Steward, *Doing Business by the Good Book*, New York: Hyperion, 2004, p. 29.
2. World Wide Technology, "David Steward, Chairman of the Board and Founder," www.wwt.com/profile/dave-steward
3. *Doing Business by the Good Book*, p. 13.
4. *Doing Business by the Good Book*, p. 12.
5. *Doing Business by the Good Book*, p. 157.
6. "2019 Fortune 100 Best Companies to Work For," www.greatplacetowork.com/best-workplaces/100-best/2019
7. Glassdoor.com, "2018 Best Places to Work: Employees' Choice," www.glassdoor.com/Award/Best-Places-to-Work-2018-LST_KQ0,24.htm
8. Matthew 7:12 and "David Steward, Chairman of the Board and Founder," www.wwt.com/profile/dave-steward
9. *Doing Business by the Good Book*, p. 118.
10. Great Place to Work, "World Wide Technology, LLC," www.greatplacetowork.com/certified-company/1100933
11. *Doing Business by the Good Book*, p. 1.

WALKER MANUFACTURING
CUTTING GRASS, NOT PEOPLE

The Lesson

A mantra for Bob and Dean Walker is "love people and use money," rather than the other way around. If that were easy, everyone would do it.

Connect, then lead. It's a basic principle in social psychology. Liking fuels leadership. Relationship feeds results. It's axiomatic.

Bob Walker has grown a business on that principle, from a regional company in the early 1990s to distributing across 31 countries today. Throughout, the man has been beloved by his employees.

But it's not because he tactically applied leadership theories. It's simply because he loved them first.

A decades-old example: How many company presidents, Christian or otherwise, wander the factory floor once a week handing out paychecks? That's unusual in a company of 200 employees, but more unusual still is that Bob knows them all by name, he stops to shake their hands and thank them for their service, and he asks about their families, most of whom he's met at one of the company events. The next week, he does it all again.

You don't get that from a textbook. The man has a personal touch that's from the heart—a heart that itself has been touched by God.

Walker Manufacturing makes commercial-grade lawnmowers, with add-ons for snow removal. Yeah, that sounds as exciting as, well, watching grass grow, but it's a challenging B-to-B niche, selling lawn care machines that cost as much as your car. To date they've sold more than 150,000 of them.

Proudly American-made with only American-made parts, veteran craftsmen in the Fort Collins, Colorado factory assemble about 30 mowers a day. They, too, have a personal touch. One guy put it this way to a film crew chronicling the Walker story: "I treat every lawnmower that I'm making like Christ is going to be getting that lawnmower. So I want to make sure that everything is just perfect on it."[1]

Clearly, at this mower company, "good enough" just won't cut it.

Not everyone at Walker is a believer, of course. There's no such requirement or expectation. But that employee's comment is a distinct echo of the front office where Bob and his brother Dean, VP of Product Development, often call God "our Senior Partner." And that itself is an echo of the founder, their late father Max, who "was careful to always recognize the Lord as his source of blessing, talent and strength."[2]

The practical expressions of their faith benefit customers, suppliers and the community at-large. Employees, though, are arguably first among the earthly stakeholders, enjoying competitive wages and great health benefits, a sizable profit-sharing bonus at Christmas, and a leadership team that's genuinely grateful for their efforts.

They hear it with every hand-delivered paycheck.

Employees also have access to an on-site chaplain because, Bob says, "We know that on any given day there is someone who is having problems of some kind, maybe outside of work. Our chaplain is the kind of person who is a good listener."[3] Along the same lines, the company offers financial counseling to employees as well as marital help, paying for marriage retreats and counseling sessions.

What employees may appreciate the most, though, is the ongoing job security. This is a seasonal business, so from an economic standpoint, the ideal is make mowers in-season and then scale back or shut down off-season. However, explains Bob, seasonal employment may fit the industry, but it doesn't fit employee needs. "People have a full-time life. Nobody has a seasonal life. So we've organized ourselves to have year-round employment."[4]

To do that, they keep production levels consistent throughout the year, rather than building more mowers some months than others. That might sound like a common sense solution, but it's uncommon in the industry because it requires retaining hundreds if not thousands of mowers in inventory. They also incur the risk of misestimating demand, rather than efficiently responding to it.

In plainer English, it's more expensive to operate the Walker way, though it's better for their people.

A dilemma? Not here. Their extensive corporate credo addresses the issue in the very first of its 18 tenets: "Operate by principles that are optimum for employees and their families." After that come the usual suspects of integrity, excellence, Sabbath-keeping, and financial stewardship.[5]

The ordering is revealing, not random. It's also rooted in scripture. Bob cites the others-first teaching of Philippians 2:4 as one basis for the primacy of employees. His voice shakes in awe of God's counsel: "When we face a decision and say *what's best for us?* scripture teaches we should be looking also to the interests of other people. It helps answer the question *what should I do?*"[6]

Their answer is to put people ahead of profits. "Love people and use money," as Bob and Dean like to say.

Here's further evidence that it's not just rhetoric at Walker. In late 2009, with the economy in a deep recession, orders dried up and inventory swelled at the company. Seeing no alternative, they began to lay off people. *Inc.* magazine recounted this crossroads moment:

"(Bob) has certain spiritual practices: regular prayer; the 15 minutes he devotes each morning to reading the Bible; the two-mile walk he takes every other day, alone. All are ways of preparing himself to receive what he describes not as an audible command, but rather as 'a quiet little voice that I hear in my mind, that tells me what I need to do.'

"What God told Bob Walker to do in late 2009 was to halt the layoffs and instead put small teams of employees to work on community-service projects around town—cutting grass, raking leaves, painting houses. Dean Walker got the same message at about the same time, and together they put the plan into action."[7]

Obviously, paying people their salaries to perform community-service did nothing to relieve the stress on Walker's financials, but it did save jobs and sustain employee families during the holiday season.

It's at times like these—under real duress, costing real dollars, in the face of real uncertainty—that we see whether our actual values match our articulated values. They did indeed at Walker Manufacturing, and the story even had a happy ending.

"Sure enough," recalled Bob, still getting choked up years later, "that was the bridge that we needed to get into January and February, and by the time we got to that point, things began to pick up a little bit. The easy thing would have been to lay people off."[8]

Just like the easy thing is to treat manufacturing employees like machines— utilitarian, disposable, replaceable. The easy thing is to treat them as costs to be minimized, instead of people created in the image of God and entrusted to the leader.

Sadly, some Christian-owned companies pay mere lip service to that theology. For Bob and Dean, it's on their lips as well as on their balance sheet, because it's in their hearts at Walker Manufacturing—a lawn care company that's equally committed to employee care.

For Further Study

David Whitford, "How This Entrepreneur Works Christianity Into His Craft," *Inc.*, July 2015. www.inc.com/magazine/201507/david-whitford/god-and-the-entrepreneur.html

"Making Beautiful Places for the Glory of God," Center for Faith and Work, LeTourneau University, October 1, 2013. Vimeo.com/75906040

Website: www.Walker.com

Notes

1. "Making Beautiful Places for the Glory of God," Center for Faith and Work, LeTourneau University, October 1, 2013. Vimeo.com/75906040 at 1:40.
2. "The Walker Story," www.walker.com/about/story
3. "Rooted in Truth and Love," *The Lookout*, December 20, 2015. Lookoutmag.com/2015/rooted-in-truth-and-love
4. "Making Beautiful Places for the Glory of God" at 2:50.
5. "What We Believe," www.walker.com/what-we-believe
6. "Making Beautiful Places for the Glory of God" at 3:20.
7. David Whitford, "How This Entrepreneur Works Christianity Into His Craft," *Inc.*, July 2015. www.inc.com/magazine/201507/david-whitford/god-and-the-entrepreneur.html
8. "Making Beautiful Places for the Glory of God" at 4:02.

POLYDECK SCREEN CORPORATION
Loving Employees through a "Caring Committee"

The Lesson

How do you make employee care a permanent reality? Assemble a "caring committee" and give them one percent of the budget.

In some ways, Peter Freissle's transformation was as radical as that of his namesake.

In the gospels, we read about Peter going from apathetic to Apostle—from a frustrated fisherman to faithful firebrand and the first to confess Jesus as the Christ. One day Jesus showed up on the dock and everything changed.

Two millennia later, Peter Freissle had a similar experience, going from autocrat to altruistic in a matter of days—from frustrated founder to faithful follower of Christ.

To back up a bit, it started with a 1994 journey from South Africa to South Carolina. Peter was working for his father's company in Johannesburg. Recently married with a child on the way, Peter asked God for a sign about what he should do and where his family should live.[1] "Not long after that," Peter told an industry magazine, "two men jumped out of a car at a red light and shot at my car with an AK-47. A bullet missed me, but went through the sleeve of my shirt. That was a clear enough sign for me."

At the time, South Africa was in a violent transition away from Apartheid. So Peter and his wife transitioned away from South Africa.

His father had a subsidiary in Spartanburg, SC, called Polydeck Screen Corporation, maker of polyurethane screens to sift the raw materials on mining sites (among other industries) into different sizes. As an example, Polydeck's screens could sift larger rocks for concrete, medium rocks for asphalt, and small particles for sand.

Sure, it might not seem like the most fascinating business, but it's an essential one and often a lucrative one. Within a few years, Peter assumed the top spot at Polydeck. His task was to sustain and grow the company, of course, but as Peter recalls, his real goal was simply to make as much money as possible.

And he did. Plenty of it as the company expanded their footprint to warehouses and dealers throughout North and South America. To get there, though, Peter and the other managers ran roughshod over employees. In fact, his people avoided Peter at all costs. Many went so far as to quit; turnover exceeded 20 percent. Things got so bad that a staffing company refused to send Polydeck any more candidates, after hearing reports of the harsh work environment.[2]

But just like with that other Peter, God showed up and everything changed for Peter Freissle. By 2006, his business was booming and so was his family, now with four children under ten-years-old. Yet all that success didn't satisfy. As Peter tells it, "I spent a lot of my life chasing the almighty dollar, and achieved the American dream, and when I achieved it, I felt empty."[3]

A friend had a potential solution, inviting him to take a silent retreat in Atlanta: a centuries-old practice known as the "Spiritual Exercises of Ignatius of Loyola."[4] Peter was unfamiliar with the retreat, but a few days of silence seemed oddly attractive, and Atlanta was just down the road. Plus, this generally fit Peter's worldview, having long been a Christian, albeit one who compartmentalized his faith. As his biographer wrote, "Peter was quite familiar with biblical principles, and he understood the concept of making God a part of his life, but he had never sat down and determined exactly what that meant."[5]

The retreat offered piercing clarity. God revealed to Peter that he had been running so fast that he could not hear his wife, nor his co-workers, nor his Creator. Now, though, mute and motionless, Peter heard God like never before.

He wrote down what he discerned, depicting his current life focus as a pie chart. About 80 percent of it was a segment that Peter labeled "ME." He had dedicated the vast majority of his time, energy and resources to his success and reputation. The other 20 percent divided into three slivers, one of which he labeled "social responsibility" and another "family." But even that might have been an overstatement. Peter realized that much of the investment in his family had been so he "could be recognized as the best father and provider for his family."[6]

On the third sliver, he wrote "God." It was a brutally honest and unexpected admission. "If you had met Peter the week before and asked him about his relationship with God," reports his biographer, "he would have told you that he had a great relationship with God and that he and his family attended church regularly. On that day he realized that it was all a lie. ... The God he had read about, talked about, and heard about all of his life, was nothing more in his life than a slice on a diagram, and a very small slice at that. ... Peter realized that this was not a mere epiphany. God did not simply speak to Peter; God had broken Peter to a point of repentance."[7]

In retrospect, Peter describes the moment this way: "I went to the retreat. God transformed my life through his mercies, through his forgiveness, and helped me to realize I didn't own the business. I didn't own anything. It was all a gift from him and I was here purely as a steward of what he gifted me. And he was going to ask me: 'What did I do with that he had given me?'"[8]

The practical takeaway? He needed to right the wrongs, first with his wife and children, and then with his employees. About the latter, says Peter, "I realized that I had to love my employees and use my work in order to glorify God. ... I've spent the rest of my life trying to please God by loving his people, my neighbors."[9]

So, reinventing his chart, Peter eliminated the narrow slices and made "God" the whole circle, with arrows pointing from God to the words "family," "business," and "society." Tellingly, his new-and-improved graphic had no category labeled "ME."[10]

Peter shared the revelation with his executive team and with Polydeck's employees. Many were skeptical. After years of heavy-handedness, their posture was basically "I'll believe it when I see it."

But did they ever, starting with a new core values statement, collaboratively designed: "We are a company grounded in the Christian values of humility, honesty, integrity, trust, respect, kindness, accountability and a sense of social responsibility. Our goal is to create eternal value by striving to honor God in all we do. This is reflected in how we conduct our business and how we care for our Polydeck family—our greatest strength." Peter even had this printed on the back of all their business cards.[11]

That was just the beginning, though. Peter knew that corporate statements don't touch culture. For something to change, he had to put money and people against the problem. Employee care had to be somebody's job and that person would need big bucks to pull it off.

Well, how about one percent of the company's multi-million dollar budget?[12] Peter tapped a leader and assembled what he called a "Caring Committee"—employees from every department—to decide how to use the money to bless employees and their families, as well as those outside the company.

The committee identified several categories of care, creating an employee "car repair fund," "home repair fund," "emergency loan fund" and "medical emergency fund," as well as a "benevolent fund" for extraordinary employee needs that didn't fit those other categories. There's also a "community charity fund" to contribute to nonprofit organizations, a "general fund" for family events, and a "reach out fund" for missions-related activities like Polydeck's employee trips to Nicaragua. They've built a school there, fed children, offered Vacation Bible School, conducted business workshops, and just shared God's love with Nicaraguan people.[13]

There's more. In the wake of 2006, Polydeck also developed what they called a "Caught You Caring" program to celebrate publicly employees who are living out the company's core values. And in the spiritual realm they offered employees a new resource library, a lunchtime Bible study, prayer groups and a corporate chaplain.

Relatedly, the company built a consulting unit called His Way at Work (hwaw.com) to export their God-centered workplace ideas to other companies. As part of that, Polydeck has boiled down its workplace initiatives a 3x3 matrix, with stakeholders on one axis (employees, families, community) and needs on the other (physical, emotional, spiritual). It's a compact tool to cultivate a culture of caring.[14]

Indeed, creating and bankrolling the Caring Committee was a masterstroke, but Peter took it one step further. Believing the old adage that "what gets measured is what gets done," his executive team built a balanced scorecard that also measured what they called Eternal ROI™ to track progress of the initiatives. They liked the term so much they even trademarked it.

A sampling of the metrics: community service hours per employee, charitable giving, employee satisfaction and turnover, number of employees involved in various caring programs (like hospital visits, marriage retreats, mission trips, prayer groups, and so on), and the number of employees and family members who have chosen to follow Jesus.

It's been nothing short of revolutionary. Turnover at Polydeck is currently three percent, not twenty-something. People just enjoy coming to work now, whereas fifteen years ago they did not. Polydeck also reports that employee productivity is up 10 percent since inception of the caring program. And perhaps most importantly for Peter, since 2006 more than 80 employees and family members have accepted Jesus as Lord and Savior—arguably the consummate definition of Eternal ROI.[15]

These outcomes didn't occur by chance. From a natural perspective, they're the result of intentionally using systems—staffing, budgeting, measurement and feedback—to produce what Peter says matters the most in his company. From a supernatural perspective, the outcomes may be God's blessing after he finally got Peter's attention on that retreat.

Sometimes you need to be silent to hear a still, small voice. But those who do, it seems, can't stay silent about it for long.

For Further Study

Steve O. Steff with Peter Freissle, *The Business Card*, Wor-K-ship Publishing, 2015. HWAW.com/wp-content/uploads/2016/09/The-Business-Card-4th-printing-July-2015.pdf

"Peter Freissle," His Way at Work, Vimeo.com/175289037

Websites: Polydeck.com and hwaw.com

Notes

1. Dennis Zeiger, "Polydeck Screen Corporation," *U.S. Builders Review*, January 14, 2015. www.usbuildersreview.com/case-studies/polydeck-screen-corporation-developing-innovative-specialty-screening-solutions-1978
2. "The Polydeck Story: A Continuing Case Study in Workplace Caring," July, 2017. hwaw.com/wp-content/up-loads/2017/07/Polydeck-Case-Study.pdf, p. 1.
3. "Peter Freissle," His Way at Work, Vimeo.com/175289037 at 0:10.

4. Steve O. Steff with Peter Freissle, *The Business Card*, Wor-K-ship Publishing, 2015. hwaw.com/wp-content/up-loads/2016/09/The-Business-Card-4th-printing-July-2015.pdf, pp. 24-25.

5. *The Business Card*, p. 25.

6. *The Business Card*, p. 26.

7. *The Business Card*, p. 27.

8. "Peter Freissle," His Way at Work, Vimeo.com/175289037 at 0:26,

9. "Peter Freissle," His Way at Work, Vimeo.com/175289037 at 1:02.

10. *The Business Card*, p. 32.

11. *The Business Card*, p. 55,

12. "The Polydeck Story," pp. 3-4.

13. *The Business Card*, p. 147. See also "Serving in Nicaragua" at Polydeck.com/blog/why-we-serve

14. "What We Do," His Way at Work, hwaw.com/what-we-do

15. "The Polydeck Story," p. 5.

TYSON FOODS
CHICKEN AND CHAPLAINS

The Lesson

For generations, Tyson has been feeding the world. Meanwhile, behind the scenes, their 100+ corporate chaplains have been feeding the soul.

They call themselves a "faith-friendly and inclusive" environment.[1] It's a curious pairing among Christian-owned companies.

Maybe even unique.

Perhaps that's because publicly-traded Tyson Foods of Springdale, Arkansas—producer of one-fifth of the country's chicken, beef and pork—is subject to shareholder scrutiny while still firmly controlled by the Tyson family.[2] Whatever the reason, Tyson's time-honored values have long served not just its owners, but the diversity of its 122,000 employees.

The primacy of employees traces its roots to the company's founder, John W. Tyson, a devout Methodist who came to Springdale in 1931 with his wife, a one-year-old child, "half a load of hay, five cents and a truck."[3] He spent the five cents on coffee and then started looking for loads to haul, securing work transporting live chickens.

Yes, that's the origin of one of the largest food companies in the world.

Over time, John began hauling longer distances, since the Midwest cities brought a higher price for chickens. On the way to those destinations, John filled-up at the gas stations that would extend credit. On the way back, after earning his money, he would pay the bill. Money was that tight.

But eventually John earned enough to buy his own hatchery, thereby creating and transporting his own inventory. In the 1940s, as public demand for chicken accelerated with the rationing of other foods and with the Baby Boom, John's company accelerated, expanding vertically into the feed business and commercial farms.[4] By 1957, John was selling 10 million chicken a year.

Fast-forward thirty years and the company was selling that many chickens *per week*, and today it's nearly quadruple that,[5] making it the largest chicken producer in the country. It also holds the second position in both beef and pork.

Clearly, the Tyson family has been a good steward from a financial perspective. A corporate biographer even called Tyson Foods "one of the most successfully managed corporations in the nation."[6] But unlike some companies that grew from the back of a truck to the front cover of magazines, the growth did not come at the expense of employees. Quite the opposite. From the days when John refused to lay off workers in tough times,[7] the Tyson family has prioritized employee care.

Case in point: When the company passed into the hands of John's son Don in the mid-1960—the man who took the company from $50 million to $10 billion in annual sales—employees still had a friend in the corner office. Though not a churchgoer, Don's style, like his father's, was to lead from "the middle of the line, not from the front or pushing from the rear."[8] He disdained suits, insisted on everyone calling him "Don," and for a while, famously charged executives twenty-five cents every time they used the word "employees" rather than "people."

It wasn't semantics. It was a disposition. A posture. A rhetorical reinforcement of workers' dignity and worth. To the press Don put it this way: "People make a business. Not numbers, not chickens, not anything else. People make a business."[9]

And historically, the implications have been impressive: competitive pay, generous profit-sharing,[10] comprehensive medical insurance, college scholarships, and a plethora of other benefits.[11] Among the perks, though, the most unusual is also among the most expensive: Tyson's team of corporate chaplains.

Actually, "team" is an understatement. No company on the planet employs as many chaplains as Tyson: 115 men and women across 22 states.

It was a third-generation innovation. In 2000, new CEO John H. Tyson, Don's son, established a chaplaincy function to offer pastoral care to workers and their families. Deeply influenced by his grandfather's faith, John H., a born-again believer, explained it this way: "I felt my calling and my responsibility was to create an environment of permission for people to live their faith—whatever that faith may be."[12]

Hence the guardrails: "Faith-friendly and inclusive."

John's charge to the chaplain team has always been to help people of faith, or of no faith, in any way they can. It's not to preach or to convert, unless the employee initiates such things. Rather, Tyson chaplains wander the work sites, being visible, building relationships, addressing issues as employees raise them.

Sometimes those issues are heavy and emotional: marital problems, addictions, an unexpected diagnosis, the death of a loved one. As one article said about Tyson, "where there is pain, there are chaplains."[13]

Also, though, where there is just ordinary need, there are chaplains: debt and budgeting, learning English, transportation issues, conflict with a co-worker. The Tyson chaplaincy is a ministry of availability, assisting people with day-to-day life.

The experience of one employee, Justin, is typical. When he first relocated to Tyson, he submitted several applications for housing, but no landlord would take him. Then, as Justin tells it: "Chaplain Abdullah was just talking to me, asking me if I had any problems or issues, and was just real warm and friendly and genuine. He pointed me in the direction I needed to go and ... within a couple days, I had a place."[14]

At the same time, the experience of Lindy is also typical. She told *The Wall Street Journal* that a company chaplain sat with her in the hospital while her young son had surgery, then comforted her after her son's death. The chaplains, said Lindy, "have faith and they pray with me, and I just love that about them. If I couldn't share my faith, I couldn't bring my whole self to work."[15]

The vast majority of the chaplains, like the flock they shepherd, are Christian, but many, like Chaplain Abdullah, are not. "We have people (chaplains) of Jewish faith," explained John H. Tyson. "We have people of Muslim faith. We got some 20 different variations of Baptists."[16]

Others as well. In that way, the structure is more akin to a military chaplaincy or a hospital chaplaincy, rather than the pastoral staff of a church.

Indeed, some companies preceded Tyson in this initiative; many more have followed. Some tap organizations like Corporate Chaplains of America for placement services; others find chaplains through their personal networks. But for all of them, Tyson Foods has become a benchmark as the company leadership represents God's love to a pluralistic workforce.

Tyson's program may also be a profitable one through higher productivity and lower absenteeism and turnover. Metrics are hard to come by. If "people make a business," though, then to care for them is to care for the business.

But rooted in their Christian heritage, ROI at Tyson is often measured more high-mindedly. Externally, their purpose is to feed the world.[17] Internally, it's to feed the soul.

For Further Study

Marvin Schwartz, *Tyson: From Farm to Market*, Fayetteville, AR: University of Arkansas Press, 1991.

Websites: TysonFoods.com, Chaplain.org (Corporate Chaplains of America)

Notes

1. "Our Purpose," Tyson Foods, www.tysonfoods.com/who-we-are/our-story/purpose-values
2. Page 16 of Tyson Foods' 2018 10-K report indicates that the Tyson family has "70.96% of the total voting power of the Company's outstanding voting stock." ir.tyson.com/reports/annual-reports/default.aspx
3. Marvin Schwartz, *Tyson: From Farm to Market*, Fayetteville, AR: University of Arkansas Press, 1991, p. 3.
4. *Tyson: From Farm to Market*, pp. 5-6.
5. Tyson Foods, "Tyson Foods Facts," ir.tyson.com/about-tyson/facts/default.aspx
6. *Tyson: From Farm to Market*, p. 37.
7. *Tyson: From Farm to Market*, p. 127.
8. *Tyson: From Farm to Market*, p. xii.
9. *Tyson: From Farm to Market*, p. xiii.
10. *Tyson: From Farm to Market*, p. 127.
11. Tyson Foods, "Compensation & Benefits," www.tysonsustainability.com/workplace/compensation-benefits
12. M. Alex Johnson, "Walking the Walk on the Assembly Line," MSNBC.com, March 24, 2005. www.nbcnews.com/id/7231900/ns/us_news-faith_in_america/t/walking-walk-assembly-line
13. Katie Clarey, "How Chaplains are Giving Tyson Foods a Major Assist," *HR Dive*, March 18, 2019. www.hrdive.com/news/how-workplace-chaplains-are-giving-tyson-foods-a-major-assist/550599
14. Tyson Foods, Inc., "Tyson Foods Chaplaincy Program," www.youtube.com/watch?v=vXj2huJEqIw at 1:25
15. Sue Shellenbarger, "Praying with the Office Chaplain," *The Wall Street Journal*, June 2, 2010. www.wsj.com/articles/SB10001424052748704853404575322742500015642, p. 2.

16. Justin Rohrlich, "Religious CEOs: Tyson Foods' John Tyson," *Minyanville*, May 19, 2010. www.minyanville.com/special-features/articles/john-tyson-christian-church-chaplain-methodist/5/19/2010/id/28276

17. Tyson Foods, "Our Story," www.tysonfoods.com/who-we-are/our-story

PART 5

THEIR POVERTY PLAN
They create jobs for people
who would not have one

Hershey Chocolate Company
Lamon Luther
Second Chance Coffee Company
Keystone Custom Homes
Tegu Toys
Sunshine Nut Company

HISTORICAL PERSPECTIVE

HERSHEY CHOCOLATE COMPANY

The Lesson

Conventional wisdom says cut back on people during a recession. Biblical wisdom may suggest investing in them instead.

"Those machines do the work of 40 men," the foreman boasted, showing the owner two excavators.

"Take them away," replied the unimpressed owner. "Hire the men."

That was the disposition of Milton Hershey, the owner in this exchange, during The Great Depression. His name is synonymous with "chocolate" in the United States. Perhaps it should also be synonymous with "compassion."

Like many successful entrepreneurs, Hershey had attempted and failed at several ventures before succeeding. Deep in debt to family members who would lend him nothing more, he finally broke through with his Lancaster Caramel Company in 1887, adding the secret ingredient of milk to the traditional caramel formula.[1]

But Milton Hershey saw something bigger on the horizon. At

185

the time, chocolate was a luxury, delicious but unaffordable. Hershey thought it possible to democratize the product, the way Henry Ford was democratizing the automobile at the time, making it available to the masses. He founded it the Hershey Chocolate Company in 1894 (the name later changed to Hershey Foods in 1968 and The Hershey Company in 2005).

Experimentation was the key, followed by automation. To do what no one else could, Hershey brought in some experienced chocolatiers and chemists. By the late 1890s, he had made real progress: His company was grossing $1 million a year (about $30 million in today's dollars) from the various caramel and chocolate products.

What really put him over the top, though, was his first-in-the-country innovation of adding milk to the chocolate. It took more than a year of trial and error to create a viable product, but once he did, Hershey sold the caramel side of the business and went all-in with chocolate.

It was an enormous risk for someone who had finally, at age 40, made a profit. But Hershey was undeterred, narrowing his product line to only the best sellers and working nonstop to perfect his chocolate recipe. In fact, Hershey may be best understood as a perfectionist inventor, obsessed with finding a better way. After several years of varying the types of cocoa beans, milk, sugar, temperature and timing, he formulated a milk chocolate that would satisfy both his pallet and the consumers' wallet.

In 1903, Hershey bought 1,200 acres of land in Derry Township, Pennsylvania, near the state capital, but more importantly, near a rail line and an abundance of fresh milk and clean water. There he built what would become the largest chocolate factory in America, as well as a model town.

Indeed, he had to build a town since so little existed there before. Curiously, Hershey's gamble—many at the time, including his wife, called it folly—became not just an experiment in low-cost candy-making, but an experiment in American industry: locating a factory in a rural rather than urban setting.

Both are now commonplace.

And when it came to his people, Milton Hershey was also far ahead of his time. In an era when wealthy business owners treated people as no different from machines, Hershey's Mennonite tradition prompted him in a different direction.

So rather than downsize, like most other businesses during the Depression of the 1930s, Hershey did the opposite, motivated by keeping people employed. Many if not most of the Derry townspeople would not have had jobs otherwise.

During that decade, Hershey's "Great Building Campaign" sustained people as it improved the town. He built what are today some of the major tourist attractions there: the ornate Hershey Theater, the Hersheypark Arena and Stadium, and the five-star Hotel Hershey, modeled after one he saw in Cairo. The luxury 200+ room facility was woefully under-utilized during those years, sometimes with just a few guests per night. But that wasn't the point. The project created jobs and it would pay for itself in the long run.

The building campaign also erected a modern office building for the factory and a community center that included two theaters, a cafeteria, a gym, a swimming pool, a bowling alley, a medical facility and a library.

Hershey also constructed the world-renown Milton Hershey School (then called the Hershey Industrial School), a further testimony to his generosity. At that school, orphan boys could get a free, first-class education and a pathway to a better life.

It's still free today. The $60 million he left in trust to that school in the early twentieth century has since grown to $14 billion, on par with Ivy League universities and enabling the school each year to provide no-cost education and housing to more than 2,000 boys and girls from difficult circumstances.

So in all, Hershey completed six major building projects during the Depression, employing 600 townspeople and many fewer excavators. It was unprecedented in the private sector then.

Fast-forward to today, a fifteen-minute drive through the town is regaling—the Chocolate World attraction, Hersheypark (the second most visited amusement park in America, behind Disney), the unique 2,600-acre school that looks like a college campus, the street lights shaped like Hershey Kiss chocolates, the occasional waft of chocolate in the air.

But from a different vantage point, the drive is a testimony. Faithful diligence, ingenuity and compassion created something extraordinary here, something enduring—something that put food on the table for generations of families, even when it may have been unprofitable to do so.

For Further Study

Nancy Koehn and Erica Helms, "Candy Land: The Utopian Vision of Milton Hershey," Case 9-805-066, Harvard Business School Press, 2005.

Hershey Community Archives: HersheyArchives.org

Notes

1. Some of the material for this story comes from Nancy Koehn and Erica Helms, "Candy Land: The Utopian Vision of Milton Hershey," Case 9-805-066, Harvard Business School Press, 2005.

LAMON LUTHER
Hiring the Homeless

The Lesson

Among the hundreds of thousands of homeless in the U.S., and the millions around the world, many are capable of exceptional work. By hiring the homeless, Lamon Luther puts quality in as it gives them a way out.

His two girls needed shoes. And some school supplies. But practically broke, the best he could do was ask his boss for help.

Fortunately, his boss was Brian Preston, owner of Lamon Luther and a big-hearted humanitarian. Brian rallied his friends and they lavished the girls with more than they needed. Then came the phone call from one of them, nine-year-old Madison.

"Brian, thank you for all the cool stuff, and thanks for letting my daddy work, because you know what? Daddy's not mad anymore and for the first time in years, he comes to see us."

It was a clarifying moment for Brian. An epiphany. "I thought we were just putting a few homeless guys to work. I thought we were just creating some opportunity for guys just to build again. But I had no idea that we were giving two little girls their father back. That's what we've seen at Lamon Luther."[1]

Rewind a few years. Brian and his wife were in a restaurant

when they overheard some people talking about a homeless community living in the woods near their house in Georgia. "I didn't think that homeless people lived in the suburbs," recalls Brian. "I thought homeless people lived in downtown Atlanta."[2]

Something inside nudged Brian to go see for himself. His family had been in poverty just recently, after his construction business tanked in the 2007 recession. Gone was their house, their car, their savings. In fact, they were one step away from living on the street—or in the woods.

Despite some cautions from well-meaning friends, Brian went to meet these guys. He learned about their needs and brought them supplies: firewood, propane, food. He built real relationships with them. There but for the grace of God…

That continued for two years, with Brian tapping friends and family members for contributions. Then it hit him: Nothing has changed for so many of these guys since I met them. Are people like me really helping? Or are we just enabling them?

So he took a relational risk, asking one of them, "What do you need? What do you *really* need?" As Brian tells it, "the guy put his beer down and looked up with his whiskey-stained eyes and said 'Brian, what we really need is a job. What we really need is an opportunity to provide for ourselves.'"[3]

These guys didn't have driver's licenses or cars or cell phones or even addresses. Nobody would hire them in that condition. They were stuck in a death spiral.

Brilliantly, providentially perhaps, Brian found a way to break that cycle. To supplement his job at a local church, he had been building and selling furniture out of his garage. It was going well, so well that he couldn't keep anything in stock. He needed a labor force; these guys needed work.

Many of them had the basic carpentry skills to do the work, too. So Brian invited one to work with him for a day. Then another day. Then another. He shared their creations on social media and within weeks, Brian was getting orders from a large design firm. Brian's employment model intrigued this firm and they loved the results. A business was born.

And the men were essentially reborn. Brian marveled at how work ignited a spark in them. Their creativity and diligence returned, as did their self-respect. Most powerfully, work gave them hope—so much hope that it became the company tagline: "Lamon Luther: Hope for the Craftsmen."

It gave them cash as well. A month into the job, Brian's first hire moved into a house. Others followed. The media became enamored. CNN did a story. So did CBS and *The Huffington Post*. Brian got invited to deliver a TED Talk. Then, all this visibility scored him a partnership with Williams Sonoma, a major high-end distributor.

It fit Brian's high-end work: Hundred-dollar cutting boards, $1,800 tables. The new supply channels generated more demand, more profits, more hires, more stories like Madison's: "Daddy isn't mad anymore."

Then there's this poignant parallel. Everything at Lamon Luther is made from what's called "reclaimed wood"—discarded pallets, old barns, old houses. They take out the rusty nails and run the wood through a cleaning and finishing process. Out comes something fruitful.

That wood has become a metaphor. When Brian says "we take broken things and reclaim them into something beautiful,"[4] he's talking about both the wood and the men.

Reclaimed wood, reclaimed lives.

Brian beams when he talks about the parallel. "Society views both as garbage, as trash. … But we believe that there's potential in the broken. … What happens in this space is that we take a broken man, and we take a broken board … and transform that into a beautiful product."[5]

And maybe transform a few families along the way as well.

For Further Study

"Hope for the Craftsman: Brian Preston at TEDx Atlanta," www.youtube.com/watch?v=V2xx4BAL5Yg

Notes

1. "Hope for the Craftsman: Brian Preston at TEDx Atlanta," www.youtube.com/watch?v=V2xx4BAL5Yg at 14:25.
2. "Social Entrepreneur Hires Homeless Carpenters," 100 Huntley Street, www.youtube.com/watch?v=_94pPmBbFiM at 2:50.
3. "Hope for the Craftsman" at 5:45.
4. "A New Legacy," Lamon Luther, Vimeo.com/87830214 at 1:40.
5. "Social Entrepreneur Hires Homeless Carpenters" at 9:00.

SECOND CHANCE COFFEE
Giving Felons a Fresh Start

The Lesson

It's possible to create a product in the top one percent with people that society says are in the bottom one percent—and along the way, restore their lives.

Imagine a for-profit company whose mission is to transition people from imprisoned to employed ... and then to empowered.

Empowered to put their past behind them. Empowered to start over. Empowered to get it right this time. Or at the very least, empowered to get their life back.

That business exists in Wheaton, Illinois. Here's why.

The United States has the highest incarceration rate in the world, with more than two million people behind bars. And according to some of the most thorough research on the issue, eight percent of all adults in the U.S.—more than 20 million people—have a felony conviction on their record.[1] When these people look for a job, what do you think awaits them?

Typically, another unscalable wall. Most employment applications ask whether you've been convicted of a crime. When you check "yes," it's game over. On to the next application, and the next.

That check mark is a scarlet letter, a life-sentence of rejections. It may be one reason the three-year recidivism rate (those going back to prison within three years of release) hovers between 37 and 50 percent.[2]

Enter Pete Leonard, an entrepreneur and software developer from Chicago. He saw first-hand the plight of a post-prison family member who couldn't get a job anywhere because of his record. It seemed so wrong to Pete, but there wasn't much he could do.

Or was there? Around the same time, Pete had been experimenting with coffee bean roasting. He had what he calls a "coffee epiphany" while on a mission trip to Brazil, experiencing freshly roasted coffee unlike anything he ever tasted. So he tried his hand at it.

His primitive first attempt at roasting involved a gas grill and a couple pots riveted together. Pete got better at the process, though, inventing more sophisticated contraptions. When he shared his creations with the neighborhood, they were so good that many offered to pay him.

Despite that, Pete had no plans for starting a business. "That was not on my radar," he recalls. "It was on God's radar; it wasn't on my radar. All I was really doing was trying to find great tasting black coffee, and eventually I got there."[3]

Then a novel idea began to percolate. Might he be able to build a coffee roasting business by employing ex-convicts, people like his family member who couldn't find work? That would give them more than a paycheck; it would give them a path to a new life.

But this would be a double-shot business. Pete also wanted to do right by the customer. His distinctive was quality—exceptional quality similar to what he experienced in Brazil. "I wanted to produce the best possible product," Pete explained to *Christianity Today* magazine, "and not guilt people into buying our coffee because of our mission."[4]

His value proposition went even further. Pete would deliver his coffee farm-fresh and Amazon-fast: You place an order today, we roast it today, you get it today. In Pete's words, from his LinkedIn page: "The business model is simple: Meticulously select beans from the top one percent of coffee in the world and then roast and deliver that coffee within hours of it being ordered."

All of that with a workforce of former felons, "employees who, because they have a label of 'felon,' are seen by society as being in the bottom one percent."[5]

An irony indeed: The bottom one percent, as some perceive, producing coffee in the top one percent. Pete called it the Second Chance Coffee Company.

Was it just a crazy caffeine high? He'd find out in 2007 as he started peddling his products online, at farmer's markets, and eventually at swanky Whole Foods Market. Cleverly, Pete named his brand "I Have a Bean," taking inspiration, of course, from "I Have a Dream," a fitting vision for his workers.

The company got traction and then grew rapidly, from one employee roasting four hours per week, to several employees roasting every day, to 24/7 roasting just to keep up with demand. Sales from their humble, side-street location now top a million dollars a year.

Sounds easy. It wasn't.

On the way to a seven-figure gross income, the logistical challenges were enormous. For example, normally it takes 18 months for someone to master the complex art of coffee roasting. You don't just put beans over heat for three minutes like popcorn. It's a delicate process, prepared in small batches with varying heat to generate unvarying consistency. So how could Pete get his people to roast beans perfectly from day one on the job?

Through sheer ingenuity. Pete invented a machine and wrote proprietary software that allowed new employees to get it right quickly. Almost comically, he named his patented roaster "The Bean Master 5000."

His competition isn't laughing, though. They're still trying to figure out how he's never lost a taste competition. It worked that well.

There were also logistical challenges in hiring. According to one industry magazine, it's a rigorous process: "Getting hired at Second Chance Coffee requires more than a rap sheet. In addition to minimum expectations like showing up on time, working hard, and taking initiative, Pete looks for candidates who are willing to take responsibility for their mistakes. An ideal employee, according to Pete, is one who is committed to turning his life around."[6]

Pete's screening process hasn't been flawless, but he's had great instincts. By the end of 2018, Pete had hired more than 50 post-prison employees who, since joining the company, have a recidivism rate of a meager four percent. In Illinois, the rate is 50 percent.

Even more impressive may be Pete's secret ingredient for leadership. It's his willingness to take a chance on people—to give them a "second chance," if you will.

A few examples.

His office manager was formerly in jail for embezzlement. But he put her in charge of the money anyway.

One of his roasting crew was coming in so early that Pete gave him a key to the building—one week into the job. The man just broke down in tears at that kind of trust.

And one of Pete's first employees, a gang-banger incarcerated for attempted murder, has now graduated from coffee roasting to inmate ministry.

It's such an instructive story for believers in business. Pete Leonard's process innovations may explain his product success. It's his social innovation, though, accepting those rejected by other employers, that explains his pastoral success.

Christianity Today captured the root issue well: "Leonard, a Christian, isn't just a coffee connoisseur. He spends just as much time thinking about the people who roast it."[7]

As a result, many of them will spend their time as confident, contributory members of society.

For Further Study

April Burbank, "The Hope Roaster: How Pete Leonard's coffee roasting startup could become the world's largest employer of former convicts" *Christianity Today*, April 23, 2013, p. 46. www.ChristianityToday.com/ct/2013/april/hope-roaster.html

"The Top 1%" Faith & Co., Seattle Pacific University. Faithandco.spu.edu/film-detail/the-one-percent-bean

---

Notes

1. Sarah K.S. Shannon et al., "The Growth, Scope, and Spatial Distribution of People with Felony Records in the United States," 1948-2010," *Demography*, Volume 54, Issue 5 (October 2017), pp 1795–1818.
2. See, for example, this research by the Pew Charitable Trust and the Bureau of Justice Statistics: "The Changing State of Recidivism: Fewer People Going Back to Prison," August 1, 2018. www.PewTrusts.org/en/research-and-analysis/articles/2018/08/01/the-changing-state-of-recidivism-fewer-people-going-back-to-prison
3. "The Top 1%" Faith & Co., Seattle Pacific University. Faithandco.spu.edu/film-detail/the-one-percent-bean at 1:35.
4. April Burbank, "The Hope Roaster: How Pete Leonard's coffee roasting startup could become the world's largest employer of former convicts" *Christianity Today*, April 23, 2013, p. 46. www.ChristianityToday.com/ct/2013/april/hope-roaster.html
5. "The Top 1%" at 4:01.
6. Jodi Helmer, "Out of Jail, Into Espresso," *Fresh Cup Magazine*, March 16, 2015. www.freshcup.com/out-of-jail-into-espresso
7. "The Hope Roaster," p. 46.

KEYSTONE CUSTOM HOMES
Alleviating Poverty through Microfinance

The Lesson

When we offer the poor mere charity, it may not really help them. At least not long-term. But when we offer them a business loan, it permanently empowers them to help themselves.

Jeff Rutt had a problem. It was dwarfed by the problems of those he was trying to help on the other side of the world, but it was a problem nonetheless. The food and clothing his company had been donating for three years may have been doing more harm than good. Paradoxically, their helping was hurting.

Some quick context. In 1992, Jeff founded Keystone Custom Homes, a home-building company in southern Pennsylvania. As a devout Christian, Jeff always tried to run his business on faithful principles, operating transparently and with integrity, offering extraordinary quality and service, ensuring that his hardworking employees got fair pay and adequate rest.

And as a devout strategist, Jeff wisely positioned Keystone between the custom and standard builders, with elements of both. "Mass customization" it's sometimes called, and when combined with Jeff's efficient culture of high productivity—it was just a norm among the people he attracted to the company—Jeff attained a favorable cost structure relative to comparable builders.

So it's only natural that the company grew and expanded geographically. The accolades, though, tell a bigger story. Keystone was, in fact, the first in the country to be named "America's Best Builder" three times. That's nothing less than the industry's most prestigious award, conferred by the 200,000-member National Association of Home Builders.[1]

But a funny thing happened on the way to the top. Jeff felt increasingly drawn to help those on the bottom, specifically those in the country of Ukraine.

He tells about it in his foreword to the book *Created to Flourish*: "After the fall of the Soviet Union, Ukraine faced a debilitating economic crisis, leaving many without enough food to eat or clothes to wear. Along with others in my church, I felt compelled to respond. There were people who were hungry, who needed shelter, who didn't have the hope of Jesus Christ."[2]

His church in Lancaster, Pennsylvania established a partnership with a church in Ukraine, and for three years, benefactors like Jeff sent containers of flour, rice, canned meat, clothing, and medical supplies. However—now full circle to the problem that opened this chapter—as much as that served immediate needs, it may have been doing long-term harm as the disposition of those receiving it went from gratitude to entitlement to dependency.

The aid from Lancaster also undercut local business owners in Ukraine who couldn't compete with free goods. At some point, Jeff's contact in Ukraine asked him to reconsider: "Isn't there a way you can help us help ourselves?"

It was an epiphany for the whole group. Jeff spent months researching and praying for a solution, eventually stumbling upon something called "microfinance"—the model of providing small loans and other financial services to people who have no access to credit, but have a vision to build a business that would lift them out of poverty.

The simplicity of the idea belies its power. Let's say a woman in a developing country has skills as a seamstress. Since she earns so little and must spend almost all of it on her family, it might take her 20 years to save up $100 to buy a sewing machine and start a real business. But if she had a loan to buy that sewing machine today, she could immediately multiply her income, paying off that loan in a year or two and giving her family a better life, maybe even hiring others eventually.

The long-term solution to poverty, as Jeff learned, was not charity, but what some call "uncharity": Instead of giving gifts, come alongside of people to facilitate their entrepreneurial goals. It's a fundamental shift in mindset toward the poor, from "you can't, you won't, you're unable" to "you can, you will, you were created for more than this"—a shift from "we can do this for you" to "you can do this for yourself."

Or as they like to say at Keystone, offering a hand-up rather than a handout.

Contrary to the stereotype, many of the poor around the world have skills and dreams and a great work ethic. To break the cycle of poverty, they just need some financial services—a $50 or $100 loan and a safe place to keep their money—and maybe some business training.

If you think that's a brilliant idea, you're in good company. A man named Muhammad Yunus won the Nobel Peace Prize in 2006 for pioneering the concepts of microfinance and for launching a bank to implement it. It's that transformational.

Learning about that model, Jeff says, was "a breakthrough moment" for him. After benchmarking microfinance organizations, he created his own, initially funded in large part by his company.

Specifically, he recalls: "While there was much I didn't know about this approach, I believed God was calling me to step out in faith. After much prayer and seeking the counsel of those around me, HOPE International was registered as a 501(c)(3) nonprofit organization in May 1997, and the next year, HOPE officially disbursed its first loans to entrepreneurs in (Ukraine)."[3]

Twelve loans in all the first year, along with Biblically-based management training for those receiving the funds, to help get them traction.

Eventually Jeff hired Peter Greer, a passionate young man with a Harvard graduate degree, to grow the organization. Peter was clearly the right man for the job. Anointed for it, even. Operations accelerated and to date, HOPE International has distributed loans to almost one-million clients in Eastern Europe, Africa, Asia and Latin America. They're jewelry makers and hairdressers, shop-keepers and bakers. Literally hundreds of other professions as well, receiving capital—the lifeblood of business—while also receiving discipleship from HOPE, the lifeblood of life.

It may be hard to get our minds around just how contributory this is, so Jeff loves to tell stories of individual impact. One of his favorites has been about Anastasia from Burundi, the third poorest country in the world. Anastasia got a $20 loan from HOPE to start a wedding business. At first, that only allowed her to buy 20 chairs to rent out for weddings, but as she made money, she was able to buy more chairs, then place settings, then baskets, then wedding dresses in small, medium and large.

Her wedding business is thriving as she works toward enrol-ling her girls in the local university—an impossibility without mi-crofinance.[4]

An impossibility, also, had she received $20 in rations. HOPE didn't *give* Anastasia anything; rather, they empowered her to pur-sue her dreams. And like 98 percent of the loans that HOPE dis-burses, Anastasia paid hers back, allowing that money to be used by others.

Now, multiply that story by one-million clients and you get some sense for the difference that people like Jeff Rutt and Peter Greer are making.

A percentage of every Keystone home sale goes to fund HOPE International. Beyond that, though, Jeff made a way for others in his profession to get involved. Homes for Hope, his second non-profit venture, invites builders and their subcontractors to do what they do best—build a house—and donate the profits to HOPE or similar organizations. Jeff's not asking them to write a check passively; he's asking them to invest themselves actively in the mission, creating a pathway to prosperity for the poor.

Have they ever. Since the late 1990s, builders across the nation have constructed more than 100 homes under this program, generating over $10 million in donations.[5] That's a lot of loans, a lot of sewing machines, a lot of Anastasias.

And that's a lot of hope from microfinance, a powerful—and permanent—answer to global poverty.

For Further Study

Peter Greer and Phil Smith, *Created to Flourish: How Employment-Based Solutions Help Eradicate Poverty*, Lancaster, PA: HOPE International, 2017.

Websites: KeystoneCustomHome.com, HopeInternational.org, Homes4Hope.org

Notes

1. See KeystoneCustomHome.com/why-keystone
2. Peter Greer and Phil Smith, *Created to Flourish: How Employment-Based Solutions Help Eradicate Poverty*, Lancaster, PA: HOPE International, 2017, p. 13.
3. *Created to Flourish*, p. 13.
4. For more stories like these, see uncharity.hopeinternational.org
5. See homes4hope.org

TEGU TOYS
Building Blocks to Rebuild Honduras

The Lesson

Creating jobs in a developing country is among the most worthy pursuits. Just be prepared to work harder than you ever have in your life.

It was kind of a fluke, a last minute request from his church. "The youth pastor is sick and can't lead the Honduras trip. Can you step in for him next week?"

Chris Haughey had a month until starting his new job at Boston Consulting Group (BCG), so he accepted. Having served in missions since he was a kid, he knew what to expect.

Or so he thought.

Little could have prepared him for his first exposure to the Honduran capital of Tegucigalpa—the extreme poverty, the malnutrition, the toxic river, the drug peddling, the alcoholism. Then there was the incessant gang violence. It's one of the most dangerous cities in the world. Everyone, it seemed, had a story to tell about friends or family being killed.

Children under 15 comprise 40 percent of the city's population. Rather than go to school, many go to the streets to shine shoes or to sell merchandise or fruit, or themselves, helping their family however they can.

Some families live next to dumpsters so they can be the first to scavenge them. Many pick through the city dump, just trying to make it through the day.

The Honduran people, Chris saw, were in dire need beyond anything he had experienced. One-third of adults are unemployed; two-thirds live below the poverty line. Honduras is the third poorest economy in the Western Hemisphere.

But in God's economy, there are no flukes. God specifically chose Chris for that mission trip in 2004. At least it seems so in retrospect.

During his first two years at BCG, Chris's clients included several Mexican companies where, he says, God prepared him to build a business in Latin America. Then in 2006, he found himself back in Honduras on a business trip where he met up with some of his missionary friends. Chris asked them: "What kind of business could we create in Honduras? What does Honduras have to offer the world?"[1]

His friends shrugged, "not that much," but Chris noticed the beautiful and underutilized hardwoods in the country, especially mahogany. He had grown up doing some woodworking, so he considered building a fine furniture business in Honduras.

Months later, while in Germany, he stumbled across a potentially better idea: wooden toy blocks.

On one hand, that seemed hopelessly anachronistic. On the other hand, Chris was a Stanford University engineer. An innovator. A problem solver. He had a smart brother, too. Will Haughey was not only an alumnus of the top-ranked Kelley Business School, he was a consultant at Goldman Sachs.

The boys put their heads together, and their hearts. Over the phone they prayed about the idea once a week.

Each came away with a peace about the direction, so they "set out to bring these classic wooden toys into the 21st century."[2] Their innovative masterstroke was magnets—magnets embedded in the blocks so they'd stick together. It allowed unlimited creativity for, as they like to say at Tegu, "kids and kids at heart." No electronics, no screens, no batteries, no instruction manuals. Just imaginative fun.

Magnetic wooden blocks, though, were just a means to a much greater end. The real goal was to improve the quality of life for individuals, families and the whole city of Tegucigalpa; to give people work and careers; to rescue kids from the dumps and dumpsters, and enroll them in school. The mission of Tegu Toys was to build Honduras, one job at a time.

It was a more sustainable solution than handouts, thought Chris: "You'd think the solution to poverty is more aid or greater charitable giving. But those are only short-term, stopgap solutions. If you care about the poor, then you're going to seek out ways to create new economic opportunities for them."[3]

That's just what these two business guys did, using the platform of a for-profit business to generate jobs and prosperity and hope, all of which gradually alleviate social problems. In fact, they went all-in, leaving their lucrative jobs and raising a million dollars in start-up capital from friends, family and others who embraced their purpose and profit potential.

By 2008, they were ready to launch, Chris running the facility in Tegucigalpa and Will handling marketing and distribution in the United States. Hiring 12 people initially, they grew to 50 in 2010 and 90 in 2013.

Today, Tegu employs 200 factory workers in addition to a U.S.-based staff. They manufacture tens of thousands of blocks every day, selling them in thousands of stores. Their block sets come in all kinds of shapes and colors, with every piece compatible. And for each toy set purchased, the company either plants 12 trees or funds a day of school for an impoverished child.[4] Customer's choice.

It's a unique niche: Eco-friendly magnetic building blocks that are "purposefully made in Honduras."

Over the next decade, positive publicity and well-deserved awards fueled their growth. *Christianity Today* listed Chris and Will among their "20 Most Creative Christians" in 2016.[5] Tegu also won the U.S. Secretary of State Award for Corporate Excellence,[6] the Krider Prize for Creativity,[7] and in 2017, the Toy Award, arguably the industry's top honor.[8]

They won plenty of others as well,[9] but the Krider tribute seemed to capture Tegu's distinctives most cogently: "By paying employees a living wage and prioritizing long-term career growth and development, rather than simple task-based jobs, Tegu brings world-class employment standards to Central America. They do all of this and still manage to create an incredibly well-designed and beautiful product."

Chris is similarly cogent when describing the deeper success: "We've seen Tegu employees come to know Christ as a result of working at the company. We've seen families get on a track of financial stability after having been out of work, and we've seen people who started with us at the age of 20 with no work skills become industrial professionals."[10]

Production manager, Lesly Aguero, adds that employees are now finding education for their kids, purchasing health care, and maybe most importantly, "they can dream and actually make those dreams a reality."[11]

Block by block, job by job, life by life, Tegu Toys has been shifting the social reality of Tegucigalpa. But then there's the business reality. Despite all the growth and awards, Chris reports that: "We've multiple times faced the company imminently going out of business, as the cash in the bank was dwindling."[12] Will elaborates: "People look at Tegu as an example of 'we've made it.' But I don't think we've made it. ... We've experienced setbacks every year along the way. Nothing has been easy."[13]

First, there was the poor timing of launching during a global economic downturn—and a Honduran military coup. Then the price of magnets spiked two years into their operation. At one point, the boys endured the unspeakable pain of having to lay off 150 workers, just to avoid bankruptcy. "Ever since Tegu was launched, it has been a grind," Will revealed at a Wheaton College chapel. "I've never once in 10 years ... felt that it was secure."[14]

It's such a good idea, and such a novel product. Why the financial challenges? Business 101: revenues minus expenses.

Tegu's commitment to Honduras has entailed oversized costs

and undersized margins. Will explains: "We have knowingly accepted less than industry-competitive margins. ... If we had been using factories in Asia, our product margins would have been more than 50 percent. In Honduras, however, they were below 30 percent" because it's not a manufacturing economy and because Tegu's pay rate is so much higher than competitors shipping from China.[15]

Bottom line: Tegu Toys never turned a profit in its first nine years of operation. And at the bottom of that ninth, Chris lost his job. The Board of Directors, consisting of the company's largest investors, made a leadership change in 2018.

Yes, they fired the founder. It doesn't just happen at Apple.

Months later, a stoic Chris Haughey told an auditorium of college students: "As you can imagine, it's been a difficult experience to walk through. ... Right now, calling looks a lot like falling."

He's not lost perspective, though, nor faith, sharing that he's exceedingly grateful to God that he got to "make a difference in the lives of hundreds of people we've employed, and their families."[16]

And Tegu continues to make a difference in those lives. Will remains at the helm and time will tell if this remarkable ministry can be sustainable. One thing is certain, though: Creating jobs in a developing country—contributory as it may be—is anything but child's play.

For Further Study

"Taylor University Chapel, Chris and Cindy Haughey," November 28, 2018. www.youtube.com/watch?v=7yVWWdasJeE

Bethany Jenkins, "Tinkering with the Toy Industry," The Gospel Coalition, December 10, 2013. www.thegospelcoalition.org/article/tinkering-with-the-toy-industry

Website: www.Tegu.com

Notes

1. "Taylor University Chapel, Chris and Cindy Haughey," November 28, 2018, www.youtube.com/watch?v=7yVWWdasJeE at 22:30.
2. "The Tegu Story: Magnetic Wooden Toys to Change a Nation" Nov. 23, 2010, www.youtube.com/watch?v=oKLwkOvn_4I at 1:15.
3. "How Do You Take Down Poverty? One Toy Block at a Time," American Enterprise Institute, April 23, 2013. www.youtube.com/watch?v=28PJPSms_xU at 0:30.
4. Kara Bettis, "Play Hard, Work Hard: How the Haughey Brothers Launched Tegu and Almost Lost Everything," *Relevant Magazine,* November-December 2015, pp. 48-49.
5. Kate Shellnutt, "CT Makers: 20 of the Most Creative Christians We Know," *Christianity Today,* June 23, 2016. www.christianitytoday.com/ct/2016/julaug/ct-makers-20-of-most-creative-christians-we-know.html
6. See "Remarks by Ambassador Nealon at a Ceremony to Recognize Tegu as a Finalist for the Secretary of State's Award for Corporate Excellence," hn.usembassy.gov/remarks-ambassador-nealon-ceremony-recognize-tegu-finalist-secretary-state-award
7. "2018 Krider Prize for Creativity," University and College Designers Association, www.ucda.com/2018-krider-prize-for-creativity
8. See www.toyaward.de/en/2017 and www.youtube.com/watch?v=y1-GYnHOzeE
9. Among some of the other awards Tegu has won are the Academics Choice Brain Toy Award, Astra Best Toys for Kids, NYIGF (New York International Gift Fair) Baby and Child Best Toy, Dr. Toy Best Green Product, and Oppenheim Toy Portfolio Gold.
10. "Taylor University Chapel, Chris and Cindy Haughey" at 29:00.
11. "How Do You Take Down Poverty?" at 1:35.

12. "Taylor University Chapel, Chris and Cindy Haughey" at 30:30.
13. "Play Hard, Work Hard."
14. "Will Haughey, Tegu," Wheaton College, October 27, 2017. www.youtube.com/watch?v=w-qv8SxOGqc at 12:06.
15. Bethany Jenkins, "Tinkering with the Toy Industry," The Gospel Coalition, December 10, 2013. www.thegospelcoalition.org/article/tinkering-with-the-toy-industry
16. "Taylor University Chapel, Chris and Cindy Haughey" at 28:00.

SUNSHINE NUT COMPANY
TRANSFORMATION IN MOZAMBIQUE

The Lesson

When the accumulation of material possessions doesn't satisfy, it's time to try it God's way. For Don and Terri Larson, that meant selling everything to start a benevolent business in Africa.

When there's an automatic weapon sticking in your ribs, you don't ask a lot of questions. You just comply.

That's exactly what Don Larson did when thugs broke into his house in Mozambique and demanded his car keys. To add to the urgency, his wife and two sons were kneeling in the driveway, held hostage by another gunman.

But then, Don did ask a question. He yelled to his wife: "Terri, where are the car keys?" to which she yelled back: "I tell you all the time to put them in the same place because someday you're going to need them and you're not going to find them. You never listen to me!"

Don would survive to remind his chuckling, TED Talk audience: "Ladies, there's a time to correct your husband. But not when he has a barrel in the side of his gut."[1]

He found his keys and the criminals took off, leaving the family physically unharmed but curiously, more resolved than ever. Rather than abandon their mission in Mozambique, they doubled down on it. "That AK-47," says Don, "didn't faze me. It actually galvanized me."[2]

Don Larson is an unusual man, and not just for his grace under pressure. In his mid-40s, he left a lucrative executive position with The Hershey Company to start a business in a poverty-stricken country.

At Hershey, he was known as "the turnaround guy," traveling the world and bringing innovation to various sectors of the business. But when his stint as Director of Cocoa Operations took him through Africa, he was appalled at the primitive living conditions, the tattered and torn clothing, and especially the farmers with crops rotting in the field. Bizarre amidst the poverty, but what those farmers really needed, Don learned, was a market.

"The plight of those farmers kept nagging me," Don recalls. "And a few years later, I went radical: I decided to sell everything I owned, move my family to one of the poorest countries in the world in Africa, and invest everything I had in a new business model."[3]

He even sold his Porsche and hot air balloon. Don, Terri and two of their children left Hershey, the self-proclaimed "Sweetest Place on Earth," and in 2011 launched a cashew company in Mozambique, among the saddest places on Earth. Decades of civil war had ravaged the nation, leaving in its wake countless widows and orphans, unsafe drinking water, an unstable government and a society where bribery, petty theft and home invasions were commonplace.

Hence the machine gun in Don's side.

By then, Don's fledgling cashew company—he selected that product because of the many cashew farms in Mozambique—was getting traction, at least in the African markets. Business people and politicians had told him he could never compete by operating in that country, but his penetrating response demonstrates why they were wrong: "I don't want to just compete. I want to win in the world marketplace."[4]

Years later, he is winning. More than 3,000 U.S. stores now carry Sunshine Nut products—stores like Whole Foods, Wegmans, Giant and Albertsons.

However, it wasn't the social mission that sold his cashews; initially, Don masked that, wanting to compete on the merits. Sunshine cashews sold because they were simply fresher than competing brands, packaged at the point of origin soon after shelling, which is uncommon in the industry. It's generated millions in annual revenue and strong profitability.

But frankly, all that is the means rather than the end. The real aspirations of the turnaround guy has been to turn around lives and communities.

It starts within. Many of his all-African staff, the vast majority Mozambicans, would not have jobs without Don's factory. He's been particularly embracing of those from difficult circumstances. "Most of my employees," explains Don, "were either abandoned or orphaned in their youth. What we were looking to do was to provide opportunity and hope for them, and transformation."[5]

He gives them careers as well, not just jobs, developing people and promoting from within. Their production manager, Benaria, is one of many examples.

When Benaria was young, his father died, his mother gave him up to his grandparents, and his grandparents beat him regularly. So as a teen he ran away, only to be mentored by one of the worst criminals in the city.

A woman rescued him from that life, giving him shelter at one of the city childcare centers, and eventually, Sunshine Nut Company hired him. That young man, says Don, has gone "from an abandoned, troubled teen to the production manager of a world-class factory. ... Benaria had no hope and no opportunity, and now he has no limitations."[6]

Besides the inreach to employees, another faith expression at Sunshine Nut Company is outreach to the farmers and community, made possible by its practice of "reverse tithing." In other words, rather than tithe 10 percent of the profits, they give away *90 percent* of the profits, channeling them through the Sunshine Approach

Foundation, which Terri runs.

One-third of that money develops the farm communities: money for schools, nutrition, health care, housing, and so on. Plus, they pay fair trade wages to their 50,000 farm family suppliers, well above market, and they're on track to plant tens of thousands of cashew trees, sustaining the farmers' income for decades to come.

Another third goes to orphan care—generous support to the established childcare centers around the country, facilities that Don and Terri visit regularly. They've also cleverly paired some of these children with widows to form family units, even buying them houses (they call them "Sunshine Houses") and registering them in the child's name. Though expensive, to Don he's just "demonstrating the gospel of Jesus Christ by taking care of the poor and orphaned."[7]

The final third of the profits goes to helping other African companies operate the way Sunshine does. It's a repeatable model, multiplying the transformational impact of Don's approach.

For the Larsons, that's the whole point: transformation. Lasting change. While traditional corporate social responsibility embraces a triple bottom line of financial, social and environmental health, "The Sunshine Approach" adds "transformation" to the objectives.

Don calls it his "quadruple bottom line," though he doesn't weigh them all equally. Transformation is at the center of it all: "We are intending in everything we do to transform the community, the employees, the villages, and orphaned and abandoned children into a better life."[8]

And maybe along the way, transform their disposition toward God. Don doesn't lead with his cross, but he does hope to point people toward it: "We're just trying to open up God's will for their lives and provide the environment where they can be satisfied and embrace the gospel when it comes. When they see God's love and they see change in their lives, they're much more open to becoming ... a true disciple."[9]

Selling everything and moving to Africa? Sticking around despite a violent home invasion? Shelling out 90 percent of profits? It may all seem a bit nutty to some. When you think about it, though, how many business people are making more of a difference than Don and Terri Larson?

For Further Study

Don Larson, "Running a Business with a Social Mission," TEDx Talks, June 3, 2015. www.youtube.com/watch?v=XB7xAEuwhDo

Robin Schatz, "Why A Former Hershey Exec Sold His Porsche To Build A Cashew Business In Mozambique," *Forbes*, July 10, 2016. www.forbes.com/sites/robindschatz/2016/07/10/why-a-former-hershey-exec-sold-his-porsche-to-build-a-cashew-business-in-mozambique

Website: SunshineNuts.com

Notes

1. Don Larson, "Running a Business with a Social Mission," TEDx Talks, June 3, 2015.
   www.youtube.com/watch?v=XB7xAEuwhDo at 1:20.
2. "Running a Business with a Social Mission" at 14:30.
3. "Running a Business with a Social Mission" at 3:55.
4. "A Kingdom Approach to Business: Interview with Don Larson," Vineyard Justice Network, September 22, 2017. vineyardjusticenetwork.org/a-kingdom-approach-to-business-interview-with-don-larson at 4:50.
5. "A Kingdom Approach to Business" at 3:40.
6. "Running a Business with a Social Mission" at 6:45.
7. "A Kingdom Approach to Business" at 10:10.
8. "A Kingdom Approach to Business" at 2:48.
9. "A Kingdom Approach to Business" at 19:35.

PART 6

$\sim$

THEIR PLANET PROTECTION
They value creation care

Herman Miller
Tom's of Maine
Oobe Apparel Design Group
Elevation Burger
Cardone Industries
Enviro-Stewards

HERMAN MILLER

The Lesson

D.J. De Pree, an evangelical Christian, was one of the first U.S. executives to claim that a business has a responsibility to care for the environment. His company, Herman Miller, has been leading the way ever since.

They're known for making high-end office furniture. Think $1,200, ergonomically-perfect desk chairs. But even if Herman Miller is not for the budget-conscious, they've long been popular with the environmentally-conscious.

For decades, the company has pursued a "triple bottom line" philosophy of financial, environmental and social responsibility. Sure, plenty of firms use that kind of language, but Herman Miller is a genuine sustainability leader, setting stratospheric goals like zero air and water emissions from manufacturing, zero hazardous waste, zero landfill, 100 percent green energy use, and buildings constructed to the strictest eco-friendly certifications.

By 2023 they expect to have achieved most of these, closing in on a once-unthinkable "zero operational footprint" and earning plenty of visibility for their efforts along the way.

What's less well-known is how far ahead of its time this company was.

They didn't just hop on the bio bandwagon and grab the reins. Their environmentalism dates back to at least 1953, long before the movement got its sea legs. In that year, owner D.J. De Pree proclaimed boldly that "Herman Miller will be a good corporate neighbor by being a good steward of the environment."[1]

It was an enigmatic statement at the time, not just because ecological concerns were on the fringe of industry, but because it was an evangelical who made the pronouncement—a group not always recognized as part of the green movement, much less on the cutting edge of it.

But D.J. saw creation care as a form of Biblical stewardship. Simple as that. The manifestations have put the company in a position of eco-leadership ever since.

Some brief background: In 1909, D.J. took a job as a clerk at the Michigan Star Furniture Company. Within a decade, he had worked his way up to the presidency. Then, in 1923, he convinced his father-in-law, Herman Miller, to buy out the company. In appreciation, D.J. rebranded it in his name.

Along with his sons Hugh and Max, D.J. went on to grow the company into what is now an internationally-acclaimed label for office and residential furniture. And they all did it on Christian principles and for a godly purpose.

The now-public company tends to mask that in its corporate history, preferring to speak of those days in euphemisms of "values," "heritage," and "inclusive capitalism," with only the occasional whiff of God language. But make no mistake: This was a family committed to pleasing God through their business, including by prioritizing sustainability.

Fittingly, the company would reaffirm that commitment in 1990, the year that D.J. passed away. When their signature product, called The Eames Chair, became a target for its use of Brazilian Rosewood—a rainforest wood—the first reaction of then-CEO Richard Ruch was that any change would "kill that chair."[2] The traditional rosewood finish made the $2,277 product distinctive. In fact, he thought, changing Eames would be akin to Coca-Cola changing its secret formula, which it did a few years earlier in the marketing debacle of the 1980s.

Despite that unsettling context, the company, under management control of Chairman Max De Pree,[3] shifted to using cherry and walnut woods from carefully managed forests.[4] As told by corporate biographer Bill Birchard, "The decision became a watershed moment. ... After all, the fate of the Eames lounge chair was at stake, and the product ... was not just Herman Miller's flagship product, but a symbol of its identity."[5]

That identity, the decision made clear, continued to place environmentalism at its core, just as D.J. De Pree had articulated four decades earlier. It was an enormous risk, but a telling one: The company was still as dedicated to principle as it was to profit.

In the end they achieved both. The new chair and the old company did fine. Moreover, the aftermath included a wave of positive press and even a congressional resolution from Michigan Senator Donald Riegel, pronouncing: "Business leadership like this is essential in our efforts to slow destruction of ... tropical rainforests. ... [Herman Miller's leaders] are to be strongly commended."[6]

Not surprisingly, perhaps, the company is not just planet-friendly, but also employee-friendly, another expression of the founder's faith. It's been that way since its earliest days, and a centerpiece has always been "employee empowerment."

The New York Times summarized it well in their obituary of D.J. De Pree: "Mr. De Pree, and later his sons, Hugh and Max, who succeeded him as chief executives at Herman Miller, were proponents of participative management, in which employees share in decision-making and profits. The system, introduced in 1950, organizes work teams, caucuses and councils that extend from top management to the lowest-level employees. Workers are encouraged to challenge their superiors' decisions and to take initiative in proposing new methods."[7]

Drilling down even further, the company was an early adopter of what were called "Scanlon Plans": If employees find a lower cost, more productive way to solve an operational problem, everyone gets rewarded with a bonus from the savings. The company thought that sort of collective gainsharing exceled traditional profit-sharing plans, where there was little connection between worker input and financial outcome.[8]

Besides that, gainsharing fit from both a faith and functional standpoint. Said Max in his international bestseller, *Leadership is an Art*, the Scanlon Plans enable "the expression of the diverse gifts of persons with an emphasis on creativity and on the quality of the process," allowing "persons and groups to reach their potential."[9]

Similarly, alongside of process ownership is employee stock ownership, another way to bless and motivate the workforce. More than just additional compensation, "employee stock ownership is essentially (another) declaration of identity," Max wrote, and thereby unleashes people to buy-in and get involved. As a result, he continued, "we are one of the few companies in the United States where 100 percent of the full-time, regular employees in the U.S. who have completed one year of service are stockholders."[10]

It was all part of the De Pree family's transcendent operating principle: *faithfulness over success*. In an oft-quoted passage, Max put it this way: "Being faithful is more important than being successful. ... Corporations can and should have a redemptive purpose. We need to weigh the pragmatic in the clarifying light of the moral. We must understand that reaching our potential is more important than reaching our goals."[11]

That's a powerful framing. Succinct and sanctified. From the environment to employees to excellent design, the De Pree family was indeed an inspirational example of doing business to honor God.

For Further Study

Max De Pree, *Leadership is an Art*, New York: Dell Publishing, 1989.

Bill Birchard, *Merchants of Virtue: Herman Miller and the Making of a Sustainable Company*, New York: Palgrave MacMillan, 2011.

Notes

1. Herman Miller, Inc., "Better World Report, 2019," www.her-manmiller.com/content/dam/hermanmiller/documents/a_better_world/Better_World_Report.pdf, p. 16.
2. David Woodruff, "Herman Miller: How Green is My Factory," *Business Week* September 16, 1991, p. 54.
3. Management of the firm passed from the De Pree family in 1995 according to Lewis D. Solomon, *Evangelical Christian Executives: A New Model for Business Corporations*, New Brunswick, NJ: Transaction Publishers, p. 104.
4. "Herman Miller: How Green is My Factory," p. 54.
5. Bill Birchard, *Merchants of Virtue: Herman Miller and the Making of a Sustainable Company*, New York: Palgrave MacMillan, 2011, p. 9.
6. *Merchants of Virtue*, p. 13.
7. Glenn Fowler, "D.J. De Pree, Who Broke Ground in Furniture Design, is Dead at 99," *The New York Times*, December 13, 1990. www.nytimes.com/1990/12/13/obituaries/d-j-depree-who-broke-ground-in-furniture-design-is-dead-at-99.html
8. *Evangelical Christian Executives*, p. 103.
9. Max De Pree, *Leadership is an Art*, New York: Dell Publishing, 1989, p. 88.
10. *Leadership is an Art*, p. 96.
11. *Leadership is an Art*, p. 69.

TOM'S OF MAINE
PIONEERING NATURAL PRODUCTS

The Lesson

Tom and Kate Chappell have always been green but gritty. Their insistence on sustainability with profitability offers important insights for any business.

It began as "$5,000 and a prayer."[1] Thirty-six years later it became a $100 million sale. Plus, the Tom's of Maine founders retained one-sixth of their company, the nation's leading brand of natural personal care products.

Indeed, Tom and Kate Chappell had come a long way from their humble beginnings of stirring a vat of detergent with a two-by-four. They couldn't find natural products for their family, so they started making them from scratch. And then they started selling them. Their first breakthrough product came in 1974—an all-natural toothpaste using calcium carbonate to remove plaque and stains.

Colgate wasn't exactly worried. How intimidating is a start-up that makes chalky toothpaste with used dairy equipment? By 2006, though, still having no answer to Tom and Kate's wildly-popular product line, Colgate made them that nine-figure offer.

If you can't beat 'em, buy 'em.

The Chappells path from getting-in to cashing-out was about as circuitous as the nearby Maine coastline. But listen for this theme: Their aim, as their mission statement said before the sale, was "to be a profitable and successful company while acting in a socially and environmentally responsible manner."

Here's how their earthy business evolved.[2] In the 1970s, natural products were part of a counter-culture, but Tom Chappell was not—at least not in the anti-capitalist, pot-smoking, Dylan-loving, Ben & Jerry's "ice-cream-for-the-people" sense. Rather, Tom was the son of a textile entrepreneur and he appreciated how businesses created jobs and products and potentially, a better world.

But growing up in that New England, Episcopalian household also sensitized Tom to the down side of business, the side that could harm people and communities and the environment. He'd soon be in a position to do it differently. More on that in a minute.

After graduating with an English degree from Trinity College in Connecticut, Tom became a top salesman for Aetna Insurance. In 1968, after an insulting raise, he and his new wife Kate moved to Maine to raise a family while Tom worked in his father's new pollution-abatement business. It was an embryonic industry at the time, since people concerned about the environment usually worked in nonprofits.

But Tom liked the idea of caring for the planet and the bottom line simultaneously. To him, contrary to the hippy rhetoric of the time, it wasn't business per se that was harmful to the environment; it was the agents of business. So Tom just needed to use the tools of free enterprise in a constructive, ethical way.

He and Kate tried their entrepreneurial hand at that in 1970, borrowing $5,000 from a friend, and later getting SBA loans and a second mortgage on their house. Frankly, it was a roll of the dice, especially since their envisioned line of natural care products—soaps, shampoos, toothpaste, detergents and so on—might be a tiny segment. Sure, there was no supply at the time, but maybe that's because there was no demand.

Tom and Kate gambled that there was. They hired a smart chemist, and in a makeshift warehouse they just started inventing natural, eco-friendly products. Unique products. In fact, Tom's of

Maine was the first in the country to make natural toothpaste, deodorant and mouthwash.

Of course, lots of people thought the couple was crazy to compete with the behemoths like Procter & Gamble, but Tom and Kate had another target in mind: people who cared about what they put in and on their bodies. Corporate America simply wasn't serving this niche yet.

Notice, the Chappells weren't activists, just innovators trying to compete on the merits of their products. They certainly shared their customers' indignation about how some companies operated, but they expressed it differently, looking to redeem business rather than to rebuke it.

It worked for several years. Tom's of Maine became a sustainable business. But by 1980, demand in the natural food community had flattened. The company was a well-regarded brand, but new growth would have to come from the larger, mainstream market that shopped in grocery stores, not health food stores.

So Tom hired a talented group of MBAs and consultants to gain entry, and commensurate with their training, and their price tag, they helped him do just that. The company grew at about 25 percent a year and by 1986, Tom's of Maine had successfully transitioned from serving "health-committed" consumers to the much wider funnel of "health-concerned" consumers.

It was all going so well. Why, then, was Tom Chappell in an existential crisis?

In his words, "In 1986, as ... Tom's of Maine was experiencing unprecedented growth, I was miserable."[3] They were hitting all their numbers, sales were skyrocketing, the company was becoming a household name ... and Tom was empty, struggling to see the broader purpose in all of this seeming success.

It's at about this point when busy leaders go on a four-day retreat, or a four-week vacation, at least if it's August. Tom Chappell, though, went on a four-year quest for answers as a part-time seminary student, while still running the company. The man who, at this point, could have been lecturing at Harvard Business School instead matriculated at Harvard Divinity School.

Rising at four a.m., he traveled to Boston a couple times a week to glean from theologians and philosophers, ancient and contemporary, trying to sort out what really mattered in corporate life. He was particularly enamored with the thinking of Martin Buber and Jonathan Edwards regarding how human beings, by our very nature, are designed to live in relationship with others. Extending that, he reflected on the web of relationships among company stakeholders, concluding that "social relationships bring responsibilities, moral as well as financial."[4]

In the end, that reinforced his belief that, as he would put it, God's goodness informs how a business should operate. Just as Tom and Kate had been operating during the 1970s, there needed to be more socially-constructive goals for their business than mere profit.

But he had allowed that simple, sanctifying idea to become diluted by the constant drip of professional managers he hired to reposition the company. Tom was grateful to that team for accelerating profits and enlarging the company's footprint, but the cost was too high. They had created a culture—again, true to their training—where the financials were the paramount, sometimes solitary, measure of success.

Tom also sensed his own culpability in this shift. And his board's. It all had to change. The very "soul of the business" was at stake, to use Tom's language.[5]

He met with his board and though not unanimous, they crafted a fresh, guiding philosophy: Tom's of Maine would operate both for profit and for the common good.

In practical terms, that meant encouraging employees to use five percent of their paid time (2.5 work weeks a year) to volunteer with nonprofits. And it meant genuine participative management, sharing decision-making power with employees. One time, years later, engineers had sketched out a $20,000 production fix, but an assembly line worker suggested a solution that cost $49. "It worked perfectly," said Tom in the late 1990s, "and we still use it. If my head of manufacturing were a tyrant, do you think that guy would have piped up?"[6]

Managing for both profit and the common good also entailed philanthropy, giving away 10 percent of pretax profits, initially to environmental causes, but then to education, the arts, and human welfare causes. It meant stepping up when emergency needs arose, too, like sending the Red Cross 50,000 bars of soap for Kosovo families during the 1999 crisis in Yugoslavia.

And with regard to the consumer, besides offering an effective, eco-friendly product, it meant admitting when they got it wrong, no matter the cost. In 1992, for example, when a new deodorant formulation caused many users to smell *worse* rather than better, Tom's voluntarily issued a recall and sent personal apology letters, costing them more than $400,000 and putting them in the red that year.

They may have lost even more in the long-run, too: Deodorant was 22 percent of their business at the time and the mounting competition in the natural products space was eager to capitalize on the blunder.

It didn't matter to Tom. Values over numbers. That was the old way and that would be the new way. "Thanks to Jonathan Edwards," he wrote, referring to his seminary training, "I realized that far from being an amoral activity aimed at maximizing shareholder interest, business was by its very nature a social enterprise and therefore a moral enterprise."[7]

And moral enterprises always take care of their customer.

Perhaps that's why the brand was worth so much to Colgate, which bought 84 percent of the company in 2006. The public respected Tom's of Maine for taking their people-centered, planet-centered values seriously, responsibilities that would continue with the new ownership.

Then there's the epilogue: At age 62, Tom was now flush with cash but hardly ready to retire. Back to his family roots, Tom set his sights on reforming the textile industry, one of the greatest polluters on Earth. His sequel company, Rambler's Way, manufactures quality clothing while maintaining a deep respect for the natural world—all the way down to how the sheep are treated in his supply chain. It's yet another lesson, to quote Tom, in how people can "do business with their hearts as well as their heads."[8]

Ultimately, Tom Chappell boils it all down to this: "I am a religious man who is passionate about conserving the environment."[9] Two companies, two generations, and two bestsellers later, he's provided strong evidence that a person can indeed be both, while making plenty of money in the process.

For Further Study

Tom Chappell, *Managing Upside Down: The Seven Intentions of Value-Centered Leadership,* New York: Marrow and Company, 1999.

Tom Chappell, *The Soul of a Business: Managing for Profit and the Common Good,* New York: Bantam Books, 1993.

Websites: www.TomsofMaine.com and www.RamblersWay.com

Notes

1. Tom Chappell, *Managing Upside Down: The Seven Intentions of Value-Centered Leadership,* New York: Marrow and Company, 1999, p. xiii.
2. Some of this information for this story comes from an interview with Tom Chappell on National Public Radio in 2018 (www.npr.org/2018/01/22/569432668/toms-of-maine-tom-chappell). Other information comes from Tom Chappell's two books, as noted within.
3. *Managing Upside Down,* p. xii.
4. *Managing Upside Down,* p. 2.
5. Tom Chappell, *The Soul of a Business: Managing for Profit and the Common Good,* New York: Bantam Books, 1993.
6. *Managing Upside Down,* p. xv.
7. *Managing Upside Down,* p. 3.

8. *Managing Upside Down*, p. xi.
9. *Managing Upside Down*, p. xv.

OOBE APPAREL DESIGN GROUP
MAKING SHIRTS FROM PLASTIC BOTTLES

The Lesson

Sometimes your big breaks come from who you are, more than what you do. The character and creativity of the OOBE guys has landed them some surprising contracts.

They make all the uniform shirts for Chick-fil-A employees. From recycled plastic.

It's a story littered with lessons. In the early 1990s, Tom Merritt and Mike Pereyo attended Clemson University. One day, they were half-listening to an infomercial from the Psychic Friends Network, a popular telephone service at the time. The guys thought the ideas sounded off-center, having recently become followers of Jesus.

So when the narrator mentioned an "out of body experience," Tom immediately offered a clever corrective: "They should have an 'Out Of Bible Experience. That's what we've had (with our conversions) and that's what they need."[1]

An "OOBE" (pronounced oo'-bē). It became their shorthand for the ultimate experience, the best day, pure joy from God's blessings.

And it remained a well-worn term for them long after graduation. Three years later, for example, Mike described his life to Tom as not having many OOBE days. Their conversation turned to a remedy. Then a radical remedy. Arguably a ridiculous remedy, since Tom had two small kids and Mike had a baby on the way: Let's quit our jobs and start a company.

They were both entrepreneurial at heart, and they both liked the idea of an outdoor clothing business, so they began brainstorming a plan. Within a few weeks, Mike called Tom to say he had incorporated. For lack of a company name, he just put "OOBE" on the form.[2]

That sort of fly-by-the-seat-of-your-hiking-pants approach came to define their first few years in business.

When they chose the clothing business, neither knew anything about it.

When deciding who should do marketing and sales and who should do design and operations, they flipped a coin.

When they visited retailers through whom they wanted to sell, they were dealing out of the back of their car.

When they finally secured office space, it was an abandoned auto body shop for $50 a month.

When they sought help from the Clemson Small Business Development Center, all they could show for their financial statements was a yellow legal pad.

And when they needed capital to survive, they took one of their tee-shirts that had been selling well to the International Dive Show in New Orleans, got a vendor booth and remarkably sold six-figures worth of business. The shirts read: "I dive. What on Earth are you doing?"[3]

Perhaps the better question, though, was "what on Earth was God doing?" Tom and Mike sought to honor God with their business, serving people with excellence and respect, and investing the arduous entrepreneurial hours. God's part, it seems, was to open doors.

And he did. God opened a door to a contract with FILA, the Italian sporting goods company. FILA heard that OOBE was a trustworthy business that put out good product, so they asked OOBE to make golf shirts for them. After realizing the request wasn't a joke, the guys gladly complied.[4]

God opened doors to other clients as well, sustaining the business for several years. But in 2005, God opened the biggest door of all for Tom and Mike: A contract to supply all of Chick-fil-A's uniform shirts.

It must have seemed like a doorway to Narnia. Consider the bizarre interview:[5]

Have you every shipped to 100,000 employees before? "No." Do you have a customer service department? "No. Unless you count me." Do you have a warehouse? "No." Can you pass financial due diligence? "Probably not." Is this contract bigger than your whole company? "Um ... yes."

Ludicrous, right? Why are we even talking to you when we have 25 others in line? Still, after a year-long process, Chick-fil-A saw something in these two guys; identifying the right people is their specialty. But the determining factor in OOBE's favor wasn't capacity or experience—clearly. Curiously, a major turning point was how Tom and Mike treated the clothing models in that interview process.

In a stealthy move, Chick-fil-A enlisted its own employees, undercover, to model the merchandise of the finalists for the contract. And afterward they asked their models, *in your interactions with these companies, which treated you with the most honor, dignity and respect when no one was looking?* [6]

It wasn't even close, and it helped OOBE win the contract.

"They aren't just entrusting their brand to us," Mike said about the surreal moment. "They are entrusting their people to us. This was where we started to get a real footing."[7]

The guys were simply being themselves—just living out their corporate mission "to love and serve people." The Chick-fil-A models felt the love and their employer reciprocated, not only awarding OOBE the deal, but helping them significantly with fulfillment.

Today, OOBE's love extends to BMW, the YMCA, Food Lion, Krispy Kreme, Verizon, Disney and many others who proudly wear their custom employee apparel. OOBE also launched its own line of clothing, available online, in Bloomingdale's, and in their flagship store on swanky King Street in Charleston, South Carolina.

But then there's that story about shirts made from plastic bottles.

In 2016, OOBE and its now long-time client Chick-fil-A partnered on an astonishing sustainability project. It's hard to imagine a comfortable, stylish shirt made entirely out of recycled plastic, but through a painstaking process, they made it a reality.

As the bottles come in from the recycling plant, they're shredded into tiny particles, sterilized, and then superheated until the plastic melts. The thick liquid gets extruded through something that looks like a showerhead and becomes a fine filament. It feels like dental floss at this point, but another iteration of stretching and twisting produces the feel of a natural fiber, which is spun into yarn, dyed, and finally woven into a Chick-fil-A polo shirt.[8]

The next time you're in Chick-fil-A, check out the right sleeve of their shirts. As of this writing, the sleeve says "Recycled Fabric" and includes a number indicating how many bottles went into making the shirt. It's currently either 9 or 19, depending on the uniform.

In the aggregate, OOBE repurposes several million bottles a year through this process. It's truly ingenious, but to sustainability advocates, it's just another example of "upcycling"—creating a higher quality product than the original.

In fact, that's analogous to what Tom and Mike have been doing all along: creating higher quality products every year through nonstop innovation. Cultivating better and better relationships with customers, employees and business partners. Upcycling business practice through Biblical values, joyful attitudes and 25 years of continuous growth.

That's a lot of OOBE days.

For Further Study

Nancy Spitler and Savannah Mozingo, "OOBE: A word, reimagined, becomes a blueprint for business and life," *Clemson World*, September 1, 2014. Clemson.world/oobe

"Sustainable Style," Chick-fil-A, www.youtube.com/watch?v=KRoRmIJo0-0

Website: www.oobe.com

Notes

1. "Head On: OOBE's Tom Merritt and Mike Pereyo," Clemson University, September 22, 2014. www.youtube.com/watch?v=lmtYZA-1ibA at 0:40.
2. This part of the story comes from Nancy Spitler and Savannah Mozingo, "OOBE: A word, reimagined, becomes a blueprint for business and life," *Clemson World*, September 1, 2014. Clemson.world/oobe
3. "The OOBE brand journey: Good guys don't finish last," *Upstate Business Journal*, October 2, 2017. Upstatebusinessjournal.com/oobe-brand-journey-good-guys-dont-finish-last
4. "The OOBE brand journey," *Upstate Business Journal*.
5. "Head On," Clemson University.
6. "The OOBE brand journey," *Upstate Business Journal*.
7. "The OOBE brand journey," *Upstate Business Journal*.
8. "Sustainable Style," Chick-fil-A, www.youtube.com/watch?v=KRoRmIJo0-0

ELEVATION BURGER
TAKING THE JUNK OUT OF JUNK FOOD

The Lesson

Fast food may be worse for us than we realize. Hans Hess found a way to mitigate that, "elevating" the health of both people and planet. The animals probably appreciate it as well.

If you can't find it, found it.

That seems to be the motto of Hans Hess after searching in vain for the healthy hamburger. In 2005, he founded Elevation Burger in Falls Church, Virginia, a restaurant serving food "that he would feel good about feeding his children."[1] Since then, the company has grown to 27 U.S. and 20 Middle East locations.

Apparently, he's feeding a lot of people's children. Here's why the parents take them, and why they love it, too.

Most burger beef in the U.S. comes from "factory farms" that raise cattle in confinement and feed them as much grain, corn and soy as they can eat. But, as Hans explains it, the animals get sick because God designed their stomach to process grass, not grain.[2] To stave off infection, feed producers add antibiotics to the meal.

Well, that fixes one issue but creates another, specifically for those of us at the end of the food chain. When we carnivores devour a Big Mac, we also ingest trace amounts of those antibiotics from the animals' food. After enough Big Macs, some think, we can develop a resistance to antibiotics, making it difficult to stop a bacterial infection when we're the ones who are sick.

Follow the logic? It's as linear as the line out their restaurant door.

Hans reasoned that if the problem begins with the livestock, so should the solution. Hence, Elevation Burger's distinctive of sourcing only 100-percent organic, grass-fed beef. No antibiotics anywhere in their supply chain. Healthier herd, healthier hamburgers.

Maybe a happier herd too, since Elevation beef is entirely free-range; that is, the animals are not raised in confinement. "Our cows live in a pasture all their life," explains Hans. "They don't live in a feedlot ever. They don't ever get antibiotics or hormones. Their feed is completely free from pesticides. The nutritional profile of the meat is outstanding."[3]

It not only sounds ethical, it's a self-evident value proposition: More nutritious beef is better than less nutritious beef.

Hans goes further, though, making a save-the-planet argument for why we should buy. His take is this: When you clear the land to grow corn and grains, "you remove the opportunity to sequester significant amounts of carbon dioxide. ... (But) when you use the animals to manage a grass pasture (i.e., let them roam and graze free-range), you actually sequester carbon dioxide, and it's not in circulation in the atmosphere, and that has an impact on global warming."[4]

The philosophy transcends his entire operation. Their restaurant floors are made of eco-friendly bamboo, their tables are compressed sorghum (a grain), their lighting is LED, their griddles are energy-efficient, and they donate their used cooking oil for conversion to biodiesel.

To Hans, a graduate of Dallas Theological Seminary, it's all an expression of the faith. "Should Christians care about the environment?" he asks rhetorically. "Absolutely. We were created in an environment, and that environment was given to us to take charge of. So if I can apply my God-given talents to reduce the negative impact I have on my environment, why wouldn't I? ... That's something God expects of me."[5]

It also seems to be an expression of leadership. Industry leadership. In 2015, national newspaper *USA Today* credited Elevation Burger with prompting McDonald's and Chick-fil-A to move away from proteins treated with antibiotics.[6]

Many other chains are following suit, at least in their rhetoric.[7] The reality will probably catch-up eventually. The point is that Hans is making a difference far-beyond his sorghum-slabbed stores.

To the business-savvy, though, it all elevates another question: What about the cost of operation? USDA-certified organic is more expensive. Grass-fed beef, hormone-free milkshakes, fries cooked in olive oil—it's all more expensive. So is the initial outlay for eco-friendly construction. Might not these laudable values put Elevation Burger at a competitive disadvantage?

Stated differently, would you pay $11 for a burger, fries and a soda in a fast-food environment? Or $14 if you substitute a shake for the soda?

Many people do, of course. No one builds an inter-continental business without strong demand and reasonable price points. But time will tell how sustainable "sustainability" can be.

Regardless the competitive challenges, the confidence of Hans Hess seems to come from elsewhere. He is worshipping God through the product he makes. Perhaps in return, God will continue to help Elevation Burger raise the bar on the food we eat.

For Further Study

Faith & Co., "Elevation," Seattle Pacific University. Faithandco.spu.edu/film-detail/eschatological-hamburgers-elevation

"Elevating Fast Food," *Faith & Leadership*, July 16, 2012. www.FaithAndLeadership.com/elevating-fast-food

Press coverage of Elevation Burger: ElevationBurger.com/press

Notes

1. "About Us," ElevationBurger.com/about-us
2. Faith & Co., "Elevation," Seattle Pacific University. Faithandco.spu.edu/film-detail/eschatological-hamburgers-elevation at 1:12.
3. "Elevating Fast Food," *Faith & Leadership*, July 16, 2012. www.FaithAndLeadership.com/elevating-fast-food
4. "Elevation" at 2:50.
5. "Elevation" at 3:06.
6. Bruce Horowitz, "Va. chain crosses over to organic chicken," *USA Today*, March 30, 2015, p. B4.
7. Kevin Kelleher, "22 Out of the Top 25 Burger Chains Graded 'F' on their Antibiotic Use, Report Says," *Forbes*, October 17, 2018. Fortune.com/2018/10/17/burger-chains-antibiotic-use

CARDONE INDUSTRIES
Remanufacturing Auto parts

The Lesson

For some companies, sustainability gets grafted on to their business. For others, like Cardone, sustainability *is* their business, rooted in Cardone's first corporate objective, "To honor God in all we do."

They rebuild enough auto parts each year to fill two ocean liners. That's two, titanic boatloads of corrosive metal they're keeping out of landfills. And another two next year.

At Cardone Industries, sustainability is not an add-on to their business. It *is* their business. They take worn out vehicle parts and make them like-new again.

More specifically, they dissemble the parts, clean them, reassemble them sometimes rewiring or adding new components, test them for compliance with performance specifications, and then sell them through auto parts stores.[1]

Not sure if it's reliable? Cardone is sure. They back every part with a lifetime warranty.

The technical term for all this is "remanufacturing." From the standpoint of environmental protection, it's a vital link in the "circular supply chain" — an ongoing cycle of production, use, restoration, and reuse. Beyond that, the process of remanufacturing uses about 86 percent less energy than creating a new part.[2]

Here's a further benefit. A longstanding objection to "green" products—those made in an eco-friendly manner—is that they're more expensive to produce (and buy) than their counterparts. But remanufactured products are green while also saving the customer lots of green: They cost 30 to 50 percent less than new products. As such, remanufacturing has become an economically attractive way to reduce landfill pollution.

Two ocean liners of reduction every year, in the case of Cardone. For decades.

The company traces its roots to the mid-1930s when Michael Cardone, Sr., started a Depression-era business, Automotive Unit Exchange (AUE), to remanufacture windshield wipers systems.[3] He was ahead of his time. The remanufacturing industry took off during World War II when scarce resources prompted the reuse of auto and truck parts. By then, AUE was well-positioned for the shift.

Cardone's business matured for 35 years until 1969, when he faced a tough choice. The 55-year-old wanted his son, also named Michael, to succeed him in leadership, but the bylaws of the company prohibited that. So, reluctantly, the founder cashed out of his thriving business, now at 700 employees, to start all over again.[4]

His new company, A-1 Remanufacturing, later rebranded as Cardone Industries, had only one product line—windshield wiper motors—and only six employees, all of them family members. Their manufacturing facility, if you could call it that, was a rented row house in a rundown section of Philadelphia, with rats the size of house cats running about in the basement.[5]

Looking for any way to sell the product, Michael Sr. convinced auto part businesses to take his remanufactured motors on consignment, only paying for the motors they sold. It got A-1 some desperately-needed traction and eventually, the company expanded to other vehicle parts.

Pretty much all of them, actually. From one product line and six employees, Cardone Industries now has 90 product lines, almost 50,000 SKUs (individual products), and 5,500 employees—what they call their "Cardone Factory Family." The company is now the largest manufacturer in Pennsylvania, as well as the largest privately-held remanufacturer in the world. And for his pioneering efforts, Michael Cardone Sr. was inducted into the Automotive Hall of Fame in 1994, alongside names like Lee Iococca, Carl Benz and Eiji Toyoda.[6]

Predominantly, the growth has come from their value proposition. Cardone was a forerunner of the disruptive innovation movement, offering same-quality parts for below-market prices.

But the Cardone family would quickly add that the increase is God's blessing on a business that, from the outset, has been dedicated to him. Says Michael Jr., who officially took over as president in 1988: "We didn't start out with that objective (to become big). ... It's just been through hard work, the Lord's blessing, and being the best at what we do."[7]

And in the third generation, the apple still has not fallen far from the tree. Michael Cardone III, currently the Executive Chairman, puts it this way: "We want to see people be successful in life, successful in work ... and we happen to believe that faith in Jesus Christ is the best way to get there. And we're not shy about talking about that and we're not shy about bringing that to the workplace."[8]

We see that overtness, for example, in their statement of corporate objectives, which follows the template from The ServiceMaster Company (pages 17-22). Cardone's four objectives are "to honor God in all we do, to help people develop, to pursue excellence, and to grow profitably."

Recall from the ServiceMaster story that the first two objectives in this template are "end" goals, while the latter two are "means" goals. That is, Cardone's *primary* goal—the reason for its existence—is "to honor God." Primary also is "to help its people develop."

That's notable: Employee before customer. Michael Jr. reconciles it this way: "In any successful business, you have to always put the customer first. ... My employees are *my* customer. That's who I have to serve, and when I serve them well, I know they're going to serve their customers well."[9]

Cardone refers to it as "servant-leadership," a sacrificial approach modeled by Jesus himself. But how real has it been there? Two illustrations among many:

The company has invested for decades in an employee chaplain team, paying more than a half million dollars each year to nurture the personal and spiritual well-being of employees. Even when times were challenging and a consultant strongly recommended cutting this cost, the family stood firm on their commitment to its people through corporate chaplaincy.[10]

Here's a second example of employee care. Michael Jr. recalls: "We found that our factory family members and their families were not getting timely health care, or the quality of health care that they deserve. We developed a partnership with a local hospital to start our own clinic. It took a lot of effort on our part, and it took an investment on our part."[11] In the long-run, though, Cardone employees have enjoyed better, more convenient health care at a lower cost to both the employees and the company.

Quite a win-win. But this kind of innovation, on behalf of employees or the environment, is what happens when Christian executives embrace the marketplace calling "to honor God in all we do."

Michael Jr. interprets that poignantly: "I'm not called to be a minister. I'm not called to be a pastor. I'm called to be a businessman. I see no difference. Work is worship."[12]

Even when the work is renovating a rusty carburetor or a health care program. Maybe especially so.

For Further Study

Michael Cardone, Sr., *Never Too Late for a New Beginning,* Old Tappan, NJ: Fleming H. Revell, 1988.

Center for Faith and Work, "Cardone," Vimeo.com/53226571

Website: www.Cardone.com

Notes

1. For more information, see "What is Remanufacturing?" Automotive Parts Remanufacturing Association, apra.org/page/Remanufacturing
2. Cardone Industries, "Remanufacturing: The Ultimate Sustainability Solution," www.Cardone.com/docs/environmental-commitment/Reman-Ultimate-Form-of-Recycling.pdf
3. Michael Cardone, Sr., *Never Too Late for a New Beginning*, Old Tappan, NJ: Fleming H. Revell, 1988, pp. 54-68.
4. *Never Too Late for a New Beginning*, p. 82.
5. *Never Too Late for a New Beginning*, p. 92.
6. Cardone Industries, "History," www.cardone.com/about-us/history
7. Center for Faith and Work, "Cardone," Vimeo.com/53226571 at 1:00.
8. Center for Faith and Work, "Cardone," Vimeo.com/53226571 at 1:31.
9. Center for Faith and Work, "Cardone," Vimeo.com/53226571 at 1:55.
10. Timothy Redmer, "Cardone Industries: Chaplain Program," *Christian Business Academy Review*, Spring 2008, pp. 62-68.
11. Center for Faith and Work, "Cardone," Vimeo.com/53226571 at 2:42.
12. Center for Faith and Work, "Cardone," Vimeo.com/53226571 at 4:15.

ENVIRO-STEWARDS
How to Make More Money
while Doing Less harm

The Lesson

Some eco-friendly solutions are also friendly to the bottom line. Consultants Enviro-Stewards have been demonstrating the connections for two decades.

It was just a few office supplies that he pilfered. And that was years ago, *and* he was just an intern at the time. Was it really that big a deal?

But Bruce Taylor couldn't shake the feeling that God was tapping him on the shoulder. The God he now believed sent his Son to die for him—the God Bruce was still resisting despite his intellectual acceptance of the Gospel story—was nudging Bruce to come clean about the historic heist.

He would later tell a Mennonite business magazine: "That little thing was much harder than going to South Sudan during the civil war or taking a leave of absence for a year."[1] It's probably because it was actually a big thing: a confession of petty theft that was also a confession of Christ.

In the years since, Bruce's faith expressions have taken a decidedly positive turn. In 2000, he founded Enviro-Stewards, a faith-informed company in Elmira, Ontario, that helps businesses be-come simultaneously more eco-friendly and more profitable. Their first core value is "we love people," so besides giving his 20 or so employees jobs and interesting work and paid time off to volunteer in the community, he also pays a minimum, "living wage" of $16.15 an hour.[2]

Their second core value is "we love our planet," and seemingly that's the essence of the business. Enviro-Stewards is a consulting company that specializes in energy efficiency, water conservation, waste reduction, and pollution prevention. They distinguish them-selves, they say, by addressing *the root cause* of excessive resource usage.[3]

That's what they did, for example, for a dairy farm client. The amount of water it takes to make cheese is simply mind-curdling. Two-thousand liters of water are required to produce one liter of milk, and five liters of milk are required to produce one pound of cheese. Doing the math, that's 10,000 liters of water per pound of cheese.

Some farms have to truck in the water at great cost and potential environmental expense. But rather than just try to reduce water consumption in each step of the process (flushing the lines, hydrat-ing the cows, pasteurizing the milk, cleaning the farm trucks, etc.), Enviro-Stewards started at the end of the process to minimize wasted cheese. As they did that, the savings went back up the pro-duction chain, entailing the use of much less water throughout. "When you save food," says Bruce, "you automatically save water and energy you used to make that food."[4]

They did the same for Campbell Company of Canada, part of the familiar Campbell's Food empire. As Bruce explained to a cap-tivated TED Talk audience in 2018, Canada discards $31 billion worth of food each year—so much that there's an entire industry dedicated to destroying food as effectively as possible. Enviro-Stewards changed six processes in the Campbell's plant to reduce food waste by 938 tons a year, saving $706,000 annually and "4,000 tons per year of embedded greenhouse gas in those vegetables and meat that would have otherwise been lost when you send it to a waste energy plant."[5]

A third example: At Southbrook Winery, which has about every green certification there is, Bruce's company showed them how to cut their energy expenses even more—40 percent more—through a waste-reducing investment that would break even in a mere four months. Their solution also removed one-third of the solar panels on the vineyard, making more space for crops and thereby increasing production.[6] As Bruce puts it, solar panels are green energy, but "there's something greener than a solar panel, and that's not using energy in the first place."[7]

The work is intricate, but the theory is inarguable. Less waste on the back end means less resource use on the front end.

The marketing challenge, though, has been formidable. Bruce sells something that most of his clients have never bought before: changes to their operation that align with environmental best practices. And besides that, who really wants an outsider to tinker with their production system? So he's had to be a good salesman.

He is, especially for a chemical engineer. Bruce's authenticity and passion are inviting, as is his company's track record. He calculates that their solutions "have saved our clients millions of dollars in operating costs, eliminated thousands of tonnes of hazardous waste, cut back natural gas usage by millions of cubic metres, and reduced millions of tonnes of greenhouse gas emissions."[8]

Beyond Bruce's pathos and proficiency, his company's awards complete the value proposition—sustainability awards from the United Nations, Clean50, B Corp and others.[9] Indeed, Enviro-Stewards seems to be doing great work, contributory work, and more of it every year.

They've also been doing great, contributory work in Africa since 2004, applying their specific skills to the problem of safe water. Bruce laments that a billion people around the globe don't have access to safe water, and that "bad water has killed more people than all wars."[10] Additionally, he cites a World Vision statistic that 45 percent of African wells will fail in the first year, although no one in these villages has parts or knowledge to fix them.

So Enviro-Stewards stepped up—not to build wells, but to train people to build something locally with local materials: bio-sand filters, where the beneficial bacteria eat the harmful bacteria.[11] Basically, the company's strategy when it comes to safe water systems is not to give a fish, and it's not even to teach someone to fish. Rather, they teach somebody to teach somebody to fish.[12] Train the trainer. It's culminated in a superior system that is fixable when it fails, thereby producing years of water from a household filtration unit.

Here again we see their penchant for solving the root problem. In Africa, it was that villagers didn't know how to help themselves. The solution naturally followed. And as usual for this company, it was a solution that fit the budget, even a budget that was close to zero.

"Engineering Change." That's this company's tagline as well as their sightline, whether in Africa or Alberta. For two decades, Enviro-Stewards has pursued a vision that some thought was impossible: loving people and planet while at the same time boosting clients' profit.

A paradigm change indeed. Environmental sustainability that also promotes economic sustainability.

For Further Study

"Business for the benefit of companies here and people around the world," *The Marketplace*, Mennonite Economic Development Associates, July/August 2019, pp. 11-13. www.meda.org/download

Website: www.Enviro-Stewards.com

***

Notes

1. "Business for the benefit of companies here and people around the world," *The Marketplace*, Mennonite Economic Development Associates, July/August 2019, pp. 11-13. www.meda.org/download

2. "Business for the benefit of companies here and people around the world," p. 12.
3. "Solutions," www.Enviro-Stewards.com/solutions
4. Jackie Sharkley, "Ontario cheesemakers work to cut down water use," *CBC News*, March 31, 2019. www.cbc.ca/news/canada/kitchener-waterloo/mountainoak-cheese-water-ontario-1.5075098
5. "Better than Charity," TEDxUW, March 8, 2018. www.youtube.com/watch?v=jBB3CkuRb7E at 5:15.
6. "Better than Charity" at 4:20.
7. "Better than Charity" at 4:07.
8. "About Enviro-Stewards," www.enviro-stewards.com/about
9. "Enviro-Stewards' Awards," www.enviro-stewards.com/about/awards
10. "Better than Charity" at 5:30.
11. "Better than Charity" at 7:40.
12. "Better than Charity" at 11:50.

PART 7

---~---

THEIR PRINCIPLE
They stand firm, regardless the cost

Wanamaker's Department Stores
Correct Craft
Flow Automotive Companies
R.W. Beckett Corporation
Masterpiece Cakeshop
Conestoga Wood Specialties

WANAMAKER'S DEPARTMENT STORES

The Lesson

We take for granted that being in business is a legitimate, contributory vocation for Christians, but that was not the assumption 150 years ago. Against staunch opposition from the pulpit, retailer John Wanamaker demonstrated that a business is itself a pulpit to transform lives.

Dwight's tone was urgent. If John remained in business, he was risking his salvation. There was that much at stake.

The business profession, Dwight claimed—multiple times now—was antithetical to the Christian life. The exact words in his letter were these: "I must ... make one more effort to get you out of your business. It seems to me that the devil wants to cheat you of your crown, and I was afraid you would lose it the way you are goin-on."[1]

The year was 1876.

The recipient of the letter was John Wanamaker, one of the great retailers in the nineteenth century. After launching a men's clothing store in 1861 and a second store in 1869, John was now poised to combine them into Philadelphia's first department store. Called Wanamaker's "Grand Depot," it was a marvel of modern construction, with a wide-open floor plan, a 12-story marble-laden atrium, skylights, high-end finishes, thick carpets, climate control, and even electricity rather than gas lighting. Wanamaker, a devout Presbyterian, saw it as an edifice to the glory of God, much like the soaring cathedrals and temples throughout history.

The author of the letter was none other than Dwight Moody, one of the great evangelists of the nineteenth century. Moody's preaching invitations took him across the United States and throughout Europe, routinely attracting crowds of up to 20,000. He was so popular that his 1875 revival in Philadelphia attracted standing-room-only crowds for 12 straight weeks in the Grand Depot, which held 12,000.

So what do you do when one of the giants of the faith insists that your soul is in jeopardy, simply because you're running a successful business?

Actually, it wasn't just Dwight Moody who objected. In those days, Christians, as well as many others in society, held big business owners in contempt. Their unethical practices, their rapacious motivations, their ostentatious living, their reshaping of American values toward consumerism—it all seemed, at the very least, incompatible with discipleship. Hence Moody's persistence, battling Beelzebub for his benefactor.

Wanamaker, though, stood firmly against this narrow interpretation of scripture, offering an alternative theology, which he later called a "businessman's gospel." To him, a business was a "pulpit," no different than Moody's, except that it reached those who might never enter a church or revival meeting.

According to corporate biographer Nicole Kirk: "Wanamaker saw his retail enterprise not as separate from religion, but as an instrument of it, as a means for achieving moral reform in business, in the city and in individuals' lives.[2] ... Wanamaker's was more than a place of employment and material consumption. It was an active site of evangelism."[3]

But his evangelistic approach was different for shoppers and employees. Shoppers met God, so to speak, though the grandeur of Wanamaker's architecture; the art gallery and concert-quality praise music performed inside, especially from on the 10,000-pipe organ; the extravagant, religious displays at Christmas and Easter; and the unusual customer-friendly sales practices across his 46 departments. Occasionally, they'd hear the religious programming from his radio station, broadcasting from the top of his building, but mostly, the evangelism of customers came in the form of a sensory experience that could lead to what Wanamaker called "moral uplift."

For employees, Wanamaker's evangelization was more paternalistic and often more direct. In his "store family," as he called them, Wanamaker "positioned himself like a father who watched over his children," writing personal notes to employees to encourage them, and to offer scriptural wisdom.[4] For his teenage employees, many dropping out of school as early as age 13 to support their families, Wanamaker created an academy. The John Wanamaker Commercial Institute trained employees not just in job skills, but in academic subjects, physical education, manners, hygiene, and most importantly, virtue.

In fact, his academy's purpose statement emphasized that "the moral welfare of the students is of special interest,"[5] and its first learning objective was "to honor God who gives us breath of life."[6] His broader hope was that these young employees would influence the morals of their parents, friends and others.

Wanamaker's employee care extended to pensions, scaled-back hours on Saturday, no Sunday work, a two-week vacation, and an employee dining room and reading room, stocked with Christian literature. He also built a rooftop athletic center with volleyball, shuffleboard, a track and tennis courts, as well as an indoor bowling alley and gym, staffed with trainers.[7]

In all, John Wanamaker filled this "pulpit" for 61 years until his death in 1922, leaving a legacy of faithful leadership and an estate of about $1.4 billion in today's dollars. His stores lived on into the 1990s.

None of that would have been possible, however, without some remarkable business acumen. Wanamaker offered ready-to-wear clothing in a society where people typically made their own clothes or paid a tailor to make them. And he displayed merchandise in an orderly, convenient fashion, in contrast to the heaps of clothing and cluttered shelves in other stores.

Wanamaker's mail-order catalog was a hit, too, and a considerable revenue stream, and he pioneered advertising, an uncommon practice for merchants at the time because of its uncertain return. "Half the money I spend on advertising is wasted," claimed Wanamaker in agreement with his competitors. "The trouble is, I don't know which half."

The marketing philosophy that may have distinguished Wanamaker the most, though, was his "Golden Rule" approach to customers. Most stores during that era would not permit customers merely to browse. If they entered, the salespeople expected them to make a purchase and even badgered them until they acquiesced. Prices in those stores varied with a customer's ability to negotiate, just like a garage sale, and no merchant accepted returns or exchanges. Worse still, in some establishments, what customers saw on the sales floor differed in quality from what they brought home.

But Wanamaker maintained a one-price-for-all system. No haggling, no harassment. What you see is what you get. And he was the first to offer a money-back guarantee. "One Price and Return of Goods!" was his stores' motto.[8]

Of course, today we shoppers take such things for granted, but they originated with people like John Wanamaker who simply treated customers the way he wanted to be treated. Basic Christian values.

Not surprisingly, perhaps, the Golden Rule approach earned Wanamaker plenty of gold, allowing him to open a New York City location in 1896 and to break ground on a magnificent new Market Street location in Philadelphia "that would advertise his Christian values and bring moral ambience to the heart of the city."[9] Constructed from 1902 to 1911, and covering an entire city block with three floors below ground and 12 above, its architect described it as "the most monumental commercial structure ever erected any-where in the world." It was indeed the largest retail space on the planet at the time, and it's still a marvel today, in use as a Macy's.[10] No less a dignitary than President William Howard Taft spoke at its dedication, the first president to participate in such an event.

Like other business leaders, Wanamaker was also a generous philanthropist, giving abundantly to Moody, Billy Sunday, and the Salvation Army, while building homeless shelters, soup kitchens, schools and churches. His greater contribution, though, may have been showing that business need not be a secular or toxic vocation.

Reframed Christianly, his business was a platform to evange-lize, to disciple, and to care for people. To get there, he and other faithful forerunners of his era (e.g., Henry Parsons Crowell, J.C. Penney, John D. Rockefeller Jr., Milton Hershey, H.J. Heinz) re-sisted great pressure—often from religious authority figures—re-jecting their incomplete perspective of Christian vocation.

And that's exactly the point. Had these narrower interpreta-tions prevailed, the practice of the Christian faith might be limited to the church, the mission field and the home. Instead, John Wanamaker's practical and public theology demonstrated that pul-pits exist on Market Street as well.

For Further Study

Nicole C. Kirk, *Wanamaker's Temple: The Business of Religion in an Iconic Department Store*, New York: New York University Press, 2018.

Notes

1. Nicole C. Kirk, *Wanamaker's Temple: The Business of Religion in an Iconic Department Store*, New York: New York University Press, 2018, p. 2.

2. *Ibid.*, p. 7.
3. *Ibid.*, p. 200.
4. *Ibid.*, p. 120.
5. *Ibid.*, p. 99.
6. *Ibid.*, p. 5.
7. *Ibid.*, p. 119.
8. *Ibid.*, p. 76.
9. *Ibid.*, p. 60.
10. *Ibid.*, p 81.

CORRECT CRAFT
Building Boats to the Glory of God

The Lesson

Their faith commitment brought them national attention during World War II. It's also made them a market leader in quality and character ever since.

There aren't many companies that can claim they helped defeat Hitler. Fewer still that did it with one day tied behind their back.

Launched in 1925 by W.C. Meloon, this Orlando boatbuilding company, with a reputation for quality and integrity, grew even through the Great Depression.[1] As a result, in the 1940s it earned government contracts to contribute to the war effort.

Correct Craft was building about 48 boats a month when the call came in. "This is classified," the Army commander told Meloon sternly. "Eisenhower will be attempting to cross the river into Germany soon, so we need as many boats as you can manufacture by the end of the month."

It was February 9, 1945. The Allies were closing in on Germany. But the muddy rapids of the Rhine River stood in their way. It was a formidable obstacle, having protected Germany from invasion since the days of Napoleon. To cross it, the Army needed "storm boats"—compact, 17-foot vessels that could skid up onto beaches full-throttle, loaded with troops.

The Meloon family quickly gathered to pray about the request and the next day committed to deliver 300 storm boats in 18 days, a seemingly impossible task for them. "We didn't know how to build 300 when we said that," W.O. Meloon, the founder's eldest son, would later admit. But they were going to rely on God to show them the way.

More than that, they were going to rely on doing it God's way, attempting to fulfill the order without working on the Sabbath. That would cost them three of the 18 work days.

The U.S. Army fired back, insisting that they operate seven days a week like everyone else. Meloon said it was non-negotiable; if need be, the Army could have the contract back. In fact, he was risking a lawsuit that could sink Correct Craft, but the Army retreated. Build all that you can build.

The company quickly expanded from 60 to 320 employees. The Army secured the necessary raw materials. On Monday, February 12, Correct Craft built their first storm boat to the detailed specs they had been given.

One down, 299 to go.

On Tuesday, the process began to improve. They built three boats. Then seven on Wednesday, despite pausing, enigmatically to some, for their usual midweek chapel service.

However, this clearly wasn't working. With only 11 boats completed in three days, the Meloon family again met that Wednesday night to ask God to show them how to complete the task.

The next day, W.O. Meloon awoke with a process idea that would speed production. They implemented it, building 13 boats on Thursday, 17 on Friday, and 21 on Saturday.

Then zero on Sunday.

Completed boats spilled out onto the street and were stacked all over the property. Production continued to accelerate, with the company building up to 42 boats in a day. Again they paused for their midweek chapel service, inviting an Army colonel to speak to them. The other three contractors, he said, were not building as many storm boats as Correct Craft—not even combined.

It was an encouragement to a weary workforce. Meloon's company tallied 240 boats in their second six-day week of production. And on February 24, four days ahead of schedule, they all cheered as boat number 306 was carted away, en route to Europe.

Then suddenly, another request: Since the other contractors had fallen short, could Correct Craft build an additional 100 boats by the end of the month? They embraced the challenge, hitting the deadline by delivering the boats in Florida fruit trucks. *National Geographic* magazine would later suggest the company had walked on water, calling those 18 days "A Miracle Production."[2]

There's also this epilogue: As it turned out, the Army couldn't use any of the boats from the other builders. The engines didn't fit right, despite those companies getting the same specs as Correct Craft. Only Meloon's boats were usable.

And apparently, those 406 boats were enough when combined with other Allied Forces vehicles. Days after delivery, George Patton's division was the first to cross the Rhine, capturing 19,000 German troops. Within weeks the Allies toppled Hitler's regime.

"Even though it was called a miracle in boatbuilding," explained W.O. Meloon, "to us, it was simply an indication that the Lord honors the obedience of His children."

That obedience extends to the modern day, touching every aspect of their operation. Briefly, here are five current expressions of the Christian faith at Correct Craft.

Profitable growth—*good stewardship*—is a fundamental expression for them. It hasn't always been smooth sailing, but Ralph Meloon, another son of W.C., clarifies their goal poignantly: "How can we be a good witness for the Lord if we're not successful in the business?"[3]

They certainly have been, growing to 1,600 employees with coast-to-coast operations. Their value proposition? The relentless pursuit of *quality*, which they also consider an expression of the faith. It could hardly be otherwise when your mission is "Building Boats to the Glory of God." Today, their Nautique brand is preeminent in the water-skiing and wakeboarding communities.

But despite their young, free-spirited target market, Correct

Craft will not partner with alcohol companies at watersports tournaments, turning away their lucrative sponsorship deals. For Correct Craft, it's just an *integrity* issue.

The same is true when it comes to their advertising. "Our ads will look a little different," says current CEO Bill Yeargin, "a little more conservative than some of our competitors' ads, but it's important to us that they be a reflection of who we are."[4] Greg Meloon, Vice-President of Marketing, translates that as models in one-piece bathing suits or modest summer clothing. In the 1990s, company president W.N. Maloon, grandson of the founder, used this Sunday standard: "If I can't take my brochure into the church and lay it on the pew and feel comfortable … I have no business printing it."[5] Today you could still project their ads and website on a church stage without offense.

Philanthropy is another faith expression at Correct Craft. Three types of philanthropy, in particular: "Global Outreach" (employee mission trips to Asia, Africa, Central America and the Caribbean to build homes, work in orphanages, and improve schools); "Local Outreach" (similar to the global outreach, but within their own communities); and what they call "Local Support" (charitable giving from one employee to another in times of need).[6] Correct Craft has long been a company that gives back.

Lastly, but historically among their highest priorities, is *evangelism*. Correct Craft's leadership has always been overt about their faith, well-beyond their mission statement, with the goal of introducing people to God—especially their employees.

"One of the opportunities that our faith culture gives us," says Yeargin, "is the ability to interact with people who would never go in a church. Employees are a great example. Each year we have employees come to faith because of our culture."[7]

Sometimes that evangelistic culture just entails being around caring people who love God. Other times it's more by design: voluntary, lunchtime Bible studies and voluntary mission trips where employees often experience God more closely—in some cases for the first time.

Stewardship, quality, integrity, philanthropy, evangelism.

There are other faith expressions as well. But like their stand against Sabbath work in the 1940s, it all flows from this boat company's unswerving dependence on God.

Correct Craft has become an industry leader by first being a follower.

For Further Study

James Vincent, *Parting the Waters: How vision and faith make good business*, Chicago, IL: Moody Press, 1997.

Websites: CorrectCraft.com and Nautique.com

Notes

1. Much of the information for this story comes from James Vincent, *Parting the Waters: How vision and faith make good business*, Chicago, IL: Moody Press, 1997.
2. "Winning the War in Supply," *National Geographic*, December 1945, p. 734.
3. "Correct Craft," Center for Faith & Work, LeTourneau University. Vimeo.com/53226570 at 6:09.
4. "Correct Craft" at 4:30.
5. *Parting the Waters*, p. 82.
6. Correct Craft website, www.correctcraft.com/who-we-are
7. "Correct Craft" at 3:00.

FLOW AUTOMOTIVE COMPANIES
GOING THE EXTRA MILE NO ONE ELSE WILL

The Lesson

What if honoring God with your business means higher expenses and lower profit per sale than your competition? For Don Flow, it means do it anyway and trust God for the results.

Once upon a time, a couple was traveling by car from the northeast to Florida. But their transmission only made it as far as North Carolina, failing after most repair shops were closed.

The only one open had a friendly mechanic who seemed empathetic when the couple explained they had limited vacation time and were hoping to get back on the road the next day.

No problem if it were flat tire. But a transmission?

The mechanic called his wife who cooked them dinner and made up some beds for the couple to spend the night at their home. The mechanic worked until 2:30 a.m. to finish the job and the astonished couple were on their way by 7:00.

It sounds like a fictitious parable, but it's actually a true story — the kind of story you hear at Flow Automotive.

The couple later wrote to the owner: "It's possible we went into a time warp and landed in Heaven. If everybody's like this, we're moving here and so is our whole town!"

The mechanic, who didn't tell anybody about that night, shrugged it off when the owner asked him about it: "Isn't that how you would treat a valued friend?"[1]

Well, yeah, but they're customers, not valued friends.

The distinction doesn't seem to exist at the 37 Flow Automotive dealerships in the southeast. And that's because the distinction doesn't exist for their leader of nearly four decades, Don Flow.

After graduating from the University of Virginia, Don told his father he wanted to go to grad school to study theology before joining their car business. Two years later, master's degree in hand, Don insisted on doing every job in the dealership at the normal rate of pay to understand from the inside both the business and the employee experience.

That went on not for four days, or four weeks, but four years. Then Don—always the learner—was off for more education, this time an MBA at Wake Forest.

Recalls Don: "When I finished (my MBA) at age 27, my dad said, 'You're in charge of this dealership. See you next year.' He really let me find my own voice and encouraged me to develop my thoughts on how to run a business."[2]

As you might imagine, someone with that much education, academic and practical, would have a few thoughts.

They were unusual thoughts, though—a philosophy entirely different than what most businesses, let alone car dealerships, adopt.

His starting point was not "how can we grow?" or "how can we increase market share?" For the theology student, the questions were far deeper: "What does a redeemed view of business look like? And within that, what's my vocational call?"

Not exactly your typical guy across the desk as you bargain for a Camry.

His answer is that a redeemed view—a God-ordained role for business in society—is that a business care in a neighborly way for customers, employees and the community in which it operates.

Let's unpack that. With respect to customers, Flow intends to be a place that keeps its promises and is worthy of customers' trust, in both service and sales. So when Flow repairs a vehicle, the owner gets one estimate. If the repair costs more than that estimate, Flow pays the difference. And if they don't fix it properly, the owner never again pays to fix that problem—plus they'll pick up your car and drop it back off to you, so you won't be inconvenienced by their mistake.

When Flow sells a pre-owned vehicle, they back that vehicle with a powertrain warranty up to 100,000 miles,[3] a three-day money back guarantee, and, strikingly, two years of free maintenance. It's expensive and unprecedented, but as Don says, "That's what you would do for a neighbor."[4]

Also, all pricing on vehicles, pre-owned and new, is "open book," meaning customers get to see what Flow paid, what they invested in preparation or reconditioning, and what their margin is.

If you want to get a laugh out of a salesperson, try asking for those numbers in your next car negotiation. They seldom provide it, since they make more money when there's asymmetric knowledge about the costs. Stated differently, it's more profitable per sale for them to hide information—and less profitable per sale for Flow to be transparent.

It's also less profitable for Flow to price everything at market, rather than the traditional approach of starting with a high list price and then creeping down. But that's exactly what they do. As always, Don Flow has a theological basis:

"We did a study and found that the people who typically paid the least for the cars were the most able to pay. Those least able to pay, paid the most. For me, it was wrong to take advantage of the least able, a clear violation of the Biblical mandate." So at Flow, "you don't have to be a tough negotiator or more educated to get a fair price. If you've got a Ph.D. or if you're a janitor, you'll pay the same price for the vehicle."[5]

With respect to employees, Don sees other Biblical mandates. "We have a saying in our company," explains Don. "'There are no little people and there is no ordinary work.' If you use Paul's metaphor for the members of a body (1 Corinthians 12), each member is important."[6]

So yes, they have nice perks—employee gyms, college scholarships for children of employees, matching funds for house down payments, good wages, an emergency fund for employees in financial trouble. "But in the end," Don is clear, "it can't be just about these things. It must extend to treating each employee as a valued, respected person."[7]

That's the kind of mindset that follows from doing every job in the dealership.

And here's the kind of growth that follows from employees feeling valued and respected: From neighborhood dealership in 1983 when Don took over, Flow Automotive has grown to 37 franchises with 1,500 employees and $1 billion in annual sales. They've won just about every customer satisfaction award that exists in the industry, and consequently, they've been highly-profitable for decades.

So with respect to the communities in which they operate, that financial success translates into generosity, whether through building homes with Habitat for Humanity, or leading a city in United Way funding, or underwriting urban education and arts programs. It's just part of a company's role in society, claims Don.

His personal passion has been revitalizing Winston-Salem, North Carolina, where the company is headquartered. Among many other contributions, that's included funding a world-class tennis facility at Wake Forest University to host an annual, international tournament, bringing visibility and economic resources to the area. Tellingly, Don insisted that it not be called The Flow Tournament, but instead, The Winston-Salem Open.

His initiative, his resources, but it's not about him.

Seemingly, nothing has been. Don Flow has reimagined and reengineered the car business to honor God, abundantly blessing customers, employees and communities in the process. "People said I must be crazy," chuckles Don. But despite the risk, he says it's just the right thing to do "if I'm really going to treat a person like my neighbor, or like a guest in my home.'"[8]

Maybe that explains why a Flow employee is willing to invite customers to be guests in his home.

For Further Study

"Don Flow: Ethics at Flow Automotive," *Ethix*, April 1, 2004. Ethix.org/2004/04/01/ethics-at-flow-automotive

"Don Flow: How Do You Live Faithfully?" *Faith & Leadership* (Duke Divinity School), February 10, 2015. www.FaithAndLeadership.com/don-flow-how-do-you-live-faithfully

"Driving Trust," Faith & Co., Seattle Pacific University, 2018. Faithandco.spu.edu/film-detail/driving-trust-flow

"2017 Distinguished Alumni Award: Don Flow," Wake Forest University, May 5, 2017. www.youtube.com/watch?v=k0CGGYA2HA4

Notes

1. "Don Flow: Ethics at Flow Automotive," *Ethix*, April 1, 2004. Ethix.org/2004/04/01/ethics-at-flow-automotive
2. "Don Flow: How Do You Live Faithfully?" *Faith & Leadership* (Duke Divinity School), February 10, 2015. www.FaithAndLeadership.com/don-flow-how-do-you-live-faithfully
3. Note: If the pre-owned vehicle has more than 88,000 miles on it, the Flow powertrain warrantee is automatically 12,000 miles. In other words, they offer a free, extended warrantee on every used car.
4. "Driving Trust," Faith & Co., Seattle Pacific University, 2018. Faithandco.spu.edu/film-detail/driving-trust-flow at 4:30.
5. "Don Flow: Ethics at Flow Automotive"

6. "Don Flow: How Do You Live Faithfully?"
7. "Don Flow: Ethics at Flow Automotive"
8. "Driving Trust" at 4:40.

R.W. BECKETT
CORPORATION
Revealing God under
the Media Microscope

The Lesson

For Christian-owned companies, it's precarious to be interviewed by the mainstream media. Despite the risk, John Beckett opened the doors to their scrutiny. Then God opened doors for him.

"We want to do a story about you."

They're among the most inviting and intimidating words a business owner can hear. Especially an overtly-Christian business owner.

On one hand, it's free publicity and a megaphone for the company's values. On the other hand, the mainstream media has been less-than-objective with faith-based companies, and once a skewed story gets published, there's little recourse.

So in 1995, when John Beckett heard those very words from ABC News, proposing a feature story for the national evening news about his company, he was guarded. "No way," John said to himself. "We're not going to let ABC News barge into the R.W. Beckett Corporation, shoot a lot of footage, extract a few sound bites and say whatever they want to say about us on national TV!"[1]

An understandable concern. During the 1980s and 90s, the media had routinely caricatured televangelists, disparaged the "Moral Majority" movement, and overall, framed public-square Christianity as a power grab. So it was hardly a stretch to assume that any news report about a Christian-owned company might follow the same narrative: A hypocritical, holier-than-thou business owner cutting ethical corners and coercing employees into conversion.

In fact, John had personally experienced this sort of parody. A regional magazine, read by much of the Cleveland business community, had done a satirical feature on the Beckett Corporation. John described the story as "lampooning some of our most important values" by, among other things, depicting him in a robe and a halo. Now, John had gotten on ABC's radar by spearheading a national effort, "taking issue with the Equal Employment Opportunity Commission after the agency had issued a set of guidelines many thought would restrict religious freedom in the workplace."

Was ABC's real motivation to undermine Beckett with a slanted story? If so, the Beckett Corporation's Bible-based approach to management could be misrepresented as one of repression rather than redemption—this time in front of millions.

However, trust in God won out. The Beckett executive team had recently deliberated how the company could make a more faithful impact on the marketplace. If they were truly to be the "city on a hill" that Jesus envisioned in his Sermon on the Mount (Matthew 5:14), then perhaps, said John, they should welcome this opportunity to appear on what was then America's most watched news program.

So they opened the door to ABC, sharing authentically how they operate their business as a ministry, and trusting God with the outcome.

Two days of filming—fifteen hours in all—culminated in a three-minute news segment. It started by highlighting Beckett employees who were enjoying benefits like paid maternity leave and college tuition. Then it segued to John's comments about the underlying philosophy: "My main mission in life is to know the will of God and to do it," he explained.

Watching from his couch in Elyria, Ohio, John breathed a sigh of relief. He had given so many jumbled answers in those interviews, but the correspondent had skillfully extracted the centerpiece of it all. John recalls: "The rest of the news piece came across wonderfully. The integrity of the company, the enthusiasm of our employees, and the relevance of our core values to the everyday world of work were presented in a clear and compelling manner."

No doubt, John's father would have been proud. Reginald W. Beckett co-founded this oil burner company in 1937, as many households were switching from coal to oil heat. The vacillating economy, and later innovations like natural gas heat, put him on a circuitous road. But in 1963, when he tapped John as an apprentice, freshly-minted from the MIT engineering program, the company was stable. Twelve employees, one million dollars in annual sales.

Only a year later Reginald died, suddenly and unexpectedly, leaving 26-year-old John in charge. Details aside, the challenge brought John to the end of himself, ultimately setting him on a path to God. And as John's faith grew, with vibrant help from his wife and his men's prayer group, so did the integration of that faith with company operations. By the time of the ABC interview, decades later, John was emerging as an eloquent spokesman for what workplace faith looks like.

The ABC broadcast accelerated his ambassadorship. In the years that followed, John taught believers in business about the joy of charitable giving. He taught them about the power of integrity and excellence in customer care—the mindset of earning the right to serve customers again. He taught them that workplace culture changes, and indeed lives change, when you remember that employees are created in the image of God.

And through it all, John taught his audiences about the fruit of faithful stewardship, offering impressive evidence. The R.W. Beckett Corporation, now a family of companies that includes gas and air products, has grown to more than 600 employees with a nine-figure annual revenue and a manufacturing footprint that includes Canada and Asia. Beyond that, the company's innovations have conserved literally billions of gallons of oil, relative to the products they sold three decades ago.[2]

As John passes the torch to the third generation, the company has become a worldwide leader in the industry. Meanwhile, two books and dozens of keynotes later, John has become a worldwide leader in the faith-at-work movement. ABC News was a catalyst.

More precisely, perhaps, John's faith was the catalyst. Despite the risk, John Beckett trusted that under the media microscope, God would be revealed.

For Further Study

John D. Beckett, *Loving Monday: Succeeding in Business Without Selling Your Soul,* Downers Grove, IL: InterVarsity Press, 1998.

John D. Beckett, *Mastering Monday: A Guide to Integrating Faith and Work,* Downers Grove, IL: InterVarsity Press, 2006.

Website: www.BeckettCorp.com

Notes

1. Quotes in this chapter come from pages 19-23 of John D. Beckett, *Loving Monday: Succeeding in Business Without Selling Your Soul,* Downers Grove, IL: InterVarsity Press, 1998.
2. The R.W. Beckett Corporation, "Beckett at 75 Years." www.BeckettCorp.com/wp-content/uploads/2015/01/Beckett75thBook.pdf, p. 18.

MASTERPIECE CAKESHOP
RECLAIMING RELIGIOUS FREEDOM

The Lesson

What happens when a business owner refuses to compromise his religious liberty? In this case, scorn, death threats, lawsuits, the loss of 40 percent of his business ... and a Supreme Court ruling that will forever fortify freedom.

For a while, Jack Phillips was a household name in the United States. Probably the most famous baker in the country. But it wasn't for the cake artist's imaginative creations or his tasty treats. Rather, Jack was known was for something he could not do.

Depending on who you ask, the issue gets framed quite differently: Jack discriminated by refusing to create a custom wedding cake for a same-sex couple, or Jack declined to create a product that violated his conscience and religious freedom.

It all started with mere 30-second interaction. In 2012, a gay couple asked Jack Phillips, long-time owner of Masterpiece Cakeshop in Colorado, to design a wedding cake for them. Jack told the couple that he would sell them anything else in the store, including pre-made cakes, but he could not customize a cake for them because of his belief that marriage is a covenant before God, between one man and one woman.

End of conversation, beginning of litigation—a six-year legal battle that would ultimately reach the nation's highest court.

At the outset, the trial court whisked away the baker's religious freedom and free speech claims, compelling Jack to create cakes with messages that violated his conscience—this despite allowing three other bakers to reject cake orders because the requested messages denounced same-sex marriage. The Commission even added some bitter icing to Jack's case: He would also have to "re-educate" his staff that Colorado law requires artists to endorse all views, and file quarterly compliance reports with the government for two years, demonstrating that he is not turning away same-sex business.[1]

The Colorado Court of Appeals upheld the Commission's ruling and the Colorado Supreme Court declined to hear the case. Jack's only chance would be an improbable appeal to the U.S. Supreme Court, which hears only about 80 cases a year of the approximately 8,000 cases filed with it. That's a one-in-a-hundred chance.

During this extended, excruciating appeals process, rather than compromise his faith as the Commission insisted, Jack stopped making wedding cakes altogether, costing him 40 percent of his revenue and six of his ten employees.

He may have lost more sleep than business, though. Besides the vandalism and ubiquitous protests outside his Lakewood shop, he says: "we had death threats, we had hundreds of phone calls and emails that were vile and vulgar and vicious." One time, Jack was at the store with his daughter and granddaughter when someone called to say they were coming to kill everyone there. "I had to have them go hide in the back," recalls Jack. "It was a crazy situation."[2]

Then there was the constant drumbeat by social and mainstream media outlets eager to vilify Jack. They built up and easily tore down strawman arguments about Jack's motivations, painting him as a poster child for bigotry and oppression.

But Jack Phillips is one tough cookie. To such things, he says "This isn't a huge cost. I mean, there are people who lose their lives for (their faith). They're just calling me names."[3]

He outlasted the persecution and surprisingly, he did get his day before the U.S. Supreme Court. In June 2018, they decided his case. Sort of.

The Court in *Masterpiece Cakeshop, Ltd. v. Colorado Civil Rights Commission*[4] didn't exactly say whether business owners can opt out of same-sex weddings. What it did say was that courts cannot devalue religion as a basis for speech and conduct, as the Colorado Civil Rights Commission had done. Seven Supreme Court justices—four conservative, two liberal and one centrist writing for the Court—directed judicial bodies to be "tolerant," "respectful," and "neutral" toward religion in free exercise cases.

As axiomatic as that sounds, in some jurisdictions it's a huge win for wedding vendors and other business owners bullied by the anti-faith animus of attorneys general, human rights commissions and state courts. Considered from another angle, had Jack Phillips lost outright, it might have been open season on Christian-owned companies, both in the courts and on Main Street. Any "mystery shopper" could walk into a pizzeria, ask whether they'll make pizzas for a same-sex wedding, and if the answer is no, they could boycott, dox, flame, sue and otherwise torment them into bankruptcy. It would be the very definition of "chilling effect."

That day has not yet come, though, in part because Jack Phillips's perseverance enabled religious liberty to triumph in this case. The *Masterpiece* ruling is not an exemption from anti-discrimination law; it's an attempt to balance the right to equal service with the right to religious expression. The State can't, by default, prefer one over the other.

However, what we don't know from the case is where the line is. At what point does religious freedom become unlawful discrimination? When can the government compel citizens to speak and act against their conscience and beliefs?

"The outcome of cases like this in other circumstances must await further elaboration in the courts," Justice Kennedy punted. But now, at least, he was punting to a level playing field.

There's an epilogue to this sordid saga as well. Actually, two.

Receiving that punted ball was the State of Colorado, which the

High Court directed to re-evaluate Jack's case in light of its opinion. It took months, but in March 2019, Colorado finally dropped all charges against Jack Phillips.

End of story? Not when you're on the front lines of a culture war. The crusade against Jack continues as some disingenuous, litigious customers have asked him for cakes they know he won't make—cakes to celebrate Satan's birthday, Halloween, or a gender transition. Because he cannot create products that, as he says, "celebrate events or express messages that conflict with my religious beliefs," he politely declines.[5]

Some of these customers go elsewhere for their cake; others go directly to a lawyer. Their strategy, it seems, is to wear him down or bankrupt him with legal costs.

But after seven years, they apparently still don't know Jack. It will take more than another half-baked lawsuit to get him to fold or to deplete his dough. In fact, through it all, his faith is more unshakable than ever. "I can trust Him," explains Jack. "God is doing what He's going to do. And if He's chosen us to be a part of that, it's quite an honor."[6]

Jack's part has certainly been no cakewalk, but it has been pretty sweet: Reclaiming religious freedom.

For Further Study

Masterpiece Cakeshop v. Colorado Civil Rights Commission, 138 S. Ct. 1719 (2018).

"Justice for Jack," Alliance Defending Freedom, adflegal.org/jack-phillips

"Masterpiece Cakeshop v. Colorado Civil Rights Commission," Timeline and resources from the Alliance Defending Freedom, www.adfmedia.org/news/prdetail/8700

Notes

1. Alliance Defending Freedom, "Colo. cake artist appeals gov't 're-education' order," July 17, 2014. www.adfmedia.org/News/PRDetail/9211
2. Meghan Keneally, "Baker who won Supreme Court case maintains he said no to cake, not couple," ABC News, June 6, 2018. ABCnews.go.com/US/baker-won-supreme-court-case-maintains-cake-couple/story?id=55660012
3. Alliance Defending Freedom, "What happened when Jack Phillips chose to follow his conscience?" adflegal.org/risk
4. 138 S. Ct. 1719 (2018).
5. Elise Schmelzer, "Masterpiece Cakeshop, state of Colorado agree to mutual ceasefire over harassment, discrimination claims," *The Denver Post*, March 5, 2019. www.denverpost.com/2019/03/05/masterpiece-cakeshop-colorado-mutual-ceasefire-over-claims
6. Alliance Defending Freedom, "Think you know all about the Colorado cake artist at the center of the Supreme Court case?" adflegal.org/jack-phillips-story3

CONESTOGA WOOD SPECIALTIES
RISKING THE COMPANY TO REMAIN FAITHFUL

The Lesson

Sometimes, honoring God entails higher costs or sharing profits or modifying operations. Other times it entails risking the entire business to do what's right.

It was litigate or liquidate.

The Hahn family never thought living out their faith convictions would require them to go to court. As keep-to-themselves Mennonites, they certainly never wanted to. But now, it seemed, the government left them with no other choice.

Since 1964, the Hahns have made custom cabinets in eastern Pennsylvania. Founded on faith and fortitude by brothers Norman and Samuel Hahn, Conestoga Wood Specialties has always offered impeccable craftsmanship at a fair price. Along the way, they've also cared for generations of employees and they've long been sensitive to environmental concerns, choosing suppliers who support sustainable forestry.

CEO Anthony Hahn, Norman's son, is straightforward: "My father started the business on Christian principles and Christian values, and it's something that we even wrote into our creed—that we want the business to continue to run on those principles."[1]

As a result, perhaps, in their first 50 years Conestoga grew from two local guys in a truck to 1,000 employees across the country.

But as a fiftieth anniversary present, a federal government gifted them an astronomical fine for resisting one aspect of a new law, the Affordable Care Act (ACA). In particular, the Hahns objected to the law's abortion-pill mandate: Employers now had to include in their employee benefit package four abortion-inducing drugs (i.e., morning after pills and other abortifacients). Since the drugs can abort a fertilized egg, those whose faith tradition says that life begins at conception cannot pay for them without violating that faith.[2]

The mandate arguably violated the United States Constitution, too, which guarantees that the federal government shall make no law prohibiting the free exercise of religion, as well as a 1990s law called the Religious Freedom Restoration Act.

Despite the dilemma for this non-litigious family, Anthony suggested that their backs were to the wall: "After talking through that for a period of time, we felt there was really no other decision to make. We weren't going to facilitate the taking of human life."[3]

The government had simply gone too far.

But the District Court disagreed, saying that Conestoga did not qualify for a religious exemption from the ACA. The Court of Appeals, in a 2-1 decision, upheld the District Court's ruling: no relief for the Hahns.

Quite the opposite, in fact. The IRS could punish them financially: One hundred dollars *per employee per day* of non-compliance. With 1,000 employees, the fine would put Conestoga out of business in a month. A half-century of service and jobs wiped out by a diktat from half of Congress.

The company could have just relented and moved on. In this area of the country, chances are that very few, if any, of their employees would ever purchase those drugs. And even if they did, the decision is ultimately on the employee, not the company — not the Hahn family. So why not quietly comply with the law and bless your customers and employees for another 50 years?

Because it was a matter of first principles.

If they surrendered, the Hahns could be helping destroy human life. So would dozens of other Christian business owners around the country who had similar cases pending. "It's not just for Conestoga," explained Anthony in his gentle manner. "We're taking a stand for other businesses as well. This is a religious liberty issue."[4]

Actually, there were even broader implications than that. If a law can require business owners, under threat of state penalty, to abdicate their bona fide religious beliefs, then the country would be moving toward a new form of governance—one that's more Pyongyang than Peoria. Next in the crosshairs could be Christian schools and churches, at least if the drift in other countries is any gauge.

The Hahn family appreciated that. They're among many in eastern Pennsylvania whose ancestors settled there seeking religious freedom. So the family didn't surrender. Instead, they appealed to the U.S. Supreme Court.

It was a long shot, typically one-in-a-hundred just to get a hearing, but it was their only shot.

Remarkably, maybe providentially, the nation's highest court did take the case, consolidating it with an identical case brought by Hobby Lobby. And in one of the highest profile cases of the term, most of the justices sided with the companies.[5]

Five justices out of nine, in fact. The decision could not have been any closer.

According to the majority opinion, the federal regulations could not be applied to closely-held, for-profit corporations whose owners—like the Hahns and the Green family of Hobby Lobby—had religious objections. In plainer English, the government overstepped by compelling Christian business owners to pay for contraceptives and abortifacients.

Case closed. Conestoga remained open.

It may seem like just another story. It's really not. Unlike business owners whose faith convictions inflate their costs or disseminate their profits, the Hahn family put *their entire business* on the line to remain faithful.

And to benefit countless others. They risked everything not just to save the company, but to save something much more. If we can't express our faith through our business, the Hahns believed, someday we may not be able to express our faith at all.

For Further Study

"Conestoga Wood, An Enemy of the State," Alliance Defending Freedom, December 19, 2014.
www.youtube.com/watch?v=pgeJQvAShuc

Burwell v. Hobby Lobby Stores and *Conestoga Wood Specialties Corp. v. Burwell*, 134 S. Ct. 2751 (2014)

Notes

1. "Conestoga Wood, An Enemy of the State," Alliance Defending Freedom, December 19, 2014.
   www.youtube.com/watch?v=pgeJQvAShuc at 1:00
2. For those who might object that Conestoga's motivation was really an anti-woman posture, Hahn retorts: "That is the furthest thing from the truth. Women are an important part of our business. We have women in various management positions, and our health plan has always been generous, including providing preventive services for women. This case is simply about whether the federal government can force us to provide life-destroying products or else face massive fines on our family business." Kathryn Jean Lopez, "Wood You Stand for Religious Freedom?" *National Review*, March 24, 2014.
   www.nationalreview.com/2014/03/wood-you-stand-religious-freedom-interview
3. "Conestoga Wood, An Enemy of the State" at 4:13.
4. "Conestoga Wood Specialties," ADF Media Relations, 2013.
   Vimeo.com/74728204 at 1:50.

5. *Burwell v. Hobby Lobby Stores* and *Conestoga Wood Specialties Corp. v. Burwell*, 134 S.Ct. 2751 (2014).

PART 8

~

THEIR PROSELYTIZING
They introduce people to God

R.G. LeTourneau, Inc.
Interstate Batteries
U.S. Plastic Corporation
Pure Flix Entertainment
In-N-Out Burger

R.G. LETOURNEAU, INC.

The Lesson

Once R.G. LeTourneau realized that a business can be a ministry, it unleashed him to change the world. Along the way, he shared that message with as many people as he could.

He invented the bulldozer. And dozens of other construction machines. For that, Robert Gilmour (R.G.) LeTourneau is known as the "Dean of Earth Moving."

That's probably not a tidbit you'll be dropping at your next social gathering, but if it's a gathering of Christians, perhaps they'd be intrigued by this: R.G., who never even made it to the eighth grade, went on to build two-thirds of the earth-moving equipment used by the Allied Forces during World War II. Then he "reverse tithed" his proceeds, donating 90 percent to Christian causes and living on 10 percent.

In fact, he continued the practice for the last three decades of his life, giving almost all of his business and personal income to the advancement of the gospel. So that might make him the "Dean of Discipleship" as well.

Here's the streamlined version of the story. To dig deeper, see

R.G.'s engagingly-written autobiography, *Mover of Men and Mountains.*[1]

Born into a Christian, church-going household in 1888, R.G. struggled to follow both his earthly and heavenly father. Regarding the latter, he recalled: "I attended (church) regularly—I had no escape—and heard a lot about God without learning a thing."[2]

Perhaps that's because he slept through most of the sermons.[3] But a revival event in his hometown of Portland, Oregon, awakened him from his slumbers, literal and spiritual.

At first, that week of messages and music in 1904 seemed unremarkable. He told his hopeful mother that he "didn't even feel a tremor of response," then quickly realized from the look on her face that he "could have hurt her less by stabbing her with a blunt knife."[4]

Wrestling with that moment all night, and with what he sensed in his heart to be the truth, R.G. at age 16 simply gave up his resistance. He described his encounter with God this way:

"No bolts of lightning hit me. No great flash of awareness. I just prayed to the Lord to save me, and then I was aware of another Presence. No words were spoken. I received no messages. It was just that all my bitterness was drained away, and I was filled with such a vast relief that I could not contain it all."[5]

A decade and a half later, R.G. reached another turning point after his infant son died. Rather than run from God, the tragedy had the opposite effect on him. "I had been paying only token tribute to God," he said of his epiphany, "going through the motions of acting like a Christian, but really serving myself and my conscience instead of serving Him."[6]

With greater commitment, though, came a greater dilemma: "To me," he lamented, "service to the Lord, to which I had just re-dedicated my life, meant the ministry or missionary work. I couldn't see myself as a minister."[7]

No, he could only see himself as a mechanic and maybe someday a business owner. Those were his skills and his interests. Reluctantly, he considered abandoning them to pursue full-time ministry.

Then, breakthrough. His pastor showed R.G. that he was already in full-time ministry: "You know, Brother LeTourneau, God needs businessmen as well as preachers and missionaries."[8]

Existential crisis averted—forever: "Those were words that have guided my life ever since. I repeat them in public at every opportunity because I have discovered that many men have the same mistaken idea I had of what it means to serve the Lord. ... I didn't realize a layman could serve the Lord as well as a preacher."[9]

It all culminated in R.G. reframing himself as "God's businessman" and pursuing a series of well-intentioned, albeit financially-precarious, entrepreneurial ventures through the 1920s. Finally, in 1929 at the age of 41, R.G. LeTourneau got it right, launching a company that would make both a profit and a better world.

An inventor by divine gifting, R.G. began designing machines to do the infrastructure work of the Depression-era United States—machines to construct roads, airports, buildings and even offshore oil platforms.

At first, though, mostly roads, since in those days, roads were still built by men with shovels and by mules dragging plows. Once R.G. offered heavy equipment to do the work, the demand was so insatiable that by 1939, the newspapers pronounced him "America's foremost creator of road-building machinery."[10] It's also why the U.S. military relied on his company to create supply lines and to help win the war.

Along the way, with a couple exceptions that R.G. humbly notes in his memoir, he returned a tithe to God from the company's growing profits—at first 10 percent, then 50 percent in the late 1930s, then 90 percent thereafter. Nine-tenths of profits, nine-tenths of the company's common stock, and nine-tenths of his annual salary went straight to his LeTourneau Foundation for distribution around the world.

Besides funding the church and missions organizations, one of R.G.'s favorite causes was education, initially vocational training in the construction trades, but later faith-based colleges. The crown jewel was LeTourneau University, which today is among the premier Christian universities in the country.

R.G. gave back in another important way as well, personally teaching business people how to honor God through their companies. His unlikely speaking ministry began innocently enough in 1935 when, after building a factory in Peoria, Illinois, the local Chamber of Commerce asked R.G. to speak to the group.

It petrified the middle school dropout. "The whole idea of standing up in front of a lot of men terrified me. ... I also knew they thought I was something of a crackpot, with wild ideas about ... being in some kind of partnership with God."[11]

But once he got up to speak, his nerves left him and he says God gave him the confidence and the words to profess what being in business for God looked like.

"I didn't get much of a hand at the conclusion of my first public speech," he remembered, but the event prompted invitations to speak at area churches, which in turn prompted more invitations from further away. Over time, he was speaking six days a week around the world to church and business groups, usually starting with the line "I'm just a mechanic whom the Lord has blessed."[12]

As such, R.G. LeTourneau was a forerunner of the modern business-as-missions movement, emphasizing not just a generic "partnership with God," but the specific use of a business enterprise to introduce people to God.

He discipled internally, too, preaching to his employees at voluntary company chapels and tapping outside speakers to encourage employees to adopt the Christian way of life. Hiring company chaplains was a related innovation. "We call it 'Christianity with its sleeves rolled up,'" he wrote, "and I am eager to testify that it is a very effective way of bringing peace among men."[13]

It's been 50 years since R.G. LeTourneau passed away, and since that time, Komatsu acquired his company. But R.G.'s legacy lives on through the untold individuals and families who turned toward God because of his missionary contributions. It lives on through the students, alumni, faculty and others blessed by his university. And most germane to this book, it lives on through the business owners around the world he's inspired to make their companies a platform for ministry.

Indeed, this master roadbuilder paved the way for a new generation of "God's businessmen," and women.

For Further Study

R.G. LeTourneau, *Mover of Men and Mountains,* Chicago, IL: Moody Press, 1967.

Notes

1. R.G. LeTourneau, *Mover of Men and Mountains,* Chicago, IL: Moody Press, 1967.
2. *Ibid.,* p. 11.
3. *Ibid.,* p. 31.
4. *Ibid.,* p. 33.
5. *Ibid.*
6. *Ibid.,* p. 85.
7. *Ibid.,* p. 109.
8. *Ibid.*
9. *Ibid.,* pp. 109-110.
10. *Ibid.,* p. 222.
11. *Ibid.,* p. 202.
12. *Ibid.,* p. 1.
13. *Ibid.,* p. 211.

INTERSTATE BATTERIES
CHARGED UP TO CHANGE LIVES

The Lesson

Those who are forgiven much tend to love God much. In Norm Miller's case, he also wants as many people as possible to experience that same love.

He had narrowly escaped his third DWI the night before, but he couldn't escape one of the worst hangovers of his life.

This, at long last for Norm Miller, was rock bottom. He had been a consistent partier since he was 14. Not unusual when you grow up in a party-town like Galveston, Texas. He had been a consistent over-indulger since around the same time. Not unusual for the son of an alcoholic. And being a traveling salesman for the last decade only exacerbated the temptations.

What happened next that morning is best described by Norm himself: "I called the office and lied, telling them I was too sick to work. Then, as I lay there in bed, the truth started to overwhelm me. Although on the outside I represented the ultimate in American success—great job, lots of money, pretty wife, cute kids, fancy car—in reality I was a drunk. My life was out of control. The realization scared me like nothing else ever had.

"In that instant of desperation, panic hit me. Terrified, I blurted out in a yell: 'God help me! I can't handle it!'

"... And he answered. He took my drinking compulsion away completely. It was instantaneous. ... I realize it does not happen that way for everyone. But it did for me and I am eternally grateful."[1]

The real irony, says Norm, is that he wasn't sure he even believed in God. But he cried out anyway and was healed.

Not unusual for agnostics who are at the end of themselves, or for a merciful God who is the beginning of everything.

Life was different after that for Norm Miller. Alcoholics Anonymous helped. A friend helped by introducing him to Christ and the Word of God. Norm's personal study of apologetics helped because he needed to be convinced intellectually. And he was: "From that moment in 1974," explains Norm, "I have never doubted my decision to put my faith in Christ."[2]

More than that, though, Norm wanted others to enjoy the same transformation that he had—the inner peace, the joy, the freedom from the bondage of addiction, the assurance of eternal life.

That included the people in his company, Interstate Batteries.

"When I became a Christian," recalls Norm, "my life changed so radically, I began to think a lot about what impact my faith should have on the job. ... I prayed about how we might proclaim Christ to all our employees and our customers as well. I wanted everyone to experience God's great love and forgiveness."[3]

In 1978, four years after his conversion, Norm found himself in a position to start making that happen. Company founder John Searcy promoted him to president (Norm would later also become the majority owner), and Norm began experimenting with several faith expressions. As a result, Interstate Batteries under Norm Miller has looked as much like a parachurch ministry as a business enterprise.

Within the company, for example, the leadership has facilitated Bible study groups before and after work, popular Christian speakers over lunch, and employee mission trips. They open company events and executive meetings with prayer, and they notify employees about prayer requests via mass email. There's an in-house library of Christian resources and historically, all new employees have received a Bible on their first day of work. None of it is required reading; it's merely an invitation.

That's an important caveat. All the faith-based activities at Interstate are optional for employees and there's no connection to job outcomes. The company emphasizes this repeatedly and underscores that it would be illegal to do otherwise. The opportunities are many, though, because Norm cares about his employees' spiritual condition.

Interstate's leadership is no less committed to the spiritual welfare of those outside the company, regularly praying for the hundreds of thousands of dealers and their families, "for each one to receive Christ and come to the knowledge of the truth,"[4] and sending them Bibles, tracts and Christian audio recordings. The company has even connected willing employees with missionary groups, to do door-to-door evangelism in Dallas.

A chaplain's office oversees it all, as well as employee counseling and some of the company's philanthropy. This is why so much happens in this realm: Norm has made it somebody's job to nurture the God-centered culture.

Still, in 2008 Norm felt led to do more. While reflecting on Jesus's call to "be my witnesses in Jerusalem, and in all Judea and Samaria, and to the ends of the earth" (Acts 1:8), Norm was prompted to invest more heavily in bringing the message of Jesus Christ to north Texas—his locality, his "Jerusalem."

So Norm teamed-up with a company called E3 Partners, asking them to develop an ad campaign that would introduce people to Jesus. Brilliantly, E3 developed the "I Am Second" concept (as in God is first and I am second): three to ten minute video testimonies by celebrities, athletes, musicians and other big names, filmed professionally and dramatically.

They were raw and they were real. And consequently, they were quickly viral.

Within six weeks, the initial films from believers like Joe Gibbs, Tony Dungy and Stephen Baldwin generated views from more than 70 countries. Today, the 100+ I Am Second testimonies have surpassed 100 million views, with traffic from every nation.[5]

Apparently, Norm's 2008 calling was instead "to the ends of the earth."

Their batteries haven't yet made it that far, but they do cover most of North and Central America. They've also entered the massive China market. So it seems the company's evangelistic priorities have not distracted it from becoming an industry leader. Quite the contrary, in the half-century from 1965 to 2015, Interstate went from selling 200,000 batteries a year to having 200,000 distributors, selling 20 million batteries a year.

The growth, Norm Miller would say, is basic stewardship and is a natural result of their corporate mission: "To glorify God and enrich lives as we deliver the most trustworthy source of power to the world"[6] ... and, perhaps, as they *introduce* the most trustworthy Source of power to the world.

Not unusual when the leader himself has tapped into it.

For Further Study

Norm Miller, *Beyond the Norm*, Nashville, TN: Thomas Nelson, 1996

Websites: www.InterstateBatteries.com and www.iamsecond.com

Notes

1. Norm Miller, *Beyond the Norm*, Nashville, TN: Thomas Nelson, 1996, pp. 42-43.
2. *Beyond the Norm*, p. 48.
3. *Beyond the Norm*, p. 129.
4. *Beyond the Norm*, p. 133.
5. See www.iamsecond.com/about-i-am-second
6. See www.interstatebatteries.com/about/our-culture

U.S. PLASTIC CORPORATION

EVERY SHARE OF STOCK TO SHARE THE GOSPEL

The Lesson

How do you give your business to God? Start by giving away all your stock.

It seemed like a good idea at the time.

In the 1930s, developing photographs required the use of silver, 80 percent of which got poured down the drain. If he could find a way to catch the excess, and then refine and resell it, he could make millions.

But a year after Stanley Tam launched his silver reclamation business, which he called States Smelting and Refining Corporation, costs still outpaced income. He had twenty dollars remaining and his father only had twelve more to lend him.

Alone in his car after another frustrating sales trip, Stanley, a Christian, cried out to God asking him why this was happening. Then, in his words, "an incredible thing happened. Just outside Columbus, the Lord seemed to say to me 'Stanley, it doesn't have to be a disappointment. You don't have to go broke. ... All you need is faith in Me.'"

When Stanley protested that he did have faith, he sensed this response: "Enough to turn your business over to Me? To let me run it for you?"[1]

Stanley wasn't sure what that meant, but one thing seemed clear. He should persevere.

So the 22-year-old got back to work, cutting costs to the bone to stretch his $32. And enough doors opened over the next few years to keep him solvent. By 1940, Stanley and his new wife Juanita were in a position to make good on that promise to God to turn over the business to Him.

Stanley's idea was to make God his "senior partner" by somehow giving Him 51 percent of the company's stock. It befuddled the lawyers he visited, having seen no precedent for such a thing. But one inventive attorney suggested creating a nonprofit foundation that would own the stock, receive the associated dividends, and then distribute the money to Christian causes.

Calling it the Stanita Foundation, a portmanteau of "Stanley" and "Juanita," Stanley forged ahead in faith. Dividends would be small at first, but, eager to introduce people to Jesus, Stanley channeled them to missionary groups.

Meanwhile, business multiplied through the 1940s thanks to Juanita's idea of using the mail rather than a car to promote and deliver the silver collectors. A novel method at the time, direct mail allowed the company during that decade to "dispense considerable funds to various aspects of Christian work" through the Foundation.[2]

Now, if you look at the title of this chapter, you might be wondering what any of this has to do with plastic. Stanley described it this way in his book *God Owns My Business*: "we got into the plastics business by accident."[3]

The story goes like this. In 1955, Stanley's company developed a new device that required a large container to collect the silver. Stumbling across plastic buckets, another new product at the time, Stanley bought a supply of them. To his surprise, clients began calling to request extra buckets—for personal use.

"One thing led to another," he wrote. "Did we have plastic tanks for sale? What about spigots? Plastic tubing? Did we have any plastic goods available? ... 'You know something?' I said to my wife one night. 'This plastic business just might outgrow the silver division.'"[4]

Did it ever. They started fulfilling the unusual requests. Business grew. They produced higher quality plastic products. Business grew more. They published a catalog. Business exploded.

Within ten years, the plastic division was grossing more than a million dollars a year, and eventually, tens of millions. It became necessary to organize it as a new business, United States Plastic Corporation. And today they distribute more than 30,000 plastic products, doing more business in a day than they used to do in a year.[5]

1955 also marked another turning point, coincidentally or providentially. It was the year that Stanley Tam gave his entire business to God.

Originally he had gifted 51 percent of the stock to the Stanita Foundation, and later bumped it up to 60 percent. Then he encountered God yet again, recalling the exchange this way:

"Stanley, what is the most important thing in the world to you?"

"To see people seek your face, Lord, as a result of the Holy Spirit's blessing on my testimony."

"Stanley, if a soul is the greatest value in the world, then what investment can you make that will pay the greatest dividends a hundred years from now?"

"What are you asking me to do, Lord?"

"Stanley, if you agree that a soul is the greatest value in the whole world and is the only investment you can make in this life that will pay dividends throughout eternity, would you be willing to go back to Ohio and become an employee of mine?"

"An employee, Lord? Isn't that what I am now?"

"We're partners now, Stanley. I want you to turn your entire business over to Me. On the cross I paid the supreme price that you might become my disciple. Are you willing to give all you have in order that others may come to know Me as you do?"[6]

Stanley agreed that night. He didn't know all the implications, and his emotions vacillated about the decision, but what he did know was that 100 percent of the stock would have to go to the Foundation—the whole business for God's saving work around the world. That would be the company's paramount purpose. Stanley's job, as an employee rather than an owner, was simply to steward it well—to make more money so they could give more money.

They have indeed. In the decades since that conversation, this faithful steward has generated charitable funding of nearly $150 million.

It's an extraordinary case study in trusting God, and one that involves evangelistic expressions beyond giving money.

For example, Stanley's companies have always included Bible tracts in the packaging. The inside cover of his product catalog has historically offered an evangelistic message. And despite his shyness and limited education, Stanley ventured into public speaking, sharing his story in 38 countries, but also locally, especially to teenagers and businesspeople.

Even their headquarters in Lima, Ohio, is a platform for witness. Covering hundreds of feet along busy I-75, the building side proclaims, in enormous lettering, "Christ is the Answer," a testimonial no passer-by can miss.

Sixty-five years after its founding, U.S. Plastic Corporation remains boldly overt and evangelistic. "While our product line, our facility and our staff have changed and grown," their website explains, "our commitment to Christ and to resourcing the Great Commission has never, and will never, change."[7]

That commitment still entails giving 100 percent of their yearly dividends to support missionary work around the globe. Their spiritual metrics for 2018 alone are stunning: 404,978 decisions for Christ, 125,229 baptisms, 31,406 churches planted in 52 countries.[8]

And it all started with a guy beaten down to his last twenty bucks, ready to surrender his business. Instead, he surrendered to God.

Looking back at age 100, Stanley described the journey this way:

"I gave God my eyes, the things I would look at, the things I would watch. My mind, the things I would think about. My ears, the things I would listen to. My mouth, the things I would talk about. My hands, the things I would handle. My feet, the places I'd go. I said 'God, you can have every bit of me.'"[9]

Every bit of his company, too. The radical humility of Stanley Tam offers an inspiring glimpse of what can happen when God owns your business.

For Further Study

Stanley Tam and Ken Anderson, *God Owns My Business*, Chicago, IL: Moody Press, 1969, 2013.

U.S. Plastic Corporation, "The Stanley Tam Story," www.youtube.com/watch?v=QxPGFlxTSro

Website: www.usplastic.com

Notes

1. Stanley Tam and Ken Anderson, *God Owns My Business*, Chicago, IL: Moody Press, 1969, 2013, pp. 36-37.
2. *God Owns My Business*, p. 67.
3. *God Owns My Business*, p. 74.
4. *God Owns My Business*, p. 75.
5. U.S. Plastic Corporation, "Still 100%" mission.usplastic.com/portfolio-items/still-100
6. *God Owns My Business*, pp. 95-96.
7. "Still 100%"
8. U.S. Plastic Corporation, "Our Story," mission.usplastic.com.

9. U.S. Plastic Corporation, "The Stanley Tam Story," www.youtube.com/watch?v=QxPGFlxTSro at 25:00.

PURE FLIX ENTERTAINMENT
FAITH THROUGH FILM

The Lesson

Surveys consistently show that movies and television are the most powerful influencers of culture. So companies like Pure Flix are using that medium to reintroduce people to God.

By the time he was 18, this Kansas boy had seen only one movie in a theater. Ironically, he would eventually produce movies seen around the world.

Growing up Mennonite was a bit of a mixed bag for David A.R. White. He developed a strong faith foundation, an exemplary work ethic, and the compassion to be a positive influence on people. Perhaps he was a bit sheltered in some respects (David jokes that the Mennonite Brethren "make the Mormons look like a pack of Hell's Angels"),[1] but it's hard to argue with results. Entering adulthood, David loved God and intended to serve him wholeheartedly.

That one theater experience from his childhood actually became a catalyst—a transgression and a transformation at the same time. In 1978, at age eight, David snuck out to see the movie *Grease*. Watching Olivia Newton-John strut around in tight leather pants produced in him two reactions: "I'm going to hell"[2] and I'm going to Hollywood. Even at that young age, he was enamored with the movie business.

At age 19, David was still enamored, dropping out of Bible college and moving to California in search of acting work. It didn't matter to him that he had no acting experience (he was, however, cast as a munchkin in his high school's musical, *The Wizard of Oz*).[3] He sensed a gentle but persistent revelation from God to be a missionary through motion pictures.

Unlike so many other hopefuls in the Land of Broken Dreams, David snagged a part in a sitcom called *Evening Shade* with Burt Reynolds and some other megastars he had never heard of. David played a high school jock and for three seasons, became a recurring character on the show. Requests tumbled in from other shows. He appeared in commercials and starred in a Christian film. David calls these his "milk and honey years."[4]

Everything stopped flowing, though, when on the set one day David put a pillow under his shirt and imitated Reynolds to amuse the studio audience. Unamused, Reynolds smacked him in the back of the head. After that, David was again imitating an unemployed actor. Even the commercial producers stopped calling.

Lesson learned. Never make the talent look bad. Or overweight.

Twenty years later, Reynolds would again team up with David in a TV show—the two had long-since reconciled. But this time David was in charge, since it was his company producing the show.

Yes, *his* company. Revelation had become reality.

The short version is this: After his expulsion from *Evening Shade*, David languished for years trying to find meaningful work. He was cast in some Christian films—productions that, in his words, "had this cheese kind of factor."[5] But despite that, David also discerned "a hunger out there for positive, inspirational, spiritual entertainment."[6]

In other words, he saw great demand but no supply. "I had an appreciation for this niche that really didn't exist," says David, "but I felt like it should exist. The Lord said: 'Why don't you do something about it?'"[7]

He did. More precisely, they did. Along with two partners, David made a few Christian films, and after getting some traction with them, launched Pure Flix Entertainment in 2005. The vision was "to influence the global culture for Christ through media."

Introducing faith through film was a genius strategy. To change the world, the efficient path is to leverage what the world is already doing—in this case, sitting in front of a screen being entertained.

Of course, Pure Flix wasn't alone in pursuing this outreach strategy. Phil Vischer did it with VeggieTales in the 1990s (see pp. 79-84 in this book). Sherwood Baptist Church was also making films at the time to advance their mission "to reach the world for Christ from Albany, Georgia." That wasn't going to happen by broadcasting their church services; instead, Sherwood chose an approach that fit the habits of their target audience. You may have seen some of the innovative results: movies like *Courageous*, *Fireproof* and their blockbuster, *Facing the Giants*, screened by millions across 58 countries in 14 languages.

Mission accomplished, Sherwood.

Yet no one seems to have executed the strategy of faith through film with the scope or success of Pure Flix. Since 2005, they've produced more than 80 films, plus a plethora of TV shows and homeschool video curricula.

You might know some of this work, too. The award-winning[8] 2014 film *God's Not Dead* really put them on the map. It put them the black, too, grossing $62 million from a svelte $2 million budget. In fact, it's still one of the five most profitable movies of all time—all movies, not just the faith genre—relative to budget. The story featured a Christian student dueling with his atheist professor over the question of God's existence. Spoiler alert: The kid gets the better of him and the audience gets Theology 101, smartly packaged as entertainment.

Secular critics trashed it; paying customers loved it. Rotten Tomatoes, one of the leaders in aggregated reviews, reported that only 13 percent of professional critics gave it a positive rating, while 76 percent of movie-goers did.[9]

So Pure Flix made a sequel depicting a Christian teacher suspended by her anti-everything-Christian administration and ultimately having to stand trial. That grossed $24 million from a $5 million budget. Another tidy ROI.

More recently, their apologetic film *The Case for Christ* and their exposé of Planned Parenthood, entitled *Unplanned*—both true stories—have also done well financially, especially for this genre, while striking a nerve among snarky critics. Some are downright apoplectic, but that's how you know you're making inroads. When you're not, you're ignored.

There's certainly no ignoring the progress of Pure Flix. Besides their consistent output of original material, they've added a streaming video service. *The New York Times* took note of its growth, marveling that "the service's nearly 250,000 paying subscribers can choose from a catalog of more than 7,500 titles."[10] It's all on-demand, available on any device, for $100 a year—comparable to Netflix and Hulu, and pretty much what you'd expect from a twenty-first century media company.

In other words, Pure Flix is now a player.

They're also a patron. Some money from each subscription goes to finance adoptions, to help military veterans, to strengthen inner-city churches, and to serve kids, abuse victims and the hungry around the world.[11]

It's an improbable story, but one that many think is long overdue. In a Christian film industry replete with bare-bones budgets, weak writing, predictable plot lines and amateurish acting, Pure Flix is taking excellence seriously. "What we're doing better," explains David, "is making more organic, real characters, so when they speak the gospel message, the characters are more believable."[12]

Consequently, perhaps, some mainstream reviewers are coming around, admitting their enjoyment of the company's work. More importantly, mainstream parents are enjoying family movie night without scrambling to cover the kids' eyes or ears.

At its core, though, Pure Flix has been about so much more than legitimizing the faith genre or offering a family-friendly alternative.

In fact, the primary reason David founded the company was evangelistic, as his initial mission statement said: "To make films that uplift and bring people to higher levels of insight about who God is and the purpose that he has for their lives."[13]

Mission accomplished, Pure Flix. They're now the largest independent Christian film studio in the world.

Mission to be continued as well. They keep cranking out better and better content every year.

And it all happened because David A.R. White—the movie-phobic Mennonite, the munchkin in the musical—is not in Kansas anymore. In faith, he followed a voice pointing him west. Ever since, he's been pointing people to God.

For Further Study

David A.R. White, *Between Heaven and Hollywood: Chasing Your God-Given Dream*, Grand Rapids, MI: Zondervan, 2016.

Website: www.PureFlixStudio.com

Notes

1. David A.R. White, *Between Heaven and Hollywood: Chasing Your God-Given Dream*, Grand Rapids, MI: Zondervan, 2016, p. 16.
2. Sasha Savitsky, "'God's Not Dead's' David A.R. White: From Mennonite to the Movies," Fox News, January 13, 2017. www.foxnews.com/entertainment/gods-not-deads-david-a-r-white-from-mennonite-to-the-movies
3. *Between Heaven and Hollywood*, p. 26.
4. *Between Heaven and Hollywood*, pp. 82-83.
5. Anthony Simon, "Pure Flix and Chill: The David A.R. White Story." Vimeo.com/249699156 at 6:20.
6. "Pure Flix and Chill" at 13:50.

7. "Pure Flix and Chill" at 14:00.
8. Emma Koonse, "'God's Not Dead' Earns Two Prestigious Awards, Sequel Film in Development," *The Christian Post*, October 30, 2014. www.christianpost.com/news/gods-not-dead-earns-two-prestigious-awards-sequel-film-in-development.html
9. See www.rottentomatoes.com/m/gods_not_dead
10. Katherine Rosman, "Forget Netflix and Chill. Try Pure Flix and Pray," *The New York Times*, April 22, 2017. www.nytimes.com/2017/04/22/style/forget-netflix-and-chill-try-pure-flix-and-pray.html
11. "Watch Movies, Make a Difference," www.pureflix.com/giving-back
12. "Pure Flix and Chill" at 18:25.
13. "Pure Flix and Chill" at 14:35.

IN-N-OUT BURGER
GOOD FOOD AND GREAT PAY,
WITH A SIDE OF SCRIPTURE

The Lesson

If you want to point people toward God, offer top-shelf quality and become one of the top employers in the country. Then they just might listen.

The southwest is known for its Tex-Mex and barbeque, but it may also have bragging rights to the best burger in the country.

And the best burger restaurant.

In a massive study of 11,000 fast-food consumers, In-N-Out swept all eight categories among hamburger chains: staff friendliness, value, quality, service speed, cleanliness, curb appeal, atmosphere, and healthy options. Not even Chick-fil-A managed to sweep its competition (close, though—they won seven of eight categories).[1]

That arguably makes In-N-Out the Chick-fil-A of burger joints. There are some differences, though. In-N-Out operates in only six states, rather than nationwide, and it does not offer franchises. That's by obsessive design, laser-focused on quality.

They ensure quality through *control*. In their model of slow, cautious expansion, the parent company owns and controls all 300+ restaurants, without recruiting or relying on franchisees.

They also ensure quality through *simplicity*. In-N-Out offers a miniscule menu—about 15 items in all, including beverages. When they added Ghirardelli hot chocolate in 2018, it was the first new menu item in a decade. The success principle is basic: Do fewer things with more excellence.

They ensure quality through *freshness*, too. Every day in each store, they bake their buns, prepare their sauce, slice their potatoes and shape their patties from ingredients that have never been frozen. No microwaves or heat lamps either. Plus, they have an open floor plan, so everything happening in the kitchen is visible to the customer. Quality through accountability, perhaps.

Add to that the cleanest bathrooms and the friendliest staff west of the Mississippi, and you see why they have an insanely loyal following.

And loyalty is lucrative. Their average sales-per-store each year, about $2 million, is well above the industry norm. In fact, the company ranks eighth on this metric among quick service restaurants in the U.S., ahead of popular burger bistros like Wendy's, Burger King, Carl's Jr., and Jack in the Box.[2]

Intriguingly, a lot of that money goes to their employees. In-N-Out long ago beefed up salaries to far-exceed federal and state minimums. They currently start employees at $13 an hour and, almost unique in the fast-food industry, and they offer a complete benefits package: a 401(k) plan, paid vacation, and dental and vision coverage for both full- and part-time employees. No wonder they attract motivated people with great attitudes.

Then there's the staggering salary for store managers—about $160,000 a year on average.[3] No, that's not a typo; it's a strategy. To deliver quality product you need quality management. So to get there, In-N-Out pays about three times the industry standard, even for someone without a college degree.

All of that might explain their top-30 ranking on the *Forbes* 2019 list of "America's Best Large Employers"[4] and the company's number four ranking by recruitment giant Glassdoor. In the latter survey, In-N-Out outranked perennial powerhouses Google, Microsoft, and Southwest Air, while no other restaurant chain even made the top 50.[5]

Quality food, care for employees, friendly service, a bodacious bottom line, and even clean bathrooms (the corporate office prefers the words "spotless" and "sparkling"). It's actually much more than a strategy. These are all expressions of the Christian faith at a company that has been faith-focused for decades.

No separation of church and plate here. Dating back to 1948 under founders Harry and Esther Snyder, and accelerating under their son Rick in 1976, Christian principles have always guided corporate principles.

Rick, in fact, was the impetus behind the Bible verses that adorn their food packaging. Unobtrusive and discreet, customers can find citations from the books of Proverbs, John, Revelation and even Nahum on the bottom of their cups, fries boxes, and burger wrappers. Most of the verses point to the goodness and trustworthiness of God.

The company has also aired a 30-second radio spot each Christmas season since 1987, using their familiar jingle, but replacing their tagline, *In-N-Out—that's what a hamburger's all about,* with an invitation: *Wouldn't you like salvation in your life?*

Many in the company advised Rick Snyder against the idea, especially in secular southern California, but this born-again believer recognized the platform he'd been given, so he boldly stood on it.[6]

All of these practices continue under the company's current president, Lynsi Snyder-Ellingson, the granddaughter of Harry and Esther. After a tumultuous past,[7] she's now a devout follower of Jesus. On the side, she and her husband, Sean, run a nonprofit called Army of Love "to minister and bring healing to broken-hearted and hurting people through Christ's love and by the power of the Holy Spirit."

It complements nicely the two nonprofits run by In-N-Out, further expressions of their Christian faith. The In-N-Out Burger Foundation (Ino4kids.org) exists "to assist children who have been victims of child abuse, and to prevent others from suffering a similar fate," and The Slave2Nothing Foundation (Slave2Nothing.org) exists "to help those enslaved by any person or substance."

It's an instructive story of evangelism through excellence. Not only does In-N-Out subtly point people toward God, its quality is about as close to burger heaven as we can get.

For Further Study

Stacy Perman, *In-N-Out Burger: A Behind-the-Counter Look at the Fast-Food Chain That Breaks All the Rules*. New York: Harper-Business, 2009.

"Lynsi Snyder," I Am Second, www.iamsecond.com/seconds/lynsi-snyder

---

Notes

1. "New Study from Market Force Information Reveals America's Favorite Quick-Service Restaurants," March 15, 2017. www.marketforce.com/consumers-favorite-QSRs-2017-Market-Force-research
2. "The QSR 50," *QSR*. www.qsrmagazine.com/content/qsr50-2018-top-50-chart
3. Melia Robinson, "In-N-Out employees can work their way up to $160,000 a year with no degree or previous experience," *Business Insider*, January 22, 2018. www.businessinsider.com/in-n-out-employee-pay-2018-1
4. Vicki Valet, "America's Best Large Employers," *Forbes*, April 17, 2019. www.forbes.com/best-large-employers
5. Rachel Gillett, "The 50 best places to work in 2018, according to employees," *Business Insider*, December 6, 2017. www.businessinsider.com/best-places-to-work-2018-2017-12
6. Zachary Crockett, "The Church of In-N-Out Burger," *Priceonomics*, September 8, 2014. priceonomics.com/the-church-of-in-n-out-burger
7. "Lynsi Snyder," I Am Second. www.iamsecond.com/seconds/lynsi-snyder

100 Best Practices of Christian-Owned Companies

The 50 companies in this project offer variety of "best practices" — effective business activities that comport with their understanding of the Christian faith. Although this is not a comprehensive list, and not all activities will align with every believer's theology, the list presents road-tested ideas that are transferable to most faith-based organizations.

Strategy and General Management

1. Mission and values statements that express a faithful purpose
2. Adopting a "Golden Rule" philosophy of business
3. Scripture attached to each core value
4. Low debt and/or a conservative debt-to-equity ratio
5. Accountability for leaders to the guiding principles of the business
6. A "balanced scorecard" to track philanthropy and employee care initiatives
7. A product that, in and of itself, is a distinctive ministry
8. Quality as a testimony and a competitive advantage
9. Focusing on a narrow product niche to maximize quality
10. Partnering with businesses that operate on common values

Integrity in Operations

11. Keeping all promises, no matter the cost
12. Voluntary recall of defective products
13. "Fair trade" payment to suppliers
14. Transparent, "open book" pricing in businesses where price negotiation is common
15. Modestly-dressed models in advertisements
16. Eco-friendly operations, buildings, furnishings, etc.
17. A supply chain that ensures proper treatment of animals
18. A supply chain that ensures care for forests
19. Replanting trees that were harvested for business operations
20. Uniforms made from recycled plastic
21. Avoiding partnerships with alcohol and tobacco companies
22. Avoiding "soft money" transactions (avoiding channeling client business to firms that offer compensation for the referral)
23. Declining to take business that would violate conscience or faith convictions
24. Taking legal recourse as a last resort when the government infringes on the free exercise of religion
25. Assessing "integrity" in the hiring process
26. Assessing "a heart for service" in the hiring people
27. Assessing willingness to advance company values in the management hiring process

Philanthropy

28. Building schools (hospitals, parks, athletic fields) for the local community
29. Building schools in poor areas of foreign countries
30. Creating vocational training programs for those who would not gain skills otherwise
31. Paying employees to work in the local community
32. Funding churches and parachurch ministries
33. Capping the owners' salaries to give away more money
34. Giving away as much product as you sell

35. Giving away ten percent of revenues from one day of operations each week
36. Giving away food (or other products from the business) to the local community
37. Creating a business specifically to generate money for a ministry or social cause
38. Creating a nonprofit / foundation to receive and distribute company profits
39. Tithing ten percent, fifty percent, or ninety percent of profits to Christian ministries
40. Giving all or part of the business, in the form of nonvoting stock, to a foundation to facilitate charitable giving
41. Assisting during humanitarian crises (natural disasters, wars, epidemics, etc.)
42. Helping people to move from slavery to freedom and self-sufficiency

Employee Care

43. Safeguarding family time by limiting evening hours
44. Remaining closed on the Sabbath
45. Reorganizing a seasonal business to provide year-round employment
46. Sensitizing managers by having them do employee jobs annually
47. Eliminating the word "employee" from policies and from manager vocabularies, replacing it with words like people, associates, partners, team members, etc.
48. Employee participation in the decision that affect them
49. Payment of a "living wage"
50. A salary for executives capped at no more than seven times the lowest paid employee
51. Ensuring everyone gets paid, even if the owner does not
52. A profit-sharing program
53. An employee stock ownership plan
54. A high-percentage match for employee pension contributions

55. An on-site health clinic
56. An on-site fitness facility
57. Paid maternity and paternity leave
58. Fees paid for marriage retreats and marital counseling
59. Building a school or a daycare center for employees' children
60. College tuition benefits for employees and their dependents
61. A complete benefit package for part-time employees
62. A no-layoff policy (sometimes sending employees to work in the community instead)
63. An emergency fund for employees in financial distress (sometimes funded by employees themselves)
64. A matching fund for down payments on employee houses
65. Creating a committee to allocate one percent of the company budget to employee care programs
66. Public praise and recognition; celebration of employee and team accomplishments
67. The CEO personally signing cards to employees for Christmas and for employee birthdays
68. The CEO and/or managers handwriting notes of thanks and encouragement to employees
69. The CEO handing out paychecks to employees with a personal thank you
70. Prioritizing career development for employees, and promotion from within
71. Hiring applicants that some consider to be "unemployable"

Evangelistic Outreach

72. Charitable giving to evangelistic causes
73. Overtness on the corporate website regarding the company's faith-based purpose
74. Christian music (often instrumental) in the workplace, store, telephone hold system, etc.
75. Christian-themed artwork on the walls
76. Scripture or other faith-based messages on door mats
77. Scriptures or scripture-based messages on product packaging

78. Evangelistic messages on the building side or on corporate signage
79. Paying for employees to participate in company-led mission trips
80. Partial payment for employee family members to participate in company-led mission trips
81. Voluntary Bible studies for employees (lunchtime, before work, after work)
82. Weekly midday chapels for employees
83. Daily or weekly devotional time as a staff
84. An on-site library of Christian resources for employees to borrow
85. Creating a website of articles, videos, etc., that equips people to live out their faith in the workplace
86. Leveraging the company's social media to point people toward God
87. Company executives speaking to business groups to share the company's principles
88. Giving new employees a Bible on their first day of work
89. Executives or other employees gathering to pray for the salvation of all their stakeholders
90. Sending Bibles, Bible tracts, recordings, etc., with invoices and payments
91. Creating evangelistic videos for the public to access online
92. Religious displays at Christmas and Easter
93. A prayer-request journal available to customers, followed by intercessory prayer by the staff
94. Newspaper ads presenting the original meaning of Christmas and Easter
95. Evangelistic radio ads and social media campaigns during the Christmas and Easter seasons
96. Establishing a Christian radio station, or sponsoring Christian radio programs
97. An executive open door policy for employees, customers, suppliers or others who want to inquire about Jesus or the Christian faith

98. Offering an evangelistic message on the back of company business cards
99. Opening and/or closing meetings, company meals, etc., with a prayer
100. Hiring full- or part-time chaplains for the workplace

For 25 years, Mike Zigarelli has been teaching and writing about the Christian way of life. Much of that work, as a Professor of Leadership and Strategy at Messiah College, has focused on how to lead faithfully in business, in sports, and in the church.

Among his books on the subject are *Management by Proverbs* (Moody), *Influencing Like Jesus* (LifeWay), and *The Minister's MBA* (B&H). You can reach Professor Zigarelli through his website, Christianity9to5.org

Made in the USA
Coppell, TX
06 January 2023